Executive Function

in the Classroom

Executive Function in the Classroom

Practical Strategies for Improving Performance and Enhancing Skills for All Students

by

Christopher Kaufman, Ph.D.
Portland, Maine

·P·A·U·L·H·
BROOKES
PUBLISHING C⁰ ®

Baltimore • London • Sydney

Paul H. Brookes Publishing Co.
Post Office Box 10624
Baltimore, Maryland 21285-0624
USA

www.brookespublishing.com

Typeset by Integrated Publishing Solutions, Grand Rapids, Michigan.
Manufactured in the United States of America by
Sheridan Books, Inc., Chelsea, Michigan.

The individuals described in this book are composites or real people whose situations are masked and are based on the authors' experiences. In all instances, names and identifying details have been changed to protect confidentiality.

Library of Congress Cataloging-in-Publication Data

Kaufman, Christopher.
    Executive function in the classroom : practical strategies for improving performance and enhancing skills for all students / by Christopher Kaufman.
        p.   cm.
    Includes bibliographical references and index.
    ISBN-13: 978-1-59857-094-6 (pbk.)
    ISBN-10: 1-59857-094-3
    1. Curriculum planning.   2. Classroom management.   3. Classroom environment.   I. Title.
LB3013.K36   2010
370.15′2–dc22   2010003639

British Library Cataloguing in Publication data are available from the British Library.

2014   2013   2012   2011   2010

10   9   8   7   6   5   4   3   2   1

Contents

About the Author

Christopher Kaufman, Ph.D., is a licensed psychologist and Lead Psychologist for the Portland (Maine) Public Schools. He also operates, with his wife Sara, a part-time business, Kaufman Psychological Services, through which he provides workshops for educators and clinicians on a range of brain-based learning topics. Dr. Kaufman was born in New York City; raised on Long Island, New York; and earned his doctoral degree in Educational Psychology (with a specialization in School Psychology) in 1993 from the Graduate School and University Center of the City University of New York. His clinical specialties include attention-deficit/hyperactivity disorder and related executive functioning disorders, learning disabilities, and pediatric anxiety disorders. He resides in Gorham, Maine, with his wife and two children.

Acknowledgments

This book would not have been possible without the sabbatical opportunity provided by the Portland (Maine) Public Schools (PPS). I remain sincerely grateful to the several PPS colleagues who took on additional work and stress during my time away. I would also like to acknowledge the numerous colleagues, students, and parents in New York City, Wyoming, New Hampshire, and Maine from whom I have learned so much since starting out, test kits in tow, so long ago. Thanks are offered here as well to my parents, Fred and Diane Kaufman, for their considerable support and encouragement across the many years. Heartfelt appreciation is also extended to Sarah Shepke and Amanda Donaldson of Paul H. Brookes Publishing Company, whose kind direction, assistance, and reassurance made the editing process far less anxiety-laden than I anticipated. Finally, I would like to extend my everlasting love and appreciation to my wife and children, whose patience and encouragement across all the months of research and writing enabled the timely completion of this project.

To my precious daughters (and finest teachers),
Mia and Sophie

And to Sara, my wife, my love, and,
quite often, my surrogate frontal lobe

CHAPTER 1

Executive Function in a Nutshell

The Core Concepts

Upon completing this chapter, the reader will be able to

☞ Define executive function

☞ State the two core strands of executive function, and describe the range of executive skills within each strand

☞ Discuss the essential roles of attention, working memory, and other executive functions in information processing

---

Executive Skill: The Human Capacity

Ponder for a moment what makes humanity distinct from the roughly 2 million known species with which people share this planet. What attributes spring most readily to mind? After quickly ticking through a range of the more obvious human traits associated with intelligence, language, cooperation, and empathy, your thoughts probably turn to those elements of human functioning that allow us to live above and beyond the base instincts that rule the behavior of creatures even just a bit farther down the food chain—that is, people's ability to be governed by more than the immediate needs of hunger, thirst, reproduction, and safety. To a far greater extent than other animal species around us, we have the capacity to know and reflect on ourselves, to establish and work toward long-term goals, and to inhibit impulses that might prevent us from achieving these goals. The so-called lesser animals live from moment to moment, reacting instinctively and immediately to the range of stimuli and circumstances around them. We, on the other hand, live considerably more planned and controlled lives, often putting aside immediate desires for the common good and the achievement of longer term objectives (e.g., academic success, a job promotion, popularity in ninth grade, a relationship with that certain someone down the hall). It is this human ability to forestall immediate gratification while planning for and persisting toward desired futures that lies at the essence of executive function.

Executive Skill Defined

Stated broadly, executive skills are those elements of cognition that allow for the self-regulation and self-direction of our day-to-day and longer term functioning. The balance of this book explores the incredible importance of these self-regulatory capacities to the learning and social/behavioral domains, but at this point all that needs to be understood is that whenever people purposefully manage their thinking or behavior to achieve some desired outcome (be it developing and presenting a lecture, artfully constructing a Dagwood sandwich, or pausing to work up a pick-up line at a singles bar), they are engaging the skills of executive function. Said even more simply, executive functions are those elements of cognition that allow both the *stop* and the *think* parts of that wonderful habit teachers try to develop in the children with whom they work: to pause (even briefly!) and review options before leaping into action. Some specialists in this field of human endeavor link the words *restraint, initiate,* and *order* to summarize the essence of executive functioning and then tie it all together with the acronym *RIO.* It is easily recalled, like all mnemonic devices, and efficiently captures the impulse control, task initiation/production, and planning/organizational elements of prefrontal cortical capacity.

Executive Function in a Nutshell

Consider the nutshell. For our purposes, it may be helpful to ponder the opening of one of the tougher nuts to crack (say, a brazil nut or a filbert). With the appropriate tools—a nutcracker or a 40-pound sledgehammer—the opening of one of these titanium-like nuggets presents little difficulty to the average adult or seriously motivated child. However, what if you lack the appropriate tools but are still desperate to consume a fistful of filberts?

Imagine a scenario in which you have been locked away, Rapunzel-like, in a tower. The only food at your disposal is a barrel of these nuts, and the only tools available are whatever basic bits of furniture and toiletries your jailer provided before throwing away the key. How can you get the confounded things open before succumbing to hunger? You begin by casting about the room for objects either large and heavy or hard and pointy. Your search initially has a random quality, but over time, as hunger mounts, you begin narrowing the quest by experimenting in your mind with a range of possibilities. Eventually, you gather up the best nut-cracking options and prepare to have at it. Before beginning, you consider the appropriate angle of attack for each whack or dig, and then sit back for a second or two after each new effort to monitor the consequences of your efforts. Being hungry and lacking appropriate tools, you experience mounting frustration as you hack away—with bits of nutshell finding their way into your eyes and every third nut winging across the floor. The impulse to chuck every single nut out the window swells in your consciousness, but it needs to be suppressed if you are to survive long enough to escape and exact sweet revenge upon your oppressor. After much trial, error, and related revision of strategies, you eventually hit upon the best means available to get the shells cracked and sit back to enjoy a well-deserved feast. Over time, your nut-cracking procedures become increasingly streamlined and proficient, leading ultimately to your ability to consume a large quantity of filbert flesh without having to give much thought to the "how-to's" of the process.

This entire scenario is governed by your executive functions. The speed at which you consume the nuts is determined by the quality of your search for potential tools (random versus planned/organized), the extent to which you learn from the experience of your initial nut-attack strategies, and the degree to which you manage frustration, anxiety, and negative impulses. Naturally, your mechanical aptitude also comes into play, as would any unorthodox nut-cracking experience you had before your imprisonment in the tower. It is the quality of your executive skills, however, that enables the marshalling of your mechanical and nut-bashing background knowledge and that keeps these skills online in working memory as you wrestle with the unusual and frustrating situation. Only after achieving filbert-cracking fluency can you engage in the process without executive function, because people generally do not need to bring executive capacity to bear in situations in which they can act by habit and routine. In this scenario, you can see the essential roles played by executive skills in approaching, managing, and completing any problem-solving process—even the "nuttiest."

The Two Core Strands of Executive Functioning

Executive function is a many varied thing, with a range of cognitive and self-regulatory concepts grouped under its broad banner (Denckla, 2007; McCloskey, Perkins, & Diviner, 2009). To simplify the discussion of this pantheon of what are sometimes called *cognitive command skills,* this book groups them under two headings: the metacognitive strand and the social/emotional regulation strand. Figure 1.1 lists the different executive skills contained within each strand. Brief discussions of each function are provided in the following sections.

The Metacognitive Strand

The metacognitive strand comprises the cognitive and academic elements of executive function that play key roles in the comprehension of information and the planning, starting, and completion of tasks. These skills enable students to *purposefully attend* to important content (even if it is boring), *select and manage the strategies* necessary to both understand it and recall it, *identify goals* for learning and assignments, *plan and organize* their work before beginning, *gauge the quality* of their progress as they work (comparing it to the goals and plans established before they started), *revise* what they are doing as necessary, *shift fluidly* within tasks and between tasks, and *manage time* so that they can finish things on schedule (Gioia, Isquith, Guy, & Kenworthy, 2000). In short, these cognitive abilities allow for the purposeful regulation/direction of learning and production. The following sections take a closer look at the elements

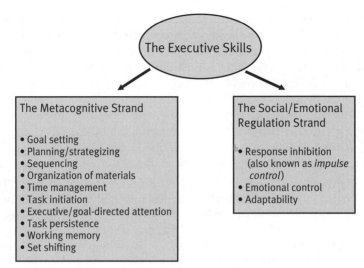

Figure 1.1.   The two core strands of executive function.

of this strand of executive function, with emphasis given to their roles in the learning process.

Goal Setting

To accomplish anything from the sublime (composing a sonnet) to the mundane (running a series of errands in the 90 minutes available while the kids are at soccer practice), people must formulate the general goals and more specific objectives that they hope to attain. The clearer the goals, the more likely they are to be achieved, because it is easier to establish the plans and strategies necessary to accomplish the desired ends if those ends are known. Goldberg (2001) talked about people's capacity for memory of the future and its relationship to goal-setting behavior; that is, the ability to identify a goal (an anticipated, or at least hoped for, future) and then hold that desired future in consciousness while determining the steps necessary to achieve it and then act on these steps. Children with less capacity for memory of the future (determined in large part by working memory skill, as discussed later) are expected to have far less ability to determine, plan for, and work toward goals than children whose foresight skills are more developed.

Planning/Strategizing

Once goals are established, plans and strategies must be selected and developed to allow for the achievement of the objectives. These also must then be held in working memory or "downloaded" from the brain onto paper or some other media in order to be followed. It is the quality—and often the specificity—of these plans and strategies that will determine in large part whether people achieve their goals.

Sequencing/Ordering

Among the key factors influencing the quality of learning and production is the ability to properly sequence the information that enters and exits the mind. Students who tend to take in facts and concepts in a poorly ordered manner will be less efficient learners than those children whose brains are skilled at absorbing information in well-sequenced ways. Those who struggle with sequencing may also have a harder time than their peers with grasping and following stepwise directions and with formulating their own plans and strategies in work situations.

Organization of Materials

Although heavily related to planning ability, the hands-on element of materials organization makes it functionally distinct from organizational skills applied largely within the mind, such as project planning. There are plenty of students who develop nicely ordered plans for their work (e.g., "I'm going to do this, this, and then this") but then fail miserably in the execution because their organization of the materials needed to study or write a paper is hopeless (e.g., "Mom, have you seen my backpack, books, paper, pens, erasers, assignment book, tape, markers, laptop? I had it all right here . . . somewhere. Now it's gone").

Time Management

Tick, tick, tick. It's amazing how time flies when you are not paying attention to it—or have a neurodevelopmental profile that makes it difficult to gauge time's passing. For many people, Parkinson's (1957) law, "Work expands so as to fill the time available for its completion," defines their daily experience because they rarely feel they have the time to get things done. The capacity to manage time is among the most essential of the metacognitive executive functions; it is very much related to goal setting, planning skills, and anxiety/stress management (Misra & McKean, 2000). To complete tasks in a timely manner (e.g., reading a book for class, writing a term paper), one must gauge with reasonable accuracy how long the task will take and then set aside the time to get it done.

Research has reported evidence of the multidimensional nature of time management skills (Britton & Tesser, 1991; Macan, Shahani, Dipboye, & Phillips, 1990). My own clinical experience suggests that time management difficulties can take two forms. One type occurs in the context of planning and organization deficiencies, and tends to result in a student often completing things at the last minute (e.g., "How am I ever going to finish this in one night? Why do I do this to myself?"). The other type is bound up in what psychologists often refer to as *deficits* in sense of time (Barkley, Edwards, Laneri, Fletcher, & Metevia, 2001), which make it difficult to accurately sense the passing of time and estimate the amount of time required to complete tasks. Individuals with this difficulty are often surprised to learn that due dates and tests are right around the corner; they have not waited to the last minute, but rather feel blindsided by deadlines (e.g., "What?!? But I thought we had 2 weeks! It's been 2 weeks? What day is it today? What happened to Wednesday?!?").

Task Initiation

Getting started on tasks and avoiding procrastination are among the most essential of all executive skills. To initiate a response to an academic direction, such as writing a daily journal entry, students must marshal their cognitive energy and organize their thinking in the moment to make decisions about where and how to begin. They must also hold these decisions and organized ideas in working memory while simultaneously initiating the mechanical aspects of production. Because task initiation also commonly involves the transition from one task to another, the ability to shift sets (see later discussion) is a major factor in getting started on subsequent activities.

Task Persistence

If you are a parent or teacher of students with executive function difficulties, you know how often academic accomplishment is inhibited by a lack of what some call "stick-to-itiveness"—an inability to keep the ball rolling, stay on track, or make it to the finish line. For many people with an executive function weakness, a lack of task persistence plays a major role in the work completion difficulties that contribute to woebegone report cards and irate bosses. The ability to remain on task with one's nose fixed firmly to grindstone is certainly dependent on other executive skills (e.g., goal-directed attention, self-monitoring capacity, time management), but it is also a function of the key cognitive energy regulation functions of the frontal lobe and its connections. A detailed discussion of the connections between the brain's energy supply routes and its executive command centers is included in Chapter 3.

Executive (Goal-Directed) Attention

Research in the fields of cognitive psychology and neuroscience has shown that there are elements of attention over which people have direct control (goal-directed or endogenous attention) and attentional elements that are involuntary in nature (Pessoa & Ungerleider, 2004). A student's self-directed attempts to initiate and sustain attention in a classroom context are a classic example of the former, whereas a person's immediate focus on the rumbles of thunder in the distance or the shape of what might be a snake in the grass represents the latter. Although automatic, involuntary attention falls outside the realm of executive function, the self-directed control and maintenance of attention (particularly in learning and performance contexts) is one of the most essential executive skills. Clearly, to be successful across school and vocational settings, students must develop a reasonable capacity to engage their attention selectively, sustain their focus independently on important activities for required time periods, and divide their attention as necessary between different essential elements of learning contexts (Pashler, 1998).

Self-Monitoring

All other metacognitive executive functions are arguably dependent on the ability to monitor what one is doing in real time. Indeed, it is self-monitoring capacity that puts the *meta* in metacognition. Successful students frequently gauge the quality of their attention, comprehension, and production in learning situations and make adjustments as necessary to maintain efficient input and productive output. If students are aware of the quality of their focus and thinking as they work, then they can tweak their cognition and environment to improve their functioning in the moment by asking questions for clarification, moving away from sources of distraction, rereading a particularly challenging section of text, or fixing a sentence that includes a syntax error, among others.

Working Memory

The crucial role played by working memory in information processing is discussed in detail later in this chapter. For now, it is sufficient to recognize that working memory serves as the cognitive workspace—or, to use Mel Levine's (2002) elegant phrase, "the mind's easel." It is the place in our conscious cognition in which people hold things before thinking about and acting on them. It also can be helpful to think about working memory as short-term memory put to work; when using working memory skills, people are not just briefly holding onto information but also are using it in some productive way (e.g., to follow directions, to make a plan, to construct comprehension).

According to Goldberg's (2001) concept of *memory of the future* (discussed previously in this chapter), it is in working memory that such projections of desired futures take place and are retained. To make a plan, you have to keep a goal in mind. If working memory capacity is too limited, the images and language associated with the goal will vanish into the ether before plans and strategies to achieve objectives can be developed. Even if the goal is retained long enough to establish plans, a "leaky" working memory will result in quickly forgotten or poorly sequenced strategies and steps that will not or cannot be followed. As the cognitive workspace, working memory also serves as the cognitive "mixing bowl" in which new information is combined with background knowledge to allow for comprehension of spoken and written language. Dehn (2008) emphasized the essential role played by working memory in the learning process, noting how it has an impact on the encoding and retrieval of information from long-term memory by serving as the essential bridge between short- and long-term memory.

Set Shifting

An essential function of the prefrontal cortex and anterior cingulate cortex (regions of the brain given considerable attention in Chapter 3) is to serve as the cognitive shifter. Said more simply, the prefrontal cortex enables a person to move with relative ease between tasks and between the steps within tasks. Because of their neuropsychological profiles, some children exhibit what Goldberg (2001) referred to as a certain stiffness of mind, in that they have greater difficulty moving within and between tasks than would be expected for their age. For these students, prompts from a parent or teacher to abandon a task (or even part of a task) are experienced as torturous and completely unacceptable directions. Possessing balky cognitive shifters, these children become routine-, schedule-, and rule-bound, and generally require considerable lead time and support to move on to other things before they are "done."

The Social/Emotional Strand

In addition to serving as the command post from which cognitive and academic functions are directed, the executive skills act as the essential modulators of functioning in the social world—or at least they should, if a person is to behave in a manner that polite society finds acceptable. The core executive skills associated with social, emotional, and behavioral regulation are discussed in this section.

Response Inhibition/Impulse Control

When was the last time you did or said something impulsively that you quickly came to regret? Assuming that you do not reside in a cave far away from the rest of the world and have yet to achieve what Buddhists refer to as "full enlightenment," you probably do not have to think long before recalling an impetuous action for which a heartfelt apology was required. An essential aspect of the human condition is the ongoing struggle to check impulses in order to live amicably with others and achieve goals. People all succeed and fail to varying degrees from day to day with the management of a range of desires—some of which might cause you to collapse on the spot from embarrassment should they reach the light of day. The capacity to inhibit angry, destructive, and self-injurious responses to environmental stimuli (e.g., "I want to eat the whole thing!") is a key factor for predicting success in school and in life. Psychologists refer to this impulse regulation capacity as *response inhibition*. It is considered by some theorists to be the primordial executive skill—the one that precedes all others (Barkley, 1997).

Emotional Control

Related to the concept of behavioral response inhibition is the executive control of emotions. The former relates to the stifling of broad range of impulses individuals must contain to survive (socially as well as literally) and succeed in life, whereas the latter refers primarily to the self-management of emotions. Although the prefrontal cortex plays no role in the creation of affect, it is responsible for managing the expression of emotions (Goldberg, 2001). Emotional control skills may not prevent you from becoming enraged or despondent when stuck in a traffic jam, but they will determine how you vent your frustration, whether by taking some deep breaths while repeating a soothing mantra or by a more maladaptive response. As Ross Greene (1998) pointed out, children come into the world with varying potentials for coping with anger and frustration. Children who have less frustration management skills than their peers may struggle profoundly in family, school, and social contexts.

Adaptability

The social/emotional facet of the set-shifting executive skill discussed earlier is often referred to as an individual's capacity for *adaptability*. Just as success with academic activities can be heavily influenced by the speed and ease with which one transitions within and between tasks, an individual's success in social/behavioral domains is at least partially determined by how well he or she can adapt to changes in routine and cope with the many curveballs life throws at everyone on a daily basis (Dawson & Guare, 2004). As the Buddhists say, life is very much about change. Those who can cope with reasonable equanimity are viewed as more "together" and socially desirable than those who stubbornly insist on sameness and melt down when their routines are disturbed.

The Roles of Executive Skills in Information Processing

Figure 1.2 shows what has come to be known among cognitive psychologists as "the milk jug of memory" (Cohen, 1997). In addition to helpfully illustrating the route information takes from the environment to the long-term memory system and back out again into consciousness (working memory), Figure 1.2 reflects some of the core information processing elements of learning and therefore serves as a handy organizer for the following discussion.

If you look to the very top of the milk jug, just above its opening, you can see acknowledgment of what all teachers know—that all learning begins with attention. Huge amounts of information enter the brain from the outside world every waking minute of every day via the senses (entering the *sensory register*, to use the appropriate bit of cognitive jargon), but people only take conscious notice of a tiny portion of this information. Can you imagine how maddening life would be if you had to actually think about every tree, bird call, stray voice, funky smell, and fabric sensation that your body encounters every day? All bits of sensory stimuli not given some direct attention degrade so fast in your mind that you have no conscious recognition of them. You see and hear these things without fully knowing that you do. When you give purposeful attention to stimuli (e.g., the cry of a mockingbird, a luscious-looking sweet roll), they are captured by your short-term memory. If you take only brief note of the bird's song but then direct your attention to something else, the short-term memory trace fades to oblivion as the new thought dominates consciousness. However, if you become so entranced and beguiled by the bird's song that you continue to think about it, holding the notes in your mind while trying to recall the name of the species linked to the call, you have

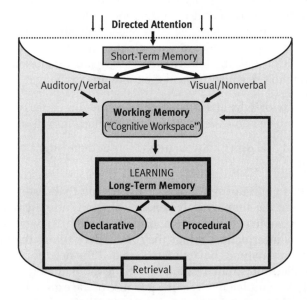

Figure 1.2. The milk jug of memory. (From *Children's Memory Scale [CMS]*. Copyright © 1997 NCS Pearson, Inc. Reproduced with permission. All rights reserved. "Children's Memory Scale" is a trademark, in the US and/or other countries, of Pearson Education, Inc. or its affiliate[s].)

thrust it into that all-important aspect of memory functioning known as *working memory*.

Looking at just these initial aspects of information processing, one can see the important role played by executive function in the larger learning process. Your capacity for selective attention enables the filtering out of the multitude of stimuli competing for notice, which allows you to focus on only important things, and your goal-directed attention skill keeps you focused on things you deem to be of value. Students equipped by their neurobiology with a comparatively strong attention skill will resist potential distractions better than classmates with less developed purposeful attention and persistence. Thus, children with strong skills will allow more learning material to enter their short-term memories. What happens to it in short-term memory brings us to the important topic of working memory capacity.

How large is the average working memory? Typically, adults can keep roughly 7 units of information in short-term memory for approximately 20–30 seconds before the information begins to fade away (Miller, 1956). Why does information fade away? Life in all of its forms continues happen around you; thus, it interferes with your ability to hold onto the information longer (e.g., forgetting a phone number before getting the chance to write it down). If ongoing attempts are made to keep things in working memory for longer periods of time via some type of recall strategy, such as purposefully picturing the information or repeating it over and over to yourself while consciously screening out all distractions, the material will remain in consciousness for a longer period of time and thus has a greater likelihood of being stored in long-term memory (Dehn, 2008).

Children's working memory capacity can vary significantly depending on their level of development and the neurobiology enabled by their DNA and experiences in life. Some children are equally skilled at holding information in short-term memory (demonstrating what is generally referred to as *short-term memory span*) and manipulating ("working on") the information once it is there. Others may display a reasonably strong short-term memory span (they can repeat a series of multiple step instructions given by a teacher), but will quickly lose the information if they must simultaneously act on it while trying to remember it, as in the following exchange:

Teacher: Taylor, why aren't you following my directions? I know you know them, because you just repeated them for me a minute ago.

Taylor: Um . . . I don't know. I guess I forgot them after I tried to start doing the stuff.

It is this notion of simultaneous processing that distinguishes working memory from the simple recall elements of short-term memory, and it helps explain why so many children—and adults, for that matter—tend to rapidly forget bits of information, things they wanted, or things they were expected to do. How many times have you recognized the need for some object, such as your wallet, and strode resolutely into the room in which you thought you left it, only to completely forget the purpose of the errand by the time you arrived at the destination? This may happen to all of us from time to time and is a function of the interference—the myriad competing thoughts and images—that can crowd out what had been foremost in working memory. Thus, the thought, *I need my glasses; I think I left them by the dishwasher,* can vanish en route to the kitchen if competing ideas or issues muscle into your consciousness. One can see that that quality of many aspects of daily functioning often is dependent on a person's ability to keep more than one thing in working memory at a time.

This capacity to store one type of information for short periods while simultaneously doing something with it (e.g., forming new ideas, acting on a plan in real time) is the essence of what Baddeley (1996) referred to as the *central executive* (self-directed, controlling) aspect of working memory. It also predicts one's simultaneous processing skill. As you will see in later chapters, many academic tasks place significant simultaneous processing loads onto children's brains. Students produce better narrative writing, for example, if they are able to hold onto and sequence their ideas in working memory while they simultaneously process the array of mechanical rules that must be followed to get thoughts on paper: spelling rules, punctuation rules, capitalization rules, syntax rules, and so forth. Similarly, children still learning to decode words can only comprehend what they read if they can simultaneously focus on both word attack and on the content of the text (LeBerge & Samuels, 1974; Penner-Wilger, 2008). Overall, the essential role that working memory capacity plays in enabling simultaneous processing is difficult to overstate. Often, children with attention and working memory problems tend to process information better if it is presented sequentially (e.g., bit by bit) because this allows them to only think about and act on one thing at a time. Figures 1.3 and 1.4 further illustrate the importance of working memory capacity and its association with simultaneous and sequential processing. In Figure 1.3, all three boys have solidly average verbal and perceptual reasoning skills and similar levels of achievement motivation, but they possess different working memory capacities. Robert, with well-above-average working memory skill, has little difficulty temporarily holding onto an array of directions and information as he engages in academic tasks. He is the student who frequently reminds the teacher of the times of special classes and daily activities (all of which appear to fit easily into his considerable working memory). Adam has

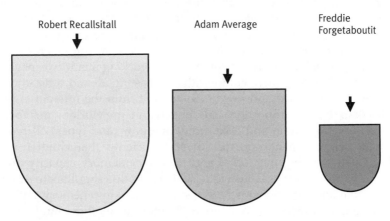

How large is the child's working memory?

Robert Recallsitall   Adam Average   Freddie Forgetaboutit

Figure 1.3. The relative working memory size of three children in the same fourth-grade class.

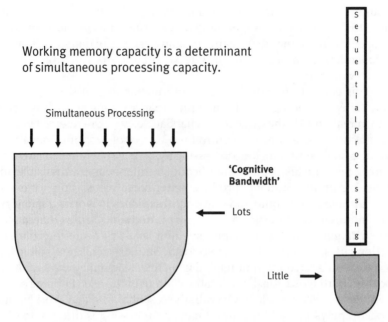

Figure 1.4. Working memory capacity is a determinant of simultaneous processing capacity.

less working memory capacity than Robert but still has sufficient ability to hold directions and information in his cognitive workspace to function in ways typical for a fourth grader. However, he sometimes forgets directions before he can act on them and has to do some rereading of text passages before he can answer comprehension questions. Freddie, with limited working memory capacity relative to developmental norms, struggles to a far greater degree than his peers to retain information provided by the teacher. He tends to easily forget the content of what he reads and the ideas he wants to convey on paper (e.g., "It's like they fly out of my head before I can finish writing them down").

In Figure 1.4, children with above-average working memory capacity relative to peer norms are often better able than their classmates to hold various types of information "online" as they think and work. Thus, they can receive and process content and directions in a more simultaneous manner than peers with less-developed working memory function. Children with a more limited cognitive workspace can still learn and produce effectively in classroom settings; however, they generally benefit from instruction that is more sequential in nature. To some extent, working memory capacity determines a child's "cognitive bandwidth." Just as broadband connections allow computers to upload and download content from the Internet at far faster rates than dial-up connections, students with large working memory capacity are able to take in and hold larger amounts (and types) of information from the environment more quickly and efficiently than children with less-developed working memory. Large working memory capacity allows for "broadband" cognitive bandwidth (which supports simultaneous processing of content and directions), whereas smaller working memory capacity contributes to narrow cognitive bandwidth and thus inhibits simultaneous processing (and is better linked to sequential, step-by-step processing).

Before moving farther down the road of information processing, it is important to highlight once again the role of working memory as the essential mixing bowl of cognition in which information from both inside and outside the brain are combined to allow productive thought to occur. It is here, in the cognitive workspace, that memories of the future (i.e., goals and plans) are formed and followed (Goldberg, 2001). It is here, too, in which people monitor their success in achieving goals, while also (via simultaneous processing) keeping the objectives and strategies for achieving them in mind. Ultimately, then, it is working memory capacity that allows and supports all the other elements of the metacognitive strand of executive function. It also has a major impact on the social/emotional strand. Children are better able to think through the range of response options available in a social problem-solving situation (e.g., "He just called me a booger-brain. What am I going to do?") if they possess both the inhibition skills to stop an aggressive response (e.g., "Well, you're a total dork and a loser!") and the working memory skill to recall and sort out choices before acting on them (Barkley, 1997).

Probing ever deeper into the milk jug of memory, one can see the important connections between working memory and long-term memory. Common sense dictates that the more a person thinks about something (i.e., mulls it over in working memory), the greater the likelihood is that it will enter the permanent storage system. This is why a child's level of engagement in the learning process is so important. Children who are just passively listening to a teacher's presentation without thinking about what is being said may be focused on the content, but they are certainly not elaborating on it in their minds. Their comprehension and longer-term retention of the core teachings in the presentation will be far less than that of students who are thinking about what is being said while it is being said.

The same is true for reading. Consider the case of Stacy and Tracy, fourth-grade girls of equal intelligence and vocabulary skill who are reading the same book about ocean mammals in the same class at the same time. Outwardly compliant and respectful, both girls are "reading" the book, but Stacy secretly finds it boring and is therefore reading passively without giving much thought to the content as it passes before her eyes. Tracy, on the other hand, thinks the book is cool because of her abiding interest in all creatures of the sea. As she reads, her executive capacity calls up from long-term memory all that she already knows and loves about seals and sea otters, and she is enjoying adding other bits of information to her personal catalog of sea mammal trivia. By virtue of her cognitive engagement in the task, Tracy is achieving a rich mix in her working memory of new information and background material, allowing the formation of questions and ideas that will foster comprehension and strong recall. To use a farming analogy, you might think of the interest and background knowledge in Tracy's memory as a well-fertilized field into which the seeds of new information can easily take root and grow into an abundant crop of concepts and ideas. Stacy's working memory, on the other hand, is likely to be far less involved in the reading process, resulting in a more minimal connection of new information with background knowledge. For Stacy, the seeds of new information and concepts that flow through her eyes would settle in generally barren soil. Some information might take root here and there, but the facts and ideas would likely wither before being established as a permanent crop in the field of her long-term memory. The level of engaged thinking (i.e., elaboration) that a child does in working memory has a huge impact on both comprehension and recall.

The bottom portions of the milk jug of memory reflect the core types of long-term memory, as well as the connections back to working memory via the retrieval process. Research has shown that the quality of storage of information in long-term memory, regardless of type, is at least somewhat dependent on the thinking that occurs about it in working memory prior to storage (Dehn, 2008; Kyllonen & Christal, 1990). In other words, people tend to hang on to information better in long-term memory if they have made some conscious attempts to remember it actively and strategically. Anyone who has ever successfully studied for a test knows this to be true. Although you will remember portions of important information if you simply review class notes and reread important passages from assigned text, your storage and recall of specific material will be far better if you use particular strategies to stamp the material into your brain. Good students tend to go to make the effort to devise content-specific mnemonic devices, flashcards, visual images, and a host of other effective study strategies because they know that their ability to access the information from memory at test time (i.e., pull it back into working memory from long-term memory) will be better if they have organized the storage of the information. Strategic working memory functioning also tends to improve the retrieval process, even if information was not encoded in long-term memory in a particularly structured way. You may more easily recall information that was acquired informally (e.g., via television, conversation) if you use some type of self-directed recall strategy. If you are trying to remember, for example, a particular factoid from a documentary watched a few evenings ago, you might consciously bring the relevant portion of the program back online in working memory and then try to zero in on the desired information. Students with comparatively sizeable working memory capacity and self-directed learning skills will be better able than their less metacognitively equipped peers to make conscious use of storage and retrieval strategies (Dehn, 2008).

So, what is the role of executive function in information processing? It simply serves as the enabler and director of the process. In the absence of executive controls, information processing would be significantly more passive in nature, with information entering consciousness from the outside world and from long-term memory in a random manner and also being stored in long-term memory in an arbitrary way. Without a central executive command function, the neurological computer would function like a ship without either captain or rudder, going hither and yon as the winds and currents dictate, picking up only those things that the sea might accidentally heave on board.

Executive Function: An Issue for Everyone

We all have executive function difficulties, at least from time to time. Each of us struggles to varying degrees with elements of attention, impulse control, organization, time management, and the larger panoply of executive skills. How people function from moment to moment depends, of course, on a range of factors such as amount of sleep, caffeine use, and duress encountered. Stress and anxiety tend to quickly grab up much of the available space in working memory (Klein & Boals, 2001; Schoofs, Preub, & Wolf, 2008), substantially affecting the amount of conscious cognition people can direct toward the myriad other things on which they must focus. Although it has become something of a cliché in the last several years, the executive load placed on people by society keeps increasing as they are compelled to juggle (i.e., simultaneously process) the demands of work, family, and the gamut of electronic devices that are now available. Some adults, by virtue of their neurobiology and life experiences, cope better with stresses to the executive systems than others, but no one is immune to the sorts of executive function–related mishaps (e.g., "Meeting? What meeting?!?") that can make some days so "interesting." The same is true for children. Regardless of the levels of executive function potential with which they enter the world, all children display varying levels of self-regulatory capacity based on their developmental levels and on the amounts and types of stresses impinging on them from moment to moment.

An essential purpose of this book is to advance the idea that executive function is an issue for *everyone,* not just children and adults with particular diagnostic labels. Just as adults tend to function best when given the levels of training and support needed to meet the executive skill requirements of their vocational roles, children do best in learning and living environments that acknowledge the work-in-progress state of their self-regulatory capacity and are structured to further enhance this capacity. Thus, teachers and school-based clinicians can help all students perform better if the adults understand the developmental nature of executive function and the ways that classrooms and other school environments can be constructed to enhance executive skill sets. (The proverb, *a rising tide raises all boats,* definitely applies here.)

Chapter 2 examines the development of executive skills from infancy though adolescence. Chapter 3 reviews the developing brain and is meant to increase the reader's understanding of the command-and-control nature of executive skills by explaining their neurological bases. Subsequent chapters discuss the assessment of these skills across the grade span; their impact on the development of literacy, math, and social skills; and the wide range of interventions that can be effective in improving the academic and social functioning of children with executive functioning weaknesses.

CHAPTER 2

The Development of Executive Skills

Learning to Stop and Think

Upon completing this chapter, the reader will be able to

☞ Summarize and discuss Russell Barkley's theories on the development of executive function

☞ Discuss the relative influence of nature versus nature (innate/genetically determined versus social/environmental factors) on the development of students' executive skills

---

Introduction

Simply stated, executive skills come from the brain's prefrontal lobes. However, the neurodevelopmental basis of executive function in children is more complex and controversial than many people may realize (see Chapter 3). Although children are born with the potential to direct and regulate cognition and behavior, no child—even those predestined to attend the most restrictive and competitive preschools—arrives on the planet with any ability whatsoever to inhibit impulses, form goals, and develop plans to achieve goals. Newborns, as any parent knows, are absolutely reactive to the range of environmental stimuli they encounter during their brief periods of wakefulness and make only the tiniest steps toward self-directed behavior during the first year of life. What happens after the first year has been described by Barkley (1997) in his treatise on executive function. This chapter provides an executive summary of Barkley's theories on development (see Figure 2.1), with an emphasis on what they mean for teachers and parents of school-age children. For a detailed presentation of his research findings on the development of executive skills and the associated theoretical implications, readers are referred to Barkley (1997), particularly Chapters 5 and 8.

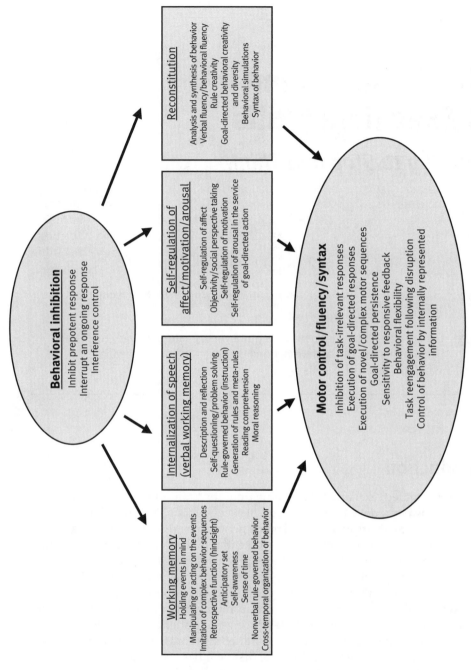

Figure 2.1. Hybrid model of executive functions. (From Barkley, R.A. [1997]. *ADHD and the nature of self-control* [p. 191]. New York: Guilford Press; reprinted by permission.)

The Growth of Self-Control

Barkley's (1997) summaries of the research on the developmental progression of executive skills conclude that children gradually become better at directing their cognition and regulating their behavior as they progress from early infancy through adolescence. It is not until late adolescence and early adulthood that the executive skills are fully developed. Only then is an individual neurodevelopmentally equipped to head out independently into the maelstrom of decisions, temptations, and potential pitfalls known commonly as life.

The developmental process of acquiring executive functioning capacity begins in the first year of life. According to Barkley (1997), this process follows a fairly predictable course that starts with the acquisition of the first bits of response inhibition (impulse control) skill. As Barkley notes, infants as young as 5–12 months show an initial capacity to inhibit a few basic impulses, such as incessant crying as a way to attract attention. Infants can also hold visual information in working memory during the very brief period of time in which the impulse is checked. As the infant progresses into the toddler years, the capacity to hold desired events and objects in nonverbal working memory increases, such that the child is able to look back in time to remember what happened the last time a particular situation occurred (e.g., being put in a playpen for a moment while Mom dashed into the bathroom) and look ahead to a probable future (e.g., Mom dashing back out of the bathroom and being picked up again).

For Barkley (1997), this emerging nonverbal working memory capacity flows from response inhibition (the primordial executive function). Children are unable to hold images of past events and expected futures in working memory unless they can first allow the thinking (imaging) to occur. As mental imaging capacity gradually expands in later infancy, a child is able to develop and practice an array of self-regulation and coping skills that were not present in the first several months of life. For example, a 3-month-old child may cry immediately on sensing any need or frustration, whereas a 12-month-old child in the earliest stages of a snit has the nascent self-regulatory capacity to cope with the source of irritation or fear, such as a mother's brief absence, by imagining her imminent return. In the meantime, the child may amuse himself or herself by playing with toes or other body parts. As motor skills develop, a child's coping skills expand to include the range of distractions provided by crawling and cruising.

In the first 12–18 months of life, a child's working memory function is largely nonverbal in nature. As basic language skills begin to develop in the early toddler years, children learn through verbal interactions to rely not just on others' actions, such as being picked up and held, but also on language for comfort and control. By about the age of 3 years, children become increasingly sophisticated in attempting to control others' behavior with language. For example, saying "I want milk" may replace vague, plaintive pointing at the refrigerator. Children also start to turn speech on themselves as a mechanism of self-control, often using the very same control words used by their caregivers. By doing this, children are taking the first rudimentary steps toward verbally regulating their own behavior. They may talk aloud to themselves about the world as they see it and what can be done to make things more to their liking.

During the preschool years, children demonstrate increased levels of internalized speech, although self-directed talk is still largely public in nature. A child's nascent efforts at verbal self-regulation are generally said aloud for all to hear (e.g., "I want to hurt him, but I'm not gonna hit again because then I'll have to sit in the thinking chair"). Although verbal working memory capacity increases at about age 4 years, children generally do not have the capacity for silent or covert self-directed speech until later in elementary school (age 9–12). Even then, however, the ability to stop and think remains a work in progress well into the adolescent years.

According to Barkley's (1997) model and the developmental research that supports it, the emergence of increasingly significant language skills in the later preschool and early elementary school years allows a child to internalize the vast array of rules that govern social behavior. With repetition and experience, these rules become stamped into children's long-term memories. Then, during situations in which a given impulse may need to be checked, children can call the rules into verbal and nonverbal working memory. To do this, however, a child needs to possess the developmentally appropriate level of impulse control skill to stop and think long enough to consider a rule.

Other executive skills include those associated with goal setting, planning/organization, and self-monitoring functions. According to Barkley's (1997) theory, these executive functions largely flow from the reconstitution element of his model. *Reconstitution* refers to the human capacity to analyze bits of information (ideas, memories, concepts) into their component parts and then synthesize them as needed to form new ideas, concepts, plans, and goals. Thus, children can be said to engage in reconstitution when they deconstruct the parts of a sentence and then reconstruct them into a different sentence. Another fairly concrete example might be recalling all the common elements of cars and then taking these elements and designing them into a new type of car. It is this capacity for reconstitution that enables older children to analyze the component parts of a social situation and then formulate their own plan for joining a game or avoiding a conflict between peers. The ability to analyze the details of an assignment and then develop a plan to complete the assignment is also an example of reconstitution. In Barkley's model, this core aspect of executive capacity becomes available to children at about age 6 years, expanding over the course of the elementary school and adolescent years. As children become increasingly skilled at analyzing and synthesizing the details of the problems and situations they confront on a day-to-day basis, their capacity for flexibility, novel problem solving, planning, and other forms of goal-directed behavior also increase. The function of the expanding working memory system across childhood enables reconstitution and thus the larger array of executive skills. The analysis of problems and the synthesis of potential options, plans, and solutions occur in working memory (i.e., the cognitive workspace).

The essential developmental points from Barkley's theory can be summarized as follows. Children enter the world with the potential to develop executive skills, but they are completely reactive to the world around them until about the age of 6 months. From that point on, the earliest types of response inhibition can be seen, with self-regulatory capacity increasing in later infancy and toddlerhood as the child's capacity for mental representation (i.e., holding pictures in working memory) increases. Once language develops and strengthens in the preschool years, children begin to rely on verbal commands to control their behavior; they ultimately turn these commands on themselves as their impulse control and verbal working memory expand. At about 6 years, children start showing the capacity for planning and other more complex forms of goal-directed behavior, which gradually expands across childhood and adolescence as the working memory process (and, as Barkley emphasizes, the ability to ignore interferences to working memory) increases. Thus, a 12-year-old child is generally far better at both stopping and thinking in social contexts and planning responses to assignments than is a 7-year-old child. Preadolescents are better at response inhibition (i.e., looking before leaping), mental representation and self-talk (holding nonverbal and verbal information in working memory), ignoring potential distractions (and thereby keeping key information in working memory), and manipulating (reconstituting) information in working memory to develop plans and goals.

Although the theoretical elements of this discussion may be unfamiliar, the notion that children develop better self-control, purposeful attention, and planning/organizational skills has been common knowledge since the dawn of formal education. This is why, for example, the executive function demands placed on ninth-grade students greatly exceed those placed on third-grade students. Society has long known that younger children require substantially higher levels of self-regulatory and metacognitive support than older children and adults; schools, community activities, and homes are therefore structured around the varying degrees of "surrogate frontal lobe" support that students require based on their developmental stage. For example, an 8-year-old child would not be allowed to drive a car, even if the child could see over the dashboard or reach the pedals, because it is known that young children do not possess the self-control, sustained attention, and decision-making capacity necessary to ward off death and destruction behind the wheel. Similarly, most parents refrain from giving their children credit cards and fully independent Internet access until some point in middle adolescence to prevent the financial problems that such liberty may produce.

Ultimately, although we recognize the wonderful qualities of children's developing minds, we also know with certainty that they remain dependent on adults' executive skills for guidance through the end of their high school years—and somewhat beyond. When children are unable to manage the executive tasks schools and society expect for given developmental levels (e.g., Theresa is unable to "sit still" in first grade, Michael is unable to sustain attention to what he reads or hears long enough in third grade to comprehend, Derek is unable to independently keep track of and complete his assignments across classes in eleventh grade), the possibility of an executive disorder may be considered.

Nature versus Nurture:
The Roles Played by Genetics and
the Environment in Shaping Executive Skills

Nature

The strong influence of genetics on the development of executive skill has been established, based largely on the wealth of family history research done on individuals with attention-deficit/hyperactivity disorder (ADHD). Multiple lines of inquiry have documented that ADHD is genetic, with some studies showing heritability rates as high as 80% from parents with ADHD to children (Barkley, 2006; Levy, Hay, McStephen, Wood, & Waldman, 1997). Approximately 32% of children with siblings diagnosed with ADHD are eventually identified with the disorder themselves, which is much higher than the 5%–7% rate of ADHD occurrence in the general population (Barkley, 1997). Monozygotic twins who were adopted and raised separately have repeatedly shown high rates of self-regulatory similarity when compared with twins raised in the same homes (Barkley, 1997).

Clearly there is little reason to doubt the strong impact that genetics has on the quality of executive skills that students show when they arrive at the first day of kindergarten. But is it all about genetics? Absolutely not. Even if you accept that genetic transfer rates of ADHD symptoms are as great as 80%, there is still a potential 20% contribution from psychosocial factors. The environments to which children are exposed also play key roles in the development and expression of executive skill. Before we put the contributions of nature aside, however, it will be helpful to consider one other aspect of Barkley's (1997) theory.

Do We Have a Self-Regulatory Instinct?

Among the more intriguing elements of Barkley's (1997) theory of executive function development is that executive skills are instinctive in nature. He contended that children enter the world genetically and biologically predisposed to develop the executive function they will eventually exhibit across childhood and adolescence, providing they are exposed to adequate environmental conditions over the course of development. Barkley drew a parallel between the instinctual nature of language capacity, the potential for which is prewired in a person's brain at birth, and the development of cognitive command skills.

Educators and clinicians may recall learning about the linguist Noam Chomsky, his famed language acquisition device, and universal grammar, which presumed the existence of brain structures at birth that were preprogrammed to allow for the rapid development of oral language skill in the absence of formal language instruction (Chomsky, 1965). Children are generally not formally taught to speak or understand their native language in early childhood, but instead acquire it by listening to and interacting with others. Barkley (1997) contended that executive skill is similarly innate, requiring only exposure to a reasonably caring world in the first few years of life to become manifest. Thus, just as children require no formal language instruction in the first 5 years of life to acquire receptive and expressive language skills (imagine how much easier it would be to parent toddlers if they did not learn the use of the words *no* and *mine* in the absence of formal instruction!), we develop the basic self-regulatory skills just by interacting in natural ways with caregivers, peers, and others. Barkley would be unlikely to contend that all expressions of executive function are innate, but has argued compellingly for the inherent nature of such core executive skills as response inhibition, working memory, and planning/reconstitution.

Nurture

If the quality of our executive skills as children and adults is substantially shaped by genetics and, as Barkley (1997) argued, we are born with a "self-control instinct," what role is played by world around us in shaping executive functioning skill? The environment plays two key roles in helping to form the executive functions. The first role is to serve as the stage on which developing children can express their burgeoning self-control/direction skills and experiment with growing executive capacities to the extent that neuro-maturation allows. Thus, as Barkley (1997) noted, a child's home and school settings should not be viewed as the true or sole originator of executive skill capacity, which stems primarily from neurological factors. Rather, the settings serve as the proving ground that allows the expression and practice of whatever inherent levels of self-regulatory skill that the child may possess. Thus, a highly impoverished language background will stymie the language development of children with otherwise intact brains at birth, because a child's innate language capacity can only acquire the language to which it is exposed. A highly chaotic, fragmented, and disorganized environment can result in the stunting of executive skill in children whose genetic potential would have led to better executive functioning in other circumstances.

A second and related role played by the environment in the development of executive capacity is to provide the specific content and form of children's executive skill. Even if the core elements of self-control are genetically and neurologically determined, the specific expression of executive skill and self-regulation (i.e., what these skills look and sound like) may be heavily influenced by the control and direction methods used by the most important models in a child's world: parents, siblings, and, increasingly, teachers and peers. This certainly holds true for language development. The quality of children's expressive and receptive language skills may be heavily influenced by the potential for language skill inherited from their parents, but the specific content and form of the language they use will be determined by their country of birth and language characteristics of their caregivers and peers. The specific means of control of others, self-regulation, and planning to which children are exposed also play major determining roles in the manner in which children's executive skills become manifest (Bernstein & Waber, 2007). Clearly, the environment plays a major role in the shaping of executive skills, with a bidirectional relationship between nature and nurture factors.

If there were no compelling reasons to view the environment as a key player in the shaping of children's executive skills, there would no rationale for the existence of this book. Unless you believe that the actions of teachers, clinicians, and parents can influence the manner in which children with executive functioning weakness operate in the world, the only intervention options are medical in nature. Psychostimulants such as methylphenidate (Ritalin), dexmethylphenidate (Focalin), and dextroamphetamine (Adderall) can be powerful tools in the treatment of executive function deficiencies. Numerous studies have documented their ability to diminish the executive dysfunction and other symptoms associated with ADHD (Barkley, 1997; Connor, 2006). In many cases, their inclusion in the package of intervention strategies is logical and laudable. What research and a wealth of clinical experience have also shown, however, is that the effective treatment of executive dysfunction in school settings should include systematic academic interventions and methods of developing internal self-control/regulation skill (Dawson & Guare, 2004; McCloskey, Perkins, & Diviner, 2009). The majority of this book is dedicated to discussions of the recommended practices for improving the academic and social/behavioral functioning of children with executive functioning weakness. To fully appreciate the strategy discussions, however, the reader should possess at least a basic understanding of the neurobiological underpinnings of executive skill. Chapter 3 presents the manner in which different brain structures operate in concert—led by the conductor, the prefrontal cortex—to enable the executive functions.

CHAPTER 3

The Neurology of Self-Regulation

Executive Function and the Brain

" The entire human evolution has been termed
'the age of the frontal lobes.' My teacher Alexander Luria
called the frontal lobes 'the organ of civilization.' "
— ELKHONON GOLDBERG (2001)

Upon completing this chapter, the reader should be able to

☞ State the essential functional distinction between the frontal lobe of the cortex and the other three cortical lobes (temporal lobe, parietal, and occipital), and discuss the importance of this distinction with regard to the frontal lobe's role in the direction of cognition and motor functioning

☞ Indicate the portion of the cortex most specialized for executive function and the approximate time in human development when this region typically reaches maturation

☞ Discuss the roles of the dorsolateral and orbital prefrontal cortical regions with regard to executive function

☞ List the other brain structures associated with attention and executive skill, and summarize the roles they are thought to play in the regulation of thinking and behavior

☞ Discuss the function of the amygdala in the formation of emotional memory and the generation of emotion

☞ Describe the changing "balance of power" between the prefrontal cortex and the amygdala over the course of childhood/adolescence and the implications of these changes for the development of emotional regulation skill

Your Amazing Brain

You possess the most complex, remarkable thing in the known universe. So do I, for that matter, as do the roughly 7 billion people with whom we share this planet. It is the human brain. As an information processing device, it is without competition. Weighing about 3.5 pounds in the average adult and comprised of hundreds of billions neurons whose connections to each other run into the thousands of trillions, it is an utter marvel of bioelectrical-chemical engineering. When one considers all that the brain does every moment of every day, the complexity and processing capacity of even the most sophisticated personal computer seems downright lame by comparison.

Of all the remarkable capacities of the human brain, the most wondrous of all is its ability to reflect on and direct itself. Because of our spectacular neurology, we are able to know, think for, and (more often than not) control ourselves. Without well-developed executive function, the human species probably would have remained mired in the fields and forests of our earliest ancestors, never to develop the civilizations, art forms, and technologies that mark mankind's greatest achievements. This chapter explores the basic neurological underpinnings of the self-regulated human mind, with emphasis given to the leading role of the prefrontal cortex (PFC) and its essential connections throughout the brain.

The Prefrontal Cortex:
Conductor of the Neurological Orchestra

Touch your hand to your forehead. Behind the skin, blood, bone, and muscle tissue that separates it from the cranial cavity is the PFC—the front-most portion of the frontal lobe (see Figure 3.1). Any discussion of the neurology of executive function should start right here. Although other brain structures play key roles in determining the quality of executive skills (particularly in children), the PFC is the area most specialized for metacognitive and self-regulatory functioning. Goldberg (2001) and Brown (2006) referred to this portion of the frontal lobes as the conductor of the brain's orchestra—a very apt metaphor indeed.

The frontal lobe is the brain's center of self-directed action and output, whereas the other three lobes of the cortex (temporal, parietal, and occipital) receive, process, and store different types of sensory information (Hale & Fiorello, 2004). Although information processed in the parietal, temporal, and occipital lobes informs so much of what you think and do, only the frontal lobe possesses the capacity to initiate movement, problem solving, and goal-directed behavior. It is the part of your brain that musters the resources available throughout the larger central nervous system to focus on and address what needs to be done as you go about your life. Thus, it is easy to see how the orchestra conductor analogy applies. A conductor does not run wildly about the orchestra plucking, blowing, and beating on various instruments to produce a played symphony, but instead stands on the podium directing the coordinated activity of the several players. The conductor does not play an instrument, but rather initiates and leads the integrated efforts of others.

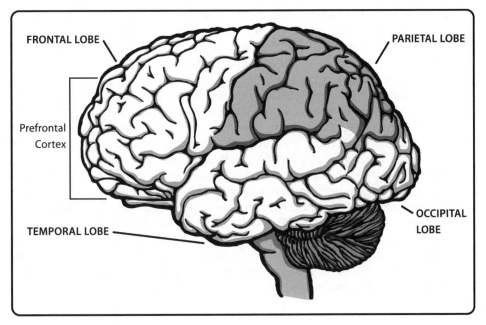

Figure 3.1.   The brain's four cortical lobes.

The role of the army general in planning and executing combat would also serve as a reasonable analogy to the functional relationship between the frontal lobe and the other areas of the cortex. Although the troops in the field may possess the specific fighting and technical skills needed to subdue the enemy, it is the general who uses these resources to devise the strategies, initiates the fight ("Charge!"), and then monitors the effectiveness of the battle plan in real time. You can pick the leadership metaphor that works best for you: the conductor, brigadier, or even chief executive officer (CEO) of a corporation. The important thing to remember is although while the other three lobes of the cortex take in and store the information obtained from the environment, it is the frontal lobe—the neurological commander—that coordinates this knowledge and puts it to use.

As Goldberg (2001) noted, the frontal lobe is on a very literal level the portion of the brain that likely houses the conscious mind. Your frontal lobe is the ultimate answer to the question, "Where are you?" The result of its functioning and myriad of connections to the rest of the brain and body is the gestalt known as *consciousness* or *self-awareness*. Drives (e.g., hunger, thirst, libido) and emotions make their way into this realm from the lower, more primitive brain centers, while past and present sensory information from the other cortical regions also compete for awareness. The prefrontal cortical regions manage this rich broth of urges, feelings, and perceptions as you go about the range of tasks (mundane, ridiculous, and sublime) that fill your days (Hale & Fiorello, 2004).

In adults, all the executive functions discussed in Chapter 1 are at least in part the product of prefrontal lobe functioning (Bernstein & Waber, 2007). Your ability to identify goals, make plans to achieve them, maintain focus on them while you execute strategies, and keep your proverbial nose the grindstone until the job is done are all mediated by the front-most portions of your brain. Impulse and emotion control centers are also housed here. For example, when you stifle the urge to yawn loudly in a boring meeting or clamp down on an angry comment that you would just love to make to an annoying coworker, your PFC is very much in play. Indeed, without this essential self-regulating portion of your neuroanatomy, you would careen from moment to moment entirely beholden to whatever drives and impulses might occur. Without it, people essentially would function like the lower animals, whose behavior is considerably more subject to basic instinctual drives. Although mankind is not the only mammal to possess a prefrontal cortex, the size of that found in human brains dwarfs those of other animals. As Korbinian Brodmann (1909) noted, the prefrontal region accounts for almost 30% of the human cortex, giving humans the comparatively strong self-regulatory capacity that has enabled the development of complex societies. This brain region occupies only about 17% of the cortex of the chimpanzee, 7% in the dog, and (remarkably, to many people who own them or have been impressed by their stealth) 3.5% in the cat (Brodmann, 1909). Such neuroanatomical comparisons of humans to the lesser mammals suggest that, in a very real sense, the human prefrontal cortex has served as the organ of civilization.

The Mechanics of the Frontal Lobe, Part I: The Bits and Pieces

Like the other three lobes that make up the cortex, the frontal lobe is actually comprised of a range of interconnected substructures that play their own roles in the direction of cognition and behavior (Lewis, 2004). Figure 3.2 illustrates these regions and their functional specialties. This section focuses primarily on the prefrontal regions of the frontal lobe. It is these regions, along with the ventral-medial areas (i.e., the anterior cingulate cortex), that are primarily associated with executive function.

Although it is often referred to as a single structure, the PFC is actually made up of a group of neocortical areas located anterior to (in front of) the motor and premotor regions of the frontal lobe (Lewis, 2004). Like all other sections of the neocortex (the wrinkled mantle of gray matter that forms the outer surface of the cerebrum), the prefrontal region is only several millimeters thick and connects to internal portions of the brain through numerous bundles of white matter (fibers composed of thousands of myelinated axons). The upper and lateral (side) portions are commonly referred to together as the *dorsolateral prefrontal cortex,* whereas the lower portion near the eye sockets is known as the *orbital prefrontal cortex.* Although each of these sections is heavily related to executive function and they substantially interact with each other as they go about their duties (Miller & Cohen, 2001), their specific self-regulatory roles differ in important ways.

Dorsolateral Prefrontal Cortex

As shown in Figure 3.2, the dorsolateral PFC is primarily responsible for the elements of executive function referred to in Chapter 1 as the *metacognitive strand.* In the mature brain, most aspects of goal setting, planning, organizing,

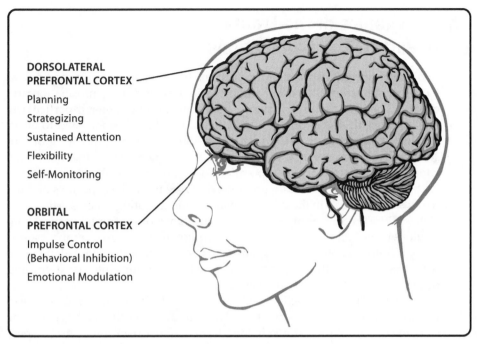

DORSOLATERAL
PREFRONTAL CORTEX

Planning

Strategizing

Sustained Attention

Flexibility

Self-Monitoring

ORBITAL
PREFRONTAL CORTEX

Impulse Control
(Behavioral Inhibition)

Emotional Modulation

Figure 3.2. The dorsolateral and orbital prefrontal cortex.

initiating, shifting, and purposeful attention are mediated here. It follows that weakness in this region—as a function of either genetics or injury—will be manifest in the types of cognitive difficulties shown by individuals with attention-deficit/hyperactivity disorder (ADHD), such as inattentiveness, planning/organizational problems, and limited working memory. Some researchers distinguish between the functional elements of the dorsal and lateral elements of the PFC. Pribram (1992), for example, noted that although the dorsal elements tend to be primarily recruited in problem-solving contexts that require determinations regarding the importance of a situation, the lateral elements are more apt to judge the levels of effort needed to accomplish goals.

Orbital Prefrontal Cortex

The orbital PFC serves as the emotional and behavioral overseer (Bloom, Beal, & Kupfer, 2003). Heavily connected to the amygdala (a key emotional processing/storage center and source of negative emotions discussed in more detail later in the chapter), the orbital PFC enables the inhibition of behavioral impulses and control of emotions. Overall, this area is the portion of the brain that supervises emotions and impulses; its absence could result in individual embarrassment or even a breakdown in society. Weakness here is generally shown in high levels of verbal and physical impulsivity and difficulties with emotional control (picture an individual who's had entirely too much to drink). It is not surprising, therefore, that the hyperactive-impulsive elements of the ADHD spectrum are often attributed to processing deficiencies in this region of the PFC and its pathways (Goldberg, 2001; Hale & Fiorello, 2004).

The Mechanics of the Frontal Lobe, Part II: The Connections

The interconnectivity of the brain's regions has already been emphasized, as have the interactions that occur among various areas during information processing. The PFC, as the primary executive functioning center, is particularly well connected. As Goldberg (2001) noted, it is directly connected to every functional unit of brain, including those associated with processing of sensory information, memory, emotions, and movement. Thus, like the highly competent CEO of a large corporation, it maintains consistent interactions with all supply and processing centers, drawing upon the capacities of these regions as necessary in the decision-making and initiating process. Miller and Cohen (2001) nicely summarized the importance of prefrontal cortical connections by noting that the PFC exerts a top-down influence over most aspects of cognition and behavior by "guiding the flow of neural activity along pathways that establish the proper mappings between inputs, internal states, and outputs needed to perform a given task."

It is the PFC's connections with the rest of the brain that enable its lead role in information processing. Its linkages to the other three lobes allow the drawing of information stored in long-term memory back into consciousness (working memory) during problem solving. For example, the PFC serves as the central executive element of visual working memory (the controlling element), while the actual imaging of information held in the mind's eye would take place in the occipital and parietal areas (Dehn, 2008). Similarly, when you pull a song or bit of verse back into awareness from long-term memory (consciously holding as much as you can recall in auditory working memory), you are using your PFC to direct the action of your temporal lobe (a key verbal storage center). Goldberg (2001) likened the role of the PFC in the information retrieval process to a hand guiding a flashlight that briefly illuminates those portions of the posterior cortical regions in which desired information is stored.

The PFC also exerts influence over the storage of information in long-term memory through its connections to the hippocampus, the brain's primary router of declarative memories (Malloy & Duffy, 2001). Whenever you purposefully hold new information in working memory, linking it to what you may already know about a particular topic, your PFC engages with the hippocampus (see Figure 3.3) and thereby increases the chance of longer term retention of the material. That is, the longer information is retained and consciously thought about in working memory, the greater the likelihood that it will be routed through the hippocampus into long-term storage. Thus, we can see the essential role played by the PFC and its connections in both the memory storage and retrieval elements of information processing.

Goldberg's (2001) notion of the PFC functioning as a hand aiming a flashlight to illuminate stored in the posterior lobes also helps us understand the relationship between the PFC and the reticular activating system (RAS). The RAS has its origins in the most primitive of the brain's regions, the brainstem, and functions as the dispenser of arousal/activation throughout midbrain and cortex. If sufficiently activated, the cortex has the resources it needs for the interactions that initiate and maintain information processing. If the

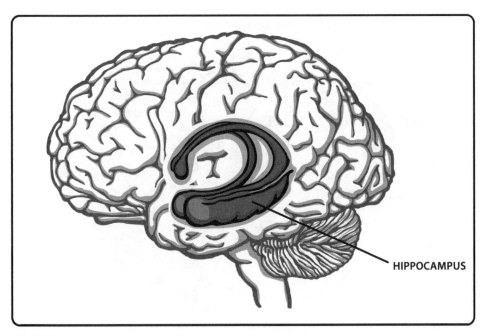

Figure 3.3. The hippocampus.

RAS is sending up insufficient levels of activation, however, the cortex is underaroused and difficulties with attention, learning, and memory can result (Andrews, 2001). The ascending RAS also excites particular sections of the cortex based on guidance it receives from the PFC. During information processing, the RAS systematically activates specific cortical regions under the direction of the PFC, allowing particular bits of information to be accessed as needed. Thus, as Goldberg (2001) noted, the RAS serves as the neurological flashlight, illuminating cortical storage sections as needed, while the PFC plays the role of the hand guiding the beam. Figure 3.4 summarizes reciprocal nature of the connections among the PFC, posterior cortex, and the ascending RAS.

Although the PFC's status as the best-connected area of cortex enables its leader/director role, its marked interconnectedness also has something of a dark side. Just as a chain is only as strong as its weakest link, the functioning of the larger brain system is dependent on the quality of functioning in all core structures. Because it interacts with all brain systems, the PFC is particularly vulnerable to the problems that might exist in other regions:

> Damage to the frontal lobes produces wide ripple effects through the entire brain. At the same time, damage anywhere in the brain sets off ripple effects interfering with frontal lobe function. This unique feature reflects the role of the frontal lobe as the "nerve center" of the nervous system with a singularly rich set of connections to and from other brain structures. (Goldberg, 2001, p. 114)

Just as a CEO's capacity to lead a large corporation can be marginalized by inadequate information flowing up from lower departments, the PFC's ability to serve as the brain's neurocognitive leader is impacted by weakness in any of the neurological systems on which it depends for energy/information and through which it must communicate its intentions.

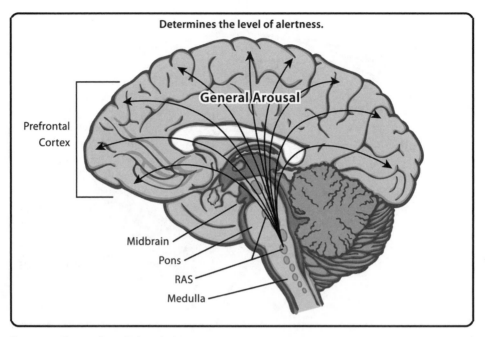

Figure 3.4. The ascending reticular activating system.

Development of the Prefrontal Cortex

Most educators know that children do not enter this world with fully developed frontal lobes. If they did, the jobs of parents and teachers would be inestimably easier. Imagine toddler years characterized not by the usual heaping amounts of egocentricity and emotional lability (i.e., tantrums), but instead by high levels of rational thought and the putting of others' needs before self (e.g., "No, I insist, dear sister—you take the red cup and I will happily make do with the yellow one"). Picture 5-year-old children who get themselves to bed at night, and then up and out to kindergarten the next morning on their own with every single thing they need secured appropriately to clothing, in pockets, and in backpacks. And while you're fantasizing, let's think for a moment about sixth graders who in early September travel with complete autonomy from class to class, moving fluidly from locker to classroom with every needed item (even pens and paper) and independently keeping track of all assignments.

In real life, however, toddlers melt down every 16 seconds (or so it seems), 5-year-old children flit from momentary pleasure to momentary pleasure (leaving a remarkably diverse debris field in their wake), and typical 11-year-old students need lots of parent and teacher support to adjust to the organizational and social minefield that is middle school. Lacking a mature PFC, children get by with whatever level of prefrontal cortical functioning their stage of development allows, leaning heavily on the regulatory capacity of their parents and teachers—their "surrogate frontal lobes." They also rely to a somewhat greater degree than adults on the self-regulatory capacity of other brain systems, as will be discussed in the next section. For now, this section looks at the growth of the frontal lobe and the impact that environmental factors can have on the developing PFC.

Among the most repeated facts about the brain is that infants enter the world with all the neurons they will ever possess (Bhardwaj et al., 2006). Although growth in virtually all other parts of the body across childhood is associated with the making of trillions of new cells, the rapid expansion of the brain that takes place soon after birth and continues to various degrees into young adulthood is actually a function of the formation of new connections among neurons. Neurodevelopment is not a process of new cell construction, but is instead the result of the elimination of unnecessary cells and increased connectivity between remaining cells (Shonkoff & Meisels, 2000). At birth, the human brain is only about a quarter of the size it will ultimately achieve (Hale & Fiorello, 2004). As infants interact with caretakers and the larger world around them, the dendrites and axons (the connecting elements) of neurons reach out to others to form synapses (interaction points) in numbers almost impossible to comprehend. By about the time children reach their early elementary school years, the brain has come close to reaching its full size, but even then neurodevelopment is far from complete. In order to mature and develop throughout childhood and into young adulthood, human brains actually cull countless millions of neurons ("use it or lose it"), leaving in place the 100 billion or so that most of us take through the balance of life. This pruning occurs so that the remaining cells and their connections form the neuroarchitecture needed for rapid, efficient processing.

Another key element of neuromaturation is the myelination of the axonal connections between cells. As axons acquire fatty sheaths of myelin, electrochemical messages travel among cells at more rapid speeds. Thus, brain growth over the course of childhood is really a function of three things: the death of unnecessary/redundant neurons, the proliferation of connections between the ones that remain, and the growth of myelin sheaths around the axons that transmit messages from one cell to the next.

As Hale and Fiorello (2004) noted, cortical maturation begins in the primary sensory zones and ends many years later in the prefrontal cortex. Research on the developing frontal cortex has shown that white matter connections between neurons and among regions increase dramatically over the course of childhood, while gray matter density peaks out in the frontal lobe at about the age of 12 (Teeter Ellison, 2005). Subsequent to the achievement of maximal size and connectivity, there is a gradual decline in synaptic density (decrease in the number of between-cell connections) over the course of middle to late adolescence as the PFC becomes increasingly refined and specialized in function (Giedd et al., 1999). What triggers the PFC to start pruning back unnecessary synapses during adolescence? Although it is likely that this refining process takes place in part as a function of genetic programming (and thus may be an intrinsic function), others have argued that the streamlining of the PFC in the years just prior to young adulthood may be a function of adolescents' interactions with the environment (Giedd et al., 1999). The contention here is that the PFC is shaped by teenagers' responses to the myriad cognitive and social challenges that the secondary years throw their way.

Can a child's environment influence the development of the PFC? Logic, not to mention increasing amounts of neuroscientific research, suggests that it can. Bernstein and Waber (2007) contend that although genetics establishes the essential brain plan at birth and clearly contributes to the growth patterns discussed earlier, interactions with the environment also play a major role in shaping the frequency and manner in which synapses are formed:

> The ontogeny of neural circuitry is crucial to these continual brain-context trans-actions. As this circuitry matures, the transactions between it and the external context deliver the young child from the tyranny of internal biology (in the form of reflexive action patterns) with respect to the child's environment. Maturation of the frontal circuitry necessarily involves ever-increasing interface with the context as executive control systems continually select behavioral options that promote the adaptive match. The developing brain has an increasing ability to differentiate contextual variables, which most likely feeds forward to promote further differentiation of context and so forth. Because contextual interaction is so critical to the successful ontogeny of brain function, the brain can—indeed, must—be exquisitely sensitive to contextual variables. (Bernstein & Waber, 2007, p. 46)

Bernstein and Waber (2007) further noted the range of research that has documented the environment's influence on the development of connections within the brains of children, adults, and nonhuman primates. Shaywitz (2003) clearly documented the impact that multisensory synthetic phonics instruction can have on the brains of readers with dyslexia, whereas Schwartz (1996) demonstrated the impact of cognitive behavioral therapy on the brains of individuals with obsessive-compulsive disorder.

Although a detailed presentation of the growing body of research on the impact of environment on developing—and even mature—brains is beyond the scope of this chapter, it is important to note that there seems little doubt that the brain–environment relationship is bidirectional. As Bernstein and Waber (2007) suggested, it is quite reasonable to conclude that development of the PFC across childhood and adolescence is significantly affected by a range of contextual variables (e.g., nutrition, family interaction styles, family organization styles, classroom instruction, trauma). Although genetics may play the leading role in determining the quality of a student's prefrontal processing (Barkley, 2006), it is important for the educational and clinical communities to understand the shaping influence of life on brain structures that enable executive function. Armed with this knowledge, you can better structure learning environments to improve/refine whatever executive skills children take with them to school and assist parents in providing more "executive function friendly" home environments.

Other Brain Regions Associated with Executive Function and Attention

Given the predominant role played by the PFC in mediating the executive functions, it is tempting to just state that the PFC is the only portion of the brain that really matters in this chapter and move on. However, as seen in the earlier discussion of the connections between the PFC and the rest of the brain, such a blanket statement would be misleading and inaccurate. Without question, the prefrontal cortical regions play the leading role in directing thoughts and behavior, but there are other brain structures that contribute to the ability to focus attention and regulate cognition and behavior.

Although numerous studies have implicated prefrontal cortical difficulties in the manifestation of ADHD symptoms in children (Barkley, 1997, 2006), research has also indicated that in children the functioning of the brain's various regions tends to be less modular (i.e., "this bit does that and that bit does this") and is instead more dynamic/interactive (Bernstein & Waber, 2007; Denckla, 2007). This is why brain injury tends to be less catastrophic in children than adults. Because many structures in children's brains are still in the process of figuring out their specific roles in the larger neurophysiological scheme, they are somewhat better able to adapt as necessary to injuries in other sections. Elliot (2003) suggested that, even in adults' brains, executive functions are not controlled entirely by specific regions but are instead regulated by more global, interacting networks. Therefore, it is important to appreciate that while the PFC may be the star in the larger executive function firmament, it is not the only player on stage. This section will review the other key brain structures associated with the abilities to focus, regulate, and control. Because the RAS was already addressed in the discussion of the PFC and its connections, its role in the enabling of attention and other executive functions will not be repeated here.

Anterior Cingulate

The cingulate cortex is a large structure that runs from the brain's frontal to posterior sections, wrapping around the corpus callosum (see Figure 3.5). In addition to serving a variety of autonomic functions, including the regulation

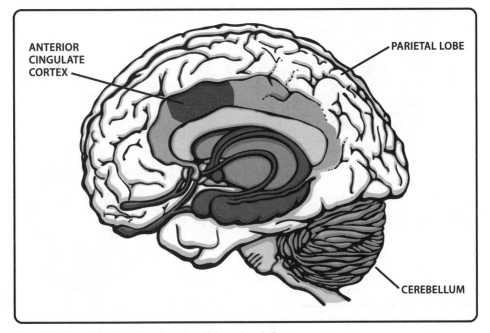

Figure 3.5.   The anterior cingulate cortex, parietal lobe, and cerebellum.

of heartbeat and blood pressure, the anterior cingulate (the front portion) has been linked by neuroscientists to a range of cognitive functions. These include the mediation of motivation, responding to novelty, self-monitoring of performance, decision making, and persistence (Posner, 1994). Given its association with elements of self-regulation, Goldberg (2001) referred to the anterior cingulate as part of the "metropolitan" (larger) frontal lobes, and noted its role (along with the orbital PFC) in "reining in" the emotional surges originating in the amygdala.

Basal Ganglia

The basal ganglia are actually a collection of forebrain nuclei at the base of the cerebral hemispheres that work closely with the frontal lobes to direct movement and basic elements of cognition (see Figure 3.6). Significantly connected to both cortical and subcortical regions, including the cerebellum (Hale & Fiorello, 2004), injury to this motor initiation area often results in interference with voluntary movements such as walking and talking (Berninger & Richards, 2002). Three sections of the basal ganglia—the caudate nucleus, putamen, and the nucleus accumbens—are known collectively as the striatum (Kiernan, 2008). Theories on the role played by the striatum and the larger basal ganglia with regard to executive function have held that it works closely with the frontal lobes (Goldberg, 2001), essentially helping to initiate the related "marching orders" generated by the PFC. Thus, it serves as a key support structure in the top-down delivery of cognitive and motor directions from

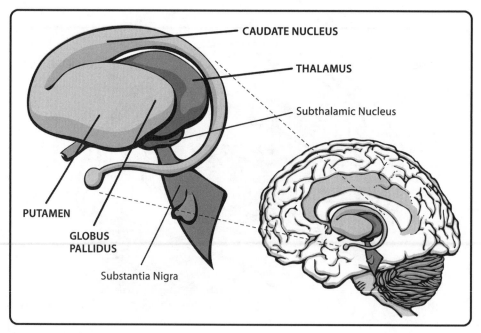

Figure 3.6. The basal ganglia.

the frontal cortex to the lower brain systems (Casey, Tottenham, & Fossella, 2002). Support for these theories comes from brain studies of children with ADHD, which have shown decreased blood flow not just to the prefrontal cortical regions, but also to pathways that connect it to the basal ganglia and the cerebellum (Barkley, 2006).

Cerebellum

A large and circular structure attached to the lower, rear-most portions of the brain (see Figure 3.6), the cerebellum's primary function was long thought to be limited to the coordination of movement and balance. A growing body of research, however, has suggested it also plays a range of important roles in the regulation of cognition (Timmann & Daum, 2007). Although it does not initiate action or thinking—the frontal lobes alone possess the power to initiate—the cerebellum and its associated brainstem connections compare the intention of movement and elements of cognition with actual performance (Best, 2001). Thus, the cerebellum's role is to serve as something of an overseer of production quality, making tweaks and changes to performance as needed to ensure the quality of output.

Parietal Lobe

The parietal regions of the cortex serve as the centers of somatosensory processing; that is, they process and store information related to tactile sense, including pressure, temperature, and movement (Hale & Fiorello, 2004). In collaboration with the occipital lobes (the center of visual processing), the parietal lobes also process spatial information and thus help you to recognize where you are at any given moment in comparison to all the things around you. In so doing, they enable both self-awareness (e.g., "Where am I in relation to everything else?") and environmental awareness ("Where is everything else in relation to me?"; Hale & Fiorello, 2004).

Weak processing in this region, either as a function of genetic transfer or injury, can significantly limit body-in-space and environmental awareness, leading to the presentation of behaviors resembling ADHD (Hale & Fiorello, 2004). Although they are not purposefully aggressive, some children have a remarkable penchant to obliviously bowl over peers or run into large objects as they run on the playground. When asked why they ploughed over some poor child found lying in a weeping heap next to the swings, these children will seem genuinely surprised that they had banged into anyone and are largely at a loss to explain what occurred (e.g., "I don't know. I guess I just didn't see her"). Although the neurological basis of this tendency to fail to observe key environmental cues may relate to prefrontal cortical weakness (manifest, for example, in high distractibility and/or motor impulsivity), an alternate hypothesis worth pursuing, as Hale and Fiorello (2004) noted, is that the problem stems from limited self- and environmental awareness associated with a parietal processing weakness. Assessment techniques to address differential diagnostic questions such as this are discussed in Chapter 4.

The Brain and Self-Control: Reining in the Amygdala

What is neurobiological source of our negative emotions? The answer, at least in general terms, is the amygdala. Found deep within the brain's mid-temporal region and linked to a range of systems associated with memory, motor functioning, and cognition, the amygdala has received significant attention in the media in recent years as a key site of emotional memory and processing. Figure 3.7 shows the location of this important structure and its connections. It is highly linked to a range of brain systems associated with survival, and is thought to have evolved in primitive brains to keep organisms away from things that were potentially deadly (i.e., fight-or-flight reflex). The amygdala's connections to the hypothalamus and the brainstem's autonomic centers allow it to initiate survival reactions as necessary. Whenever you find yourself moving quickly and automatically away from a potentially danger-ous situation (e.g., lighting strikes nearby and you instinctively dive for cover), your amygdala is working in concert with your autonomic nervous system to drive the action. Similarly, when you feel intense anger welling quickly through your brain and body in response to provocation, your amygdala is functioning with your hypothalamus to whip up the rage.

Although the amygdala's role as our fight-or-flight center continues to have value, the ease with which we may experience intense fear and anger may cause problems for all of us. When anxiety or rage overwhelm our abil-ity to think and problem solve in a rational manner, we are experiencing what some mental health professionals refer to as an *amygdala hijack* (Goleman, 1995), in that our higher-order cognitive abilities have been temporarily superseded by the lower brain systems associated with emotional generation. Children, by virtue of their less mature neurodevelopment, experience these

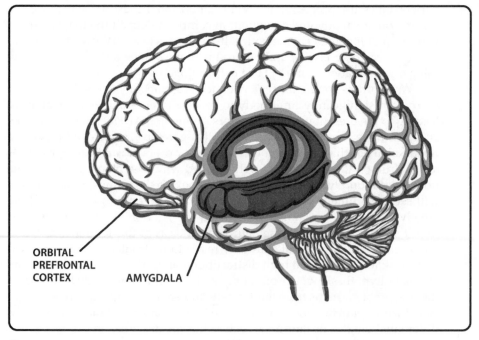

ORBITAL
PREFRONTAL
CORTEX   AMYGDALA

Figure 3.7.   The orbital prefrontal cortex and amygdala.

emotional hijackings far more often than adults, with younger age being associated with greater frequency (2- and 3-year-olds melt down numerous times per day, whereas older adolescents—despite the seeming frequency of their emotional tempests—may only "lose it" once or twice in a period of several days). In the classroom, amygdala hijackings may take the form of intense fear or anger reactions to certain academic task demands or rage reactions on the playground associated with peer-to-peer altercations.

Research on the amygdala suggests that in addition to triggering strong emotions in response to environmental stimuli, it is also the place in the brain where much of our "emotional baggage" is stored (Cahill, Babinsky, Markowitsch, & McGaugh, 1995; Goldberg, 2001). In other words, it is where fears and resentments literally reside and emerge from when conditions are right. Because of its strong connections to the hippocampus (the primary router of information from working memory to longer term memory) and other memory structures, the amygdala is also heavily associated with emotional conditioning (Richter-Levin, 2004). Thus, the amygdala is the brain center that learns to link fear and anger with particular ideas, content areas, skills, or experiences. You may know students who developed fears associated with certain subjects or academic activities after struggling with them over a period of time (e.g., math anxiety). Some students with ADHD or Asperger syndrome have such an intense conditioned fear of narrative writing tasks that the mere presentation of a writing prompt quickly results in them shredding all written language materials on their desks. Other children learn to associate the playground with pain or fear because of the consistent bullying experienced there, and consequently avoid going outside for recess whenever possible.

Even if students' emotional reactions to specific environmental triggers do not result in dramatic outbursts, fearfulness, and/or intense frustration in instructional settings can have a significant impact on cognition. It is hard for people to think clearly when they are frightened or angered. Think back to the last time you attempted to read something when upset and you will likely recall the futility of the effort. Your eyes probably scanned the text and moved from line to line, but comprehension did not occur because your conscious mind remained focused on the source of anxiety or irritation. Intense emotion inhibits cognition by consuming significant amounts of working memory. When you are upset, your "cognitive desktop" is largely taken up by the negative emotions and related thoughts surging into consciousness from the amygdala and other lower brain structures, leaving little room for focus on cognitive tasks (Klein & Boals, 2001). Therefore, upset children are often unable to be attentive in class or engage in their work until the source of their irritation/anxiety has been addressed. This also helps to explain the difficulties that chronically traumatized students have with focusing and producing in classroom contexts. Fortunately, as they move from childhood to adulthood, people develop increasing capacity to wrestle control of the cognitive desktop (working memory) away from amygdala-driven emotional content.

As noted earlier, the brain regions associated with managing the emotional impulses that surge from the amygdala are the orbital PFC and anterior cingulate. As Goldberg (2001) noted, there are strong connections between these regulating mechanisms and the reptilian brain's emotional centers, which allow the frontal systems at least some measure of control over the base emotions and drives that would otherwise direct behavior from moment to moment. The design of our neuroarchitecture therefore gives the role of emotional generation to the amygdala and associated limbic structures, whereas orbital prefrontal and anterior cingulate regions function as the overseer of these regions. Young children enter the world with fully developed and functional emotion generating systems, and therefore possess the capacity at birth to experience fear and rage in heaping helpings.

Because the orbital regions of the PFC are not fully mature until the latest stages of adolescence in the early 20s, the portion of the brain most charged with the task of regulating the expression of strong emotions is not equipped to do so until children have already left the high school years behind. Therefore, K–12 teachers and school-based clinicians everywhere are working with a client base that is experiencing (and demonstrating) a mismatch of power between fully developed emotion-generation systems and only partially developed prefrontal control systems. Thus, when a typical kindergarten or first-grade student feels slighted by the behavior of a peer or the rebuke of a teacher, negative emotions will surge; the student's nascent orbital prefrontal cortical capacity will have limited ability to prevent the likely meltdown. Even as children progress well into their teenage years, they remain more susceptible than typical adults to emotional outbursts and impulsive actions as a function of their still-incomplete orbital prefrontal maturation.

Mom: "Michael, why on earth did you punch a hole in your bedroom wall?! What were you thinking?!"

Michael (age 14):   I don't know, Mom! All right?! I was really mad and I came up here and I guess I just lost it! I'm sorry, okay!?"

If all children struggle to some extent with emotional and behavioral control as a function of a mismatch of power between the fully functional amygdala and the still-developing orbital prefrontal region, what can be expected from the multitude of children whose neurological self-regulatory mechanisms are less developed than those of most peers? You can expect exactly what you see from so many of these children: comparatively high levels of easily frustrated, angered, and frightened behavior combined with comparatively little ability to manage these negative emotions when they occur. Children with relative developmental weakness in prefrontal cortical regions (or in the connections between the PFC and other brain systems essential for self-regulation) exhibit significant levels of oppositionalism, noncompliance, and disruption in school contexts because they lack (relative to peer norms) emotion/behavior self-regulation capacity. Although these children often possess the same levels of generalized intelligence as their peers, they function emotionally and behaviorally in manner more consistent with an earlier developmental level (Barkley, 2006).

Putting It All Together: What We Know About the Neurological Bases of Executive Skill

The cognitive skills known commonly as the executive functions have a credible and comprehensible neurodevelopmental basis. Although neuroscience has a long way to go before clearly establishing all of the neurological un-derpinnings of executive function, research conducted over the last,30 years has revealed much about the brain's inner workings that, prior to the advent of neuroimaging technology, could only be guessed at via autopsies of pa-tients with brain injuries and studies of animal brains (Sousa, 2003; Teeter-Ellison, 2005). Because long-term retention of technical information tends to be aided by summarization and chunking, listed here are some of the essen-tial points made in this chapter.

1. The frontal lobe is the brain's action/direction cortex, whereas the other three lobes serve as centers of receptive, sensory processing. Said more simply, the frontal lobe specializes in output, while the other three lobes are all about input.

2. The front-most area of the frontal lobe, the PFC, was the last to develop from an evolutionary perspective. The human PFC is proportionally larger than that of all other species, and is the portion of the brain that endows humanity with the capacity for higher order reasoning and compara-tively strong governance of drives and emotions. As Luria (1973) aptly noted, it has served as the "organ of civilization."

3. Some specialists in prefrontal cortical functioning, including Elkhonon Goldberg, have used the analogy of an orchestra's conductor in describ-ing the PFC's relationship to the rest of brain (particularly the other cor-tical regions). Applying this analogy, the other structures become the various instrumentalists in the band, each with its own processing skills and specialties. The PFC, as the director and regulator of cognitive and behavioral action, serves as the conductor of the neurological symphony by leading and coordinating the activity of the other players. Other lead-ership analogies that readily apply would be the commander of an army or the CEO of a corporation.

4. The metacognitive elements of executive function are primarily medi-ated by the dorsolateral (upper and side) portions of the PFC, while the orbital PFC (in collaboration with the anterior cingulate) allows for the self-regulation of emotion and behavior. Although something of an over-simplification, it is generally accurate to note that the metacognitive dif-ficulties of individuals with ADHD involve processing deficiencies in the dorsolateral PFC (and/or its connections with other brain systems), while the hyperactive/impulsive traits of ADHD relate to processing weaknesses in the orbital prefrontal regions (and/or its connections to other regions).

5. Although the PFC is the primary brain region associated with executive function, it is by no means the only neurological system that affects at-tention and self-regulation. Brain scan studies have revealed the sub-stantial role played by the cerebellum in coordination of the execution/ implementation of elements of cognition, including executive functions. Research has also highlighted the manner in which the basal ganglia serve the frontal lobes in the top-down direction of behavior. Portions of the parietal lobe have also been implicated in the ability to be aware of (and attend to) yourself in relation to the environment. Finally, as noted,

the RAS plays an essential role in arousing the prefrontal lobes to allow for attention and executive functions.

6. The RAS originates in the brainstem and projects through the thalamus deep into the brain. It serves a vital role as the cortex's excitation and arousal management system, enabling through its connections the workings of the various brain centers. Insufficient activation of the frontal lobes by the RAS is thought to contribute to attention and executive function difficulties, whereas overactivation may result in motor excess (hyperactivity), excessive startle responses, and hypervigilance. It is also important to remember that the RAS helps to illuminate (recall Goldberg's flashlight metaphor) sections of the posterior cortical lobes in which long-term memories are stored.

7. The PFC's ability to lead and direct cognition and behavior is enabled by its marked interconnectivity with other brain systems. The dark side of all these connections, however, is that the PFC is vulnerable to weakness in other regions or in connections between regions. Thus, as Goldberg noted, executive functioning weaknesses may be due to processing deficiencies in the prefrontal cortical regions, but can also be associated with processing problems in other areas of the brain (problems that drag down the action of the PFC).

8. The amygdala, an almond-shaped structure in the medial temporal lobe, is an important source of negative emotions. A primitive neurological structure located in what is often referred to as the *reptilian brain*, the amygdala serves as the trigger of fight-or-flight reactions and can exert major influence over cognition and behavior. The orbital PFC and the anterior cingulate rein in the lower brain's emotion generation center, allowing the inhibition of impulses that might otherwise lead to the expression of considerably higher levels of aggression than our species already exhibits.

CHAPTER 4

Beyond Neuropsychological Testing

What Teachers Should Know About the Assessment of Executive Function

Upon completing this chapter, the reader will be able to

☞ List the range of assessment methods used to assess students' executive function and discuss the comparative strengths and weaknesses of these methods

☞ Describe the essential limitations of most neuropsychological tests of executive function, and indicate why they cannot be relied on to validly reflect students' executive capacity in real-life learning settings

☞ Discuss the roles teachers can and should play in the assessment of students' executive skills

☞ Describe some of the ways in which weakness across several of the executive skill areas may be expressed in students' learning and performance in the classroom

All Hail the Wise and Mighty Test

We live in a test-happy society. We tend to like our concepts objectively defined and tightly measured, so we can know with at least a reasonable degree of confidence, for example, the amount of radon in our basements or cholesterol in our blood vessels. Americans are increasingly data-driven people whose decisions across so many domains of life are determined by that which can be counted or measured. To a large extent, we have become accustomed to the quantification of many of the phenomena that have an impact on our day-to-day existence. Is your car running roughly? No worries. Mechanics are now equipped with a gamut of computerized equipment that can test the engine and often pinpoint the problem. Have a few bare spots on your lawn? Annoying to be sure, but only a phone call is needed to the local cooperative extension or lawn care professional to initiate a diagnostic soil testing process. These days, it seems like there is test for just about every problem life throws at us.

School psychology (not to mention the larger psychoeducational assessment industry) may owe its very existence to society's ongoing use of objective tests. Although recent shifts in practice trends and special education law have encouraged the delay of formal testing until data have been collected regarding children's responses to specific interventions, the belief among educators and parents that struggling learners should be "tested" remains widespread. Our society has become accustomed to a medical perspective of learning and social difficulties, as well as the ready availability of formal and reliable tests for most medical conditions. Therefore, the educational community (and beyond) has long believed that tests can help to shed light on the nature of children's learning weaknesses, just as formal medical tests can identify specific physical pathologies.

Is this assumption correct? For the most part, yes. Although standardized tests have their clear limitations, general intelligence and the majority of psychological processes that underlie academic skills can be reliably and validly assessed using tests readily available to psychologists, in combination with an array of other data sources (Dawson & Guare, 2004). What about the executive functions? Can they be validly assessed by the assortment of neuropsychological tests of executive skill published each year? The answer to this question, as this chapter will hopefully make clear, is largely no. Please note that the position advocated here does not encourage the swift chucking into recycling bins of all formal tests of executive function. They have their uses and can be effectively included in a larger, multidimensional assessment process. The main point, however, is that formal executive functioning tests cannot be relied on as the true or even best indicator of a student's attention and executive functioning profile. Thus, unlike other academic and cognitive difficulties, executive skills weaknesses are often not effectively identified by a one-to-one testing process (Brown, 2006; Dawson & Guare, 2004).

It is important for educators to understand not only the marked limitations of formal tests of executive function, but also the key roles classroom staff can play in the more authentic assessment of students' metacognitive and self-regulatory skills. This chapter considers the range of executive function evaluation techniques, with particular emphasis given to the parts that classroom staff can—and indeed, should—play in the assessment process.

Methods of Assessing Executive Skills

Because of their variety and complexity, the executive skills are among the more difficult elements of human cognition to validly assess. Fortunately, there are an array of evaluation methods that can be employed by school-based teams of educators and clinicians seeking to understand the scope and severity of children's executive functioning difficulties. Used collectively, with emphasis given to what students do in the real world as opposed to more artificial testing settings, these techniques can often tell us a great deal about a student's areas of executive strength and weakness. This section examines the major methods of assessing executive skills, with some discussion given to the potential benefits and limitations of each technique.

A veritable abundance of formal tests of executive skill are available for use by appropriately trained psychologists across school and clinical settings. Most have been designed to assess one or only a narrow band of related executive functions. They are often administered by psychologists in cases in which particular executive skill weaknesses are suspected or as part of a larger battery of executive function measures.

Table 4.1 presents some of the more common types of neuropsychological tests of the executive functions. These tests represent only a fraction of the broader array of tests of executive functions available to psychologists. As the popularity of the executive skill concept has soared across the educational and clinical communities, researchers, clinicians, and publishing companies have jumped eagerly into the executive function test development business. However, the relative profusion of neuropsychological tests of executive functions generally cannot be counted on to validly assess the metacognitive and self-regulatory skills of children and adolescents. Although they have some effective uses, as will be discussed later, their limitations are significant. These limitations should be borne in mind not just by all psychologists using them but also by parents, educators, and physicians—the primary consumers of psychological evaluation reports.

Limitations of Neuropsychological Tests of Executive Function

By far the most significant limitation of virtually all formal tests of executive function is their undetermined ecological validity (Sborbone & Long, 1996). *Ecological validity* refers to the extent to which a test's findings can be considered to have bearing on real-world settings. Standardized tests of academic functioning generally have fairly high external and ecological validity because the reading, math, and written language skills measured by these instruments have strong associations with the academic skills students use in actual learning settings. A child demonstrating very poor oral reading fluency on a standardized measure of oral reading skill, such as the Gray Oral Reading Test, Fourth Edition (GORT-4), is also likely to display significant levels of dysfluency when reading aloud in school and home contexts. Both the examiner and person reading the evaluation report can have confidence that the GORT-4 results generalize well to real-life literacy settings. As Lezak (1995) and Dawson and Guare (2004) concluded, the nature of formal testing environments and the neuropsychological measures of executive function themselves greatly limit the degree to which findings of formal tests of executive capacity can be generalized beyond the testing context. Many psychologists share these concerns, which can be summarized as follows:

- *Executive skill weaknesses are less apt to be shown in one-to-one testing contexts.* The individualized and supportive nature of testing sessions essentially manages the attention, task initiation, and self-monitoring problems

Table 4.1.   Neuropsychological tests of executive function

Type of test	Example	Task structure	Executive skills assessed
Continuous performance tests	Conners' Continuous Performance Test, Second Edition (Conners & MHS Staff, 2000) Test of Variables of Attention (Corman & Kindschi, n.d.)	Most continuous performance tests are computer administered. They generally require students to sustain attention for about 20 minutes to repetitive stimuli flashed on the screen and to press the spacebar (or button) only when specific stimuli are shown.	Goal-directed attention Impulse control
Cancellation tests	Cancellation subtest of the WISC-IV (Wechsler, 2003) Visual Attention subtest of the NEPSY-II (Korkman, Kirk, & Kemp, 2007)	Similar to continuous performance tests, most cancellation tests are paper-pencil tasks that require the student to cross out ("cancel") only certain types of stimuli as quickly as possible in pages crowded with a broader range of stimuli.	Goal-directed attention Impulse control
Color-word interference tests	Stroop Color-Word Interference Test (Golden, 1978)	Require students to rapidly read aloud a series of color names (e.g., red, blue, green, red, green). The catch is that each color name is printed in a color different from the name (e.g., "red" is printed in blue).	Goal-directed attention Set shifting/cognitive flexibility Impulse control
Complex figure drawing tests	Rey Complex Figure Test (Meyers & Meyers, 1995)	Require students to copy with pencil on paper one complex, abstract/ geometric figure.	Visual planning/ organization
Mazes	Elithorn Mazes subtest of the WISC-IV Integrated (Kaplan et al., 2004)	Require subjects to draw lines from starting points inside of a series of increasingly complex mazes to specific ending points.	Visual planning Cognitive flexibility Impulse control
Tower tests	Tower of Hanoi Tower subtest of the NEPSY	Require subjects to reproduce target patterns by moving balls or rings among three towers (pegs) of varying size while adhering to task rules.	Visual planning Visual sequencing Cognitive flexibility
Trail-making tests	Comprehensive Trail Making Test Trail Making subtest of the Delis-Kaplan Executive Function System (Delis, Kaplan, & Kramer, 2001)	Require students to locate and sequentially connect (draw lines between) numbered or lettered dots on a page, with the speed and accuracy of performance monitored by the examiner.	Goal-directed attention Divided attention Visual planning Set shifting

Table 4.1. *(continued)*

Type of test	Example	Task structure	Executive skills assessed
Wisconsin Card Sorting Test (WCST; Grant & Berg, 1993)	WCST WCST 64-Card Version	Requires the sorting of cards on which various colored geometric shapes are printed. The subject is initially directed to sort the cards according to the patterns (concepts) on four stimulus cards, but is then required to alter the sorting concepts at various intervals based solely upon feedback from the examiner about the accuracy of the sorting.	Set shifting Cognitive flexibility Goal-directed attention Working memory skill

Key: WISC-IV, Wechsler Intelligence Scale for Children–Fourth Edition; NEPSY-II, A Developmental Neuropsychological Assessment, Second Edition.

children exhibit in real-world settings. In the highly controlled testing context, the examiner focuses the student to the task at hand, explicitly prompts the beginning and ending of activities, and continuously monitors the child's performance (Dawson & Guare, 2004). In classroom and homework environments, however, children are far more dependent on their own initiation and sustained attention/monitoring and are subject to a far greater array of potential distractions.

- *Most formal tests of executive function are highly structured, predictable, and directed by the examiner.* As Dawson and Guare (2004, p. 12) noted, "the need for planning and organization on the part of the student is reduced, if not in many cases eliminated." The brevity of the tests (several require no more than a few minutes of sustained executive processing) also makes them rather poorly aligned to classroom tasks that require far longer periods of self-directed cognition.

- *The demands of tests of executive skill tend to link poorly to classroom learning and performance.* Many classroom assignments are structured around somewhat ambiguous response formats that require students to make decisions, establish plans, organize materials, and generally direct their own performance over somewhat lengthy periods of time. As Dawson and Guare (2004) indicated, it is open-ended assignment contexts such as these in which executive skills are most in demand. The majority of formal measures of executive skill, however, require a rather narrowly defined response type that might be limited to the pressing of a button, crossing out of figures, or connection of dots. Although successful completion of the Rey Complex Figure Test (RCFT; Meyers & Meyers, 1995; see Figure 4.1) and a 20-page term paper both involve planning and organization, it may be unrealistic to assume that a student's performance on the rather brief and narrowly defined RCFT can be validly generalized to the student's struggles with term paper completion.

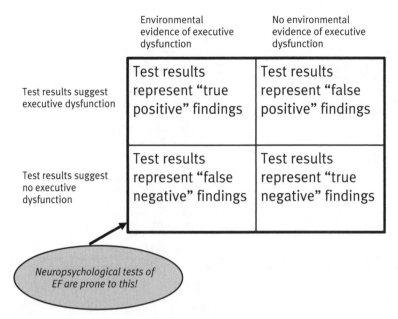

	Environmental evidence of executive dysfunction	No environmental evidence of executive dysfunction
Test results suggest executive dysfunction	Test results represent "true positive" findings	Test results represent "false positive" findings
Test results suggest no executive dysfunction	Test results represent "false negative" findings	Test results represent "true negative" findings

Neuropsychological tests of EF are prone to this!

Figure 4.1. Problems can occur with results of neuropsychological tests of executive functions.

Other problems with neuropsychological tests of executive functions relate less to the tests and more to the interdependent nature of several executive skills (Brown, 2006). For example, attention problems rarely exist in isolation within any child's executive functioning profile, but instead influence and are influenced by a host of other executive functioning difficulties. Real-life learning and social contexts rarely (if ever) require children to use only one or two executive functions, but instead demand the fluid synchrony of a range of executive skills. Actual school settings also elicit a variety of motivational and emotional responses that can substantially affect a student's ability to self-direct cognition and behavior (Meltzer & Krishnan, 2007). Given the complex and interdependent nature of the executive/self-regulatory skills in classroom and playground settings, the logic of examining various executive functions one by one in highly contrived testing contexts seems very much open to question (Brown, 2006).

Viewed together, the limitations of the formal measures of executive function are such that it becomes very difficult to invest much faith in the meaningfulness of their findings outside of individualized testing contexts. It is common, in my experience, for students with unambiguous executive skill struggles in the real world to show little sign of these problems when tested for them, earning average (or at least close to average) scores on formal tests of executive function. Psychologists can interpret these results in one of two ways: 1) that apparent executive function difficulties in classroom settings must be due to something other than genuine executive skills weaknesses, or 2) that many students with substantial executive function difficulties in real-world environments are able to perform well on formal tests of executive function because of the nature of individualized testing and the formal executive function tests themselves. As suggested in the previous discussion, it is the second of these interpretations that is the more compelling. As Dawson and Guare (2004) noted, the "absence of evidence" of executive skill weaknesses reflected in the findings of formal executive function tests cannot be confidently viewed as "evidence of absence" of executive dysfunction. Thus, users of these instruments (and readers of their reports) must bear in mind the relatively strong likelihood of false-negative results—findings that fail to identify executive weaknesses in one-to-one testing contexts that are clearly apparent in classrooms and other real-world settings (see Figure 4.1).

Despite the clear limitations of available neuropsychological tests of executive function, they should not be considered entirely useless and avoided altogether. Although problematic for all the aforementioned reasons, the tests have some value. They provide trained examiners with up-close observations of executive dysfunction—if the student's executive functioning difficulties are actually exhibited in one-to-one testing settings. In other words, when children's profiles of executive dysfunction are such that they exhibit obvious executive skills deficiencies in individualized testing contexts, the neuropsychological tests of executive function allow observations to be made of performance patterns that may have relevance to classroom functioning (Dawson & Guare, 2004). The quantitative results (i.e., standard scores) can also be helpful in these cases because they may help to confirm or even clarify the nature of the executive skill struggles shown in home and school environments. However, when there is a clear mismatch between a child's executive functioning in real-life settings and performance on the formal tests of executive function, the clinical value of the test results plummet.

Because neuropsychological tests cannot be consistently relied on to reveal the scope and severity of a student's executive difficulties, it is essential for systematic evaluations of executive skill to obtain data from a variety of sources (Barkley & Edwards, 2006; Chaytor, Schmitter-Edgecombe, & Burr, 2006; Gioia, Isquith, Guy, & Kenworthy, 2000). The next sections examine the executive function assessment methods that are considered to be externally and ecologically valid and therefore produce data that can be linked to the intervention process.

Interviews and Case Reviews

Among the most helpful ways of assessing children's executive skills is to talk not just to children about their executive strengths and weaknesses, but also to their parents and teachers (Barkley & Edwards, 2006). Although interview data must be interpreted with caution because of the subjective bias of all interviewees (Parry & Drogin, 2007; Somers-Flanagan & Somers-Flanagan, 2002), much can be gained by talking directly to children, as well as to those who raise and educate them. Indeed, of all the data generated by a systematic evaluation process, information obtained from questions about students' past and present functioning is among the most helpful in identifying the scope/severity of their executive struggles and then linking the profile to related interventions. Systematic interviews are also great ways to study the goodness of fit between children's executive skill sets and the classroom and social environments in which they must operate. The semistructured interviews that I recommend for use with students, parents, and teachers in assessing executive skills are provided in Appendixes 4.1–4.3. Clinicians and educators who are adequately trained to conduct clinical interviews should feel free to photocopy and use these interview formats. Please note, however, that these interviews reflect only the subset of questions related to executive function that should be put to students, parents, and teachers as part of a comprehensive evaluation process.

Rating Scales

Standardized behavior rating scales are another method of collecting information about executive functioning from the student, as well as from parents and teachers. Unlike interviews, which are generally unstructured (i.e., the examiner asks whatever questions seem fitting) or semistructured (i.e., the examiner follows a preset list of items or questions, but may also ask follow-up questions and can change the order as necessary), rating scales are standardized. The printed surveys allow for the computation of standard scores (i.e., scores reflecting a comparison of a student's executive functioning profile to national developmental norms).

The strengths of these scales include their ease of use and ability to quantify the scope and severity of a student's executive skill weaknesses relative what is considered typical for large groups of peers from around the country. The downside of the behavior rating scales relates primarily to their vulnerability to subjective bias (Hinshaw & Nigg, 1999). Although all published scales are constructed to fairly high levels of psychometric rigor, some of the items are vaguely worded and are therefore subject to responder biases and interpretations. The rating scale systems most commonly used by school psychologists to assess executive function include the following:

- Behavior Rating Inventory of Executive Function (BRIEF; Gioia et al., 2000). As its title reflects, the BRIEF is entirely devoted to the assessment of executive function and is available in student, parent, and teacher forms. Standardized on samples of children age 5–16 years, the parent and teacher forms ask respondents to rate, on a 3-point scale, how often a child performs each of 86 items associated with a range of metacognitive and self-regulatory executive functions. The student form of the BRIEF is similar and asks older children and adolescents (age 11–18 years) to rate on the same 3-point scale how often they perform 80 behaviors related to the core executive skills.

- Behavior Assessment System for Children, Second Edition (BASC-2; Reynolds & Kamphaus, 2004) is a broadband rating scale system that also includes parent, teacher, and student self-report versions. Unlike the BRIEF, which focuses exclusively on the executive functions, the BASC-2 also asks respondents to rate a student's abilities/tendencies across domains of behavioral, emotional, and adaptive behavior functioning. In addition to assessing the traditional symptoms of attention-deficit/hyperactivity disorder (ADHD), this instrument also examines other aspects of a student's executive functioning including adaptability, anger/emotion control, and social skills. The parent and teacher versions also include a content area subscale made up of items related to planning, self-maintenance of goal-directed activity, and the ability to respond appropriately to environmental feedback.

- Brown Attention Deficit Disorder Scales (BADDS; Brown, 1996). The BADDS was designed to extend rating scale assessments of ADHD symptoms beyond the traditional domains of attention and hyperactivity to executive difficulties that might be less apparent. There are now child, adolescent, and adult versions of this instrument, all of which are structured around the six executive function clusters that make up Brown's theory of ADHD: organizing, prioritizing, and activating to work; focusing, sustaining, and shifting attention to tasks; regulating alertness, sustaining effort, and processing speed; managing frustration and modulating emotions; utilizing working memory and accessing recall; and monitoring and self-regulating action (Brown, 2005).

Classroom Observations

Nothing is quite like watching children's executive skills in action in the settings in which executive functions have greatest importance. Although the developers of formal tests of executive function make claims about their instruments' ability to study elements of self-directed cognition in one-to-one testing contexts, it is often only when we carefully watch youngsters in real-life situations that we are afforded a true sense of the scope and severity of their executive struggles, as well as the learning and social settings that trigger these difficulties (McIntosh, Vaughn, Schumm, Haager, & Okhee, 1993). Classroom observations (regardless of who conducts them) are most effective when the observer keeps the following questions in mind:

1. What does the observed behavior imply about the target child's areas of comparative strength and weakness?

2. How good is the fit (match) between the child's profile of comparative strengths and weaknesses and setting in which the observation occurs?

3. What does a child's behavior in a particular setting reflect about what he or she needs to learn in order to be more functional in the setting?

4. How might the setting be changed (via accommodations and modifications) to be better linked to the child's profile?

By focusing on these questions while observing students, you can look beyond the fairly simple question of what a child is doing (or not doing) in given school contexts to the range of strategies that might address the difficulties he or she exhibits; that is, you can expand your mindset from the more limited perspective of data gathering to the more productive mindset of problem solving.

One does not need to be a psychologist to observe and try to pinpoint a child's executive function difficulties and the settings in which they cause particular challenge. Although the considerable cognitive and logistical demands of teaching can make it hard to devote much time to the careful watching of any one student, the sheer amount of hours teachers spend with their charges across the year in real-life academic and social contexts provides them with a rich and valid data set from which conclusions can be drawn about executive function profiles. If knowledgeable about executive skills and their impact on academic and social functioning, teachers, in collaboration with school-based clinicians and parents, can be highly instrumental in developing intervention strategies that really help students do better across settings.

Table 4.2 lists several of the metacognitive and emotional/self-regulatory executive functions, as well as some of the behaviors students might exhibit if their executive function profiles include difficulties in these areas. Naturally, this list of possible problem behaviors is far from comprehensive; it is meant to only provide a sampling of the types of struggles students might show across the various executive function subdomains. The reader is also cautioned to bear in mind, as was noted earlier in this chapter, that a child's executive functioning profile rarely includes only one or two executive skill difficulties, and instead consists of weaknesses across a range of domains that may interact and amplify each other in actual school environments (McCloskey, Perkins, & Diviner, 2009). For example, a fourth-grade boy who consistently alienates himself from peers because of the tendency to barge into others' games and conversations may do so partly as a function of impulse control difficulties, but may also have skill weaknesses with regard to the "reading" of social situations and planning appropriate ways of entering social activities. Many students may struggle with developing such right-of-entry thoughts (e.g., "Maybe I can get myself into this game if I say I'll be the scorekeeper or if I find another person who also wants to play so the teams stay even"). When developing effective problem-solving strategies, it is important to note more than that a child has difficulty with social skills, or even that the social struggles appear related to impulse control and social planning deficits. The specific manner in which these deficits cause difficulties for the student across school settings should be determined.

Work Sample and Performance Reviews

Sometimes the information most helpful in revealing the key elements of a student's academic profile comes not from the pages of formal evaluation reports, but instead from the most direct and ecologically valid source: classroom performance samples (Knight & Yorke, 2003; Leslie & Jett-Simpson, 1997). As many experienced classroom and special education teachers know, if you listen closely to a student's oral reading patterns and take careful note of performance and error patterns across domains of reading comprehension, spelling, written language, and math, there is often a wealth of information that can be mined for clues to the nature of a child's academic struggles. Patterns and profiles of executive dysfunction can also show themselves in work sample reviews.

For example, several years ago a classroom teacher stepped abruptly into my office and slapped on my desk a reading comprehension worksheet page completed that very morning by a student in her class, who I was slated to evaluate the next day. With a look of certainty and triumph in her eyes, the teacher said

> There! If you want to see what's up with Peter [a pseudonym] and his reading, just take a look at his answers on that page! You can see that he got most of the matching parts wrong at the top, not because he didn't know or remember the facts, but because he didn't follow the directions properly and just rushed through it, and didn't line up his arrows to the right answers. Peter's a sweet

Table 4.2. Domain of executive function and behaviors teachers might see

Domain of executive function	Behaviors/tendencies teachers might see
Goal-directed attention	Difficulties sustaining attention in nonpreferred task settings
	Easily distracted by external stimuli (e.g., extraneous noises, other students' comments, items in desk or in classroom)
	Easily distracted by internal stimuli (e.g., stray thoughts, fantasies/daydreams, obsessive interests)
	Requires numerous cues/reminders to remain focused and on-task
	Complains about difficulties sustaining attention (e.g., "My mind keeps wandering," "I can't help thinking about other stuff," "I just can't focus when other people are talking around me")
	Single-word decoding is not problematic, but oral reading fluency characterized by numerous word deletions and changes (difficulties reading connected text)*
	Oral reading fluency also characterized by the tendency to skip whole lines of text without noticing*
	Math error patterns reflective of the tendency to make numerous "careless" errors
	Written work contains numerous "careless" mechanical errors (e.g., misspelling of words the student can spell in isolation)*
Goal setting, decision making, prioritizing	Difficulties identifying long-range goals (e.g., "I have no clue what I want to do after high school")
	Seems "rudderless" and appears to live from moment to moment
	Is highly "field dependent" (behavior is largely determined by what is happening in immediate environment, rather than being inner directed)
	Requires significant support with identifying goals and making decisions about the topics longer-term projects (e.g., "I don't know what to choose")
	Requires significant support with making decisions about class work (e.g., "I never know what to write about in my journal," "I don't know which group to join")
	Seems somewhat lost or aimless in other decision-making contexts such as library time and art
	Struggles with identifying starting places for assignments (e.g., "What should I do first?")
	Often fails to complete work because of difficulties determining the portions/elements of assignments that should be given priority (e.g., spends far too much time on minor details)
Planning, organization, sequencing	Classroom work and homework reflect a consistent lack of planning (student's work reflects the clear tendency to just "wing it" and "fly by the seat of his/her pants")
	Written work lacks a sense of narrative flow and organization (e.g., one random thought after another)
	Significant struggles with planning in assignment contexts in which planning is required (e.g., when outlines must be developed or graphic organizers completed)
	Difficulties managing the details and sequence of assignments, such that the student begins tasks in the middle or at some vaguely defined point rather than logical starting place
	Difficulties breaking larger assignments into smaller, more manageable units
	Student often seems overwhelmed by task demands that, if organized and sequenced, should not be so challenging
	Frequent inability to solve math problems because of difficulties following algorithm steps
	Reading comprehension deficits appear associated with difficulties organizing/sequencing (child remembers the important details but does so in a disjointed, poorly sequenced manner that defeats higher order understanding)

(continued)

Table 4.2. *(continued)*

Domain of executive function	Behaviors/tendencies teachers might see
Task initiation	Difficulties starting tasks across a variety of academic settings (*key question:* If worse in some settings than others, what aspects of the settings in which the child particularly struggles seem poorly aligned to his/her needs?)
	Student often "just sits there" when other students have started working (may know what needs to be done and what he/she wants to do, but can't seem to "get the ball rolling")
	Often completes tasks successfully and well once is given help starting (does fine once he/she gets going, the problem is with "getting off the dime")
Task persistence, problem solving	Starts tasks reasonably well, but often seems to quickly "run out of steam" and stops working
	Appears to fatigue quickly in academic contexts
	Written work may be reasonably well planned and sequenced, but tends to be rather brief ("That's all I can do" or "That's all I can think of")
	Gets adequate amounts of sleep (by parental and self-report), but often seems sleepy or tired in class, particularly in the afternoons (seems more easily "spent" by academic work than peers)
	Needs frequent teacher cues/reminders to keep working
	Is unable to cope independently with even very minor difficulties (appears to have very limited independent problem-solving skills)
	Frequently "shuts down" (stops working) when individualized help is not immediately/consistently available
Time management	Consistently struggles with gauging the amount of time needed to complete tasks (e.g., "I didn't know it would take so long," "I just thought I could do it in one night")
	Requires more time than peers to complete tasks
	Is often surprised to learn about imminent due dates (e.g., "What?! I thought the test was next week?!")
	Can tell time, but never seems to know the time or seems surprised by the time (e.g., "It's 5:00?! Already?!")
Self-monitoring	Written work contains numerous spelling and other mechanical errors
	Written work reflects the tendency to omit small words (e.g., *the, a, is*)
	Expresses a strong reluctance to edit work
	Oral reading fluency characterized by numerous insertions, deletions, and changes
	Oral reading fluency characterized by the tendency to skip whole lines of text without noticing
	Math work contains numerous "careless" errors (e.g., misread signs, failure to accurately regroup)
	Often seems genuinely surprised when told about numerous errors in work
Working memory	Often forgets/unable to follow multiple-step directions
	Often forgets what he or she wants to say after starting talking
	Often forgets the details of reading while reading or soon after finishing
	Is able to answer factual/explicit questions (e.g., *Who? What? Where? When?*), but struggles with recalling more complex details, making predictions, and drawing inferences
	Often appears to forget what he or she is looking for in desk or backpack ("Wait, what was I looking for in here?")
	Lack of writing production related to the tendency to forget ideas or sequences of thoughts soon after writing tasks are started (e.g., "I forget what I wanted to say")
	Spells words well or at least reasonably well in isolation (i.e., spelling test contexts) but makes numerous spelling errors in narrative writing

Table 4.2.   (*continued*)

Domain of executive function	Behaviors/tendencies teachers might see
	Patterns of math errors appear associated with the tendency to forget entirely or incompletely recall algorithms (the procedures/steps need to solve math problems)
Set shifting, adaptability	Expresses marked frustration with changes in schedule or usual routines (e.g., "But we always have computer time at 10:00!!")
	Resists moving from one activity to the next (e.g., "I can't stop this until I'm done!")
	Tends to "get stuck" in phases of assignments or on particular thoughts and resists prompts to move onto other phases
	Has ritualized social habits/roles and resists encouragement to try other things (e.g., "But I'm always the pitcher in kickball!" "But I always sit next to Michael!!")
Impulse control (response inhibition)	Calls out frequently in class
	Often says or does things that he or she quickly regrets
	Often says or does things that embarrass others
	Often acts as if unencumbered by the thought process
	Often denies behavior (e.g., "I didn't do it," "It wasn't me") even when caught in the act
	Often has difficulty explaining why he or she does things (e.g., "I don't know why I threw the book, I just did it")
	Oral reading characterized by the tendency to guess impulsively at words based on the first letter and the tendency to insert words that are not in text
	Math error patterns reflective of the tendency to "leap" quickly to answers without pausing to recall or problem solve
Emotional control	Becomes easily frustrated by situations that would not likely frustrate peers (low frustration threshold)
	Often cries, whines, or expresses frustration in other ways that appear excessive to the situations at hand (low frustration tolerance)
	Becomes easily angered by the behavior of others
	Often becomes verbally and physically aggressive when angered
	Often appears overwhelmed by both positive and negative emotions
	Is generally remorseful after exhibiting anger/aggression

*May also reflect working memory or self-monitoring difficulties.

kid, but he never checks his work before he hands stuff in! When I asked him about it just now, he was surprised he got any of it wrong because he had thought it was so easy. And look at the bottom part. He got most of the facts right, but he blew all the more inferential questions because he didn't think them through. It's like he's only able to keep ideas in his mind for a few seconds before it all blows away into the air.

What this veteran teacher was noting, in essence, was the student's impulsive, poorly self-monitored work patterns, as well as his apparent difficulties in classroom contexts holding directions and content long enough in working memory to process it properly. Given these performance patterns—about which the teacher had a strong degree of confidence—the logical place for us to start in framing interventions for this student was with strategies that 1) helped him to understand and hold onto directions before and during tasks, 2) required him to systematically check the accuracy of his work on his own and then with classroom staff before calling it finished, and 3) assisted him with visualizing and personalizing important content from reading assignments to enable its longer processing in working memory (i.e., making "text-to-self" and "text-to-world" connections; see Chapter 6).

Several of the descriptors in Table 4.2 reflect the kinds of patterns that teachers can pick up from performance and work sample reviews rather than behavioral observations. Chapters 5–7 discuss in more detail the literacy and math error patterns that research, logic, and clinical experience suggest are associated with executive struggles. Using information from these chapters and their own deductive reasoning skills, teachers will be able to look for signs of the influence of the various executive skills on a student's academic difficulties. When children struggle across any academic domain, it is essential to look closely at the specific manifestations of the struggle (e.g., work samples, behaviors, student comments) for indications of where in the course of information processing that breakdowns might be occurring. It is also important to share data and hypotheses about specific children with the learning specialists available in your school; clarification of hypotheses and the development of related strategies often ensue from such discussions. Even if a child is not suspected of having ADHD or some other condition that raises red flags about the quality of his or her executive functioning, it is important to look for the impact of executive challenges on the student's learning. These difficulties frequently co-occur with and can therefore amplify other learning struggles (Barkley, 2006). For example, it is common for children with letter-sound association and related sound-blending weaknesses (i.e., a type of reading disorder commonly known as *phonological dyslexia*) to also experience attention, working memory, and other executive struggles that compound their reading and spelling problems (Dehn, 2008; Willcutt et al., 2001).

By closely watching a child's behavior and studying work samples, you may gain important insights into the scope and severity of the struggles, which may have clear implications for possible intervention strategies (Swicegood, 1994). Careful observation of the student and his or her work samples also allows for the examination of the extent to which instructional settings are linked to the student's learning needs. In Peter's case, it seemed apparent from the work sample review conducted by the teacher that the child's particular executive function profile was poorly aligned to worksheets that included the independent following of written directions and required inferential processing without first helping the student elaborate reading content in working memory.

☞ Case Example

Consider the case of 13-year-old Ricky, a seventh-grade student. Ricky was referred for evaluation in the fall of his seventh grade year after being placed by his parents in a private school for students with learning disabilities. His mother explained that they elected to remove Ricky from the public middle school he had been attending after his grades dropped "to disastrous levels" and he started refusing to attend school. They sought a comprehensive evaluation of his learning and social needs to determine the next steps for Ricky.

Parent Interview/Case History Data

Ricky was the product of an uneventful, full-term pregnancy and normal delivery. All verbal and motor milestones were met on or close to schedule. His mother recalled that although Ricky was somewhat shy in his preschool and early elementary school years, he was also described by teachers as being more easily distracted than most classmates and as having more difficulty "sitting still." As a function of Ricky's social reticence and reported hyperactivity, his parents elected to delay his entrance to kindergarten by a year. Although his shyness continued into his early elementary school years, Ricky had no difficulties making and maintaining friendships.

Ricky's kindergarten and first-grade teachers expressed varying levels of concern about his difficulties sustaining attention, approaching and completing tasks independently, and remaining seated during activities in which this was expected. Because his early reading and writing skills were well below those of most classmates at the start of his first-grade year, Ricky was enrolled in his school's Title I reading program. His mother recalled that although Ricky did not appear to have obvious difficulties learning letter sounds and sight words, "he had a hard time applying this knowledge when he actually needed to read — it was like he was only able to focus on one word at a time and couldn't string the words together." Ricky tended to resist reading and writing tasks throughout his elementary school years, and would often attempt to draw in his literacy journals rather than write in them.

Although Ricky's hyperactivity diminished as he moved into the middle elementary school years, teachers continued to express concerns about his limited attention skills, as well as his difficulties following multiple-step directions and recalling key elements of books and discussions. An initial psychoeducational evaluation conducted by the school district found that although Ricky's phonological processing, word reading, and basic arithmetic skills were close to grade level (and generally commensurate with his intelligence), his reading fluency, comprehension, and written language skills were substantially below grade level. Based on these findings, Ricky was found eligible for special education services as a student with a specific learning disability toward the end of his fourth-grade year.

Despite the resource services he received throughout fifth grade, Ricky continued to perform well below grade level on literacy tasks and expressed considerable resistance when compelled to read or write. He often complained about easily forgetting what he was reading as he was reading (e.g., "Why should I even try if I'm just going to forget it anyway?"). Ricky's academic performance and related frustrations worsened over the course of his first year in middle school. He rarely completed assigned readings, and only completed writing assignments with considerable parent prompting. His mother said, "It was like pulling teeth to get him to get much of anything on paper — he had the ideas and could think things through, but just couldn't get his thinking organized when he tried to write." Ricky complained often to his parents about having to attend resource-room classes.

Teacher Interview Data

Interviews with Ricky's former teachers at the public middle school indicated that although they generally found him to be a polite and cooperative youngster, they were also quite concerned about his distractibility, difficulties following directions, tendency to start tasks incorrectly, and marked reticence to seek help when he needed it. As a group, the teachers expressed particular frustration with Ricky's frequent refusal to attend resource classes.

Ricky's private-school teachers noted his significant difficulties with processing and following directions. One teacher said, "Even if the directions are written down, he'll forget them and have difficulty following them unless reminded about the steps. And if the directions are even somewhat vague, he can really struggle." Teachers also reported his difficulties knowing when to use his academic skills: "It's like he has a really hard time directing his own learning. He's just so passive and reluctant as a learner, unless he has a crystal clear road map to follow." Other specific concerns expressed by the faculty of this school included the variable nature of Ricky's attention across small-group settings (e.g., "You can see him fade in and out a lot") and his marked difficulties with the organizational/sequencing aspects of the writing process. With regard to reading, the teachers reported that although Ricky's single-word decoding skills were reasonably strong, his oral reading fluency remained "balky" and his comprehension was characterized by significant difficulties drawing inferences. One teacher stated, "Ricky tends to respond to questions in a literal and concrete manner, and has a hard time grasping the big picture."

Student Interview Data

Ricky noted that although he clearly missed his friends and the greater variety of athletic and social opportunities at his old school, he was happier with the level of individual support he was receiving in the smaller private-school setting. He emphasized the embarrassment he often experienced in the public middle school when teachers would attempt to provide him with individual help in larger class setting and when he was compelled to attend resource classes. Ricky readily admitted to being easily distracted by the activities of others: "If other kids are talking around me in class and I'm supposed to work—forget it." He also stressed his difficulties remembering things when he was reading and writing: "It's just really hard for me to think about the stuff I'm reading while I'm reading it and so I don't."

Ricky described reading as boring, and noted generally avoiding books at home unless his parents really compelled him to read: "And so then I'll try and pick up books about things I'm interested in, but even then I'll usually stop after only a few minutes." Ricky noted that although he could be a better writer if he tried harder, he found most written language tasks to be highly tedious and overwhelming: "They're just too much for me. I can't get my thoughts organized and I just can't face it, and so I don't do it." He denied significant difficulties with organizing and keeping track of materials, and noted that his organizational difficulties were limited to the task level, "like with how to do things."

Classroom Observation Summary

Ricky was observed in two contexts as part of this evaluation process. In the first, he and three other students in the school's writing lab edited brief essays they had written on computers. The second observation took place in a language arts class in which the six students in the class took turns reading aloud from the same text and then discussed a series of teacher-directed comprehension questions. Although he sighed every few several seconds during the editing task (as if finding the process quite tedious), Ricky seemed consistently on task during the 20-minute writing period. The students were required to edit their work using a systematic editing process (COPS [Capitalization, Organization, Punctuation, Spelling]; see Chapter 7 for description of this and related approaches) before printing their draft and submitting it to the teacher.

Ricky's attention to the task was more variable during the reading and related discussions in the subsequent language arts class. Although he appeared to consistently follow along when the teacher read, he tended to play with his pen or fidget with other small items in his desk when peers were reading. Ricky's oral reading was somewhat more halting and erratic than most classmates, with several small words omitted and some longer words changed. He also read in a fairly rushed manner with little to no inflection or apparent notice of punctuation. Consistent with the teachers' reports, Ricky was generally more successful during the comprehension discussions at answering basic factual questions than those that required a deeper (more inferential) level of processing.

Rating Scale Data

Ricky's responses to the range of self-report scales included in this evaluation process suggested that he viewed himself as a socially competent individual with significant difficulties with attention, impulse control, and working memory. His rating scale responses also reflected a marked antipathy for school in general and literacy tasks in particular. Consistent with his student interview responses, Ricky's responses to the self-report scales reflected a preference for hands-on learning environments to more traditional literacy-based activities. He also rated most items related to academic and generalized anxiety at moderate to strong levels.

Ricky's mother's responses to the parent rating scales characterized him as exhibiting a range of executive function difficulties relative to peer norms, with particular weakness indicated in the areas of working memory, goal-directed attention, and independent task initiation and organization. She tended to place greatest emphasis on her son's difficulties with retaining and following directions, avoiding distractions while working, and organizing/sequencing his thoughts in production contexts. The parent rating scale data also reflected Ricky's longstanding academic anxiety and rather limited frustration tolerance with regard to reading and written language activities.

Faculty from both the public middle school and smaller private school were asked to complete teacher rating scales in this case. Response patterns were similar from both sets of teachers, in that Ricky was consistently described as exhibiting marked struggles with working memory, task organization, attention, task initiation, problem solving, and self-monitoring relative to peer norms. The public school teachers also expressed moderate to more significant concerns about Ricky's anger and frustration in learning contexts. Although the private-school teachers did not note any concerns about Ricky's frustration tolerance or management, they did report the ease with which he became anxious in academic contexts.

Summary of Neuropsychological Test Findings

Ricky's performance on the Wechsler Intelligence Scale for Children, Fourth Edition showed him to be of generally average intelligence, with no obvious weaknesses across domains of verbal or nonverbal cognitive ability. Comparative weakness (standard scores within the low-average range) was indicated on measures auditory working memory (i.e., digit span tests) and visual processing speed (i.e., cancellation tests). His performance across a range of neuropsychological tests of executive function was also not suggestive of significant executive deficits relative to developmental norms. He made no more omission or commission errors on the Conners Continuous Performance Test than would be expected for a boy his age. His performance on the

Comprehensive Trail Making Test was suggestive of some difficulties with divided attention and processing speed, although the obtained standard scores did not fall significantly below the average range.

His responses to the 64-card version of the Wisconsin Card Sort Test resulted in average scores across all measured indices. Ricky exhibited his greatest struggle with the copy phrase of the RCFT; he appeared to have difficulty organizing a strategy to copy the complex figure and employed a somewhat scattered/random part-to-whole approach. The findings of standardized measures of academic achievement were reflective of solidly average word reading, word attack, phonological processing, spelling, and math reasoning skills (i.e., the ability to apply math skills and concepts to the solving of applied problems). Below average ability was indicated in the areas of reading comprehension and written language, although his skills in these areas were actually higher than predicted by parents and classroom staff.

Conclusions

The picture that emerged of Ricky from the summarized data set was of a youngster of generally average intelligence whose considerable academic struggles appeared to be primarily a function of two factors: 1) significant weaknesses across a range of executive function domains, with greatest struggle shown in the areas of working memory, sustained attention, task initiation/organization, problem solving, and frustration tolerance; and 2) academic anxiety and related maladaptive avoidance strategies. Although it is common for students with learning struggles to develop school-related fears, Ricky's particular emotional and personality style was such that he had extremely limited acceptance of his academic difficulties and the remedial supports teachers attempted to provide him in school. Rather than avail himself to the forms of assistance that were available to him in public school, he tended to literally run from them and essentially tried to cope with his academic difficulties by, to use his own words, "not thinking about them."

Although the formal tests of executive function included in this case provided only tepid support for the presence of executive deficits, Ricky's performance in real-life academic settings (including homework contexts) provided unambiguous evidence of significant executive skills weakness relative to developmental norms. His working memory and attention limitations appeared to have particular impact on the development of his literacy skills, inhibiting the acquisition of reading fluency, reading comprehension, and narrative writing abilities. Ricky's relatively slow processing speed (suggested by some of the formal test findings) may have also contributed to his learning struggles.

Recommendations

☞ *Use Demystification to Reduce Anxiety and Increase Engagement*

Ricky's longstanding tendency to run (sometimes literally) from academic interventions was grounded at least in part in marked fears of being globally damaged and impaired. To reduce these anxieties and improve his willingness to engage in remedial activities, a thorough "demystification" of his neurodevelopmental profile was required. Although Ricky showed some insight into the nature of his reading comprehension, writing, and other executive function difficulties, he did not seem to understand the focal nature of these weaknesses and the linkages between his profile and the remedial strategies attempted by school staff. To move beyond the rather negative image he had developed of himself as a student and the maladaptive behavior patterns that accompanied these self-perceptions, it was necessary to demystify Ricky's neuro-development profile and help him recognize his strengths, the limited (as opposed to global) nature of his weaknesses, and the steps he could take to improve his situation.

☞ Develop Specific Academic Goals to Increase Buy-in to the Remedial Process

Children do not want to fail at either school or life. Students with significant learning disabilities often become grounded in maladaptive coping patterns, such as work avoidance, because they come to see failure as inevitable (e.g., "I give up. I'm a total screw-up and I'll never be able to do this"). Once helped through the demystification process to understand the limitations of their weaknesses areas (i.e., to grasp that they are not globally impaired), they are often willing to engage in at least some dis-cussion of the goals they hope to achieve in school and in life. Once framed, these goals then can become the basis for improving students' engagement in the problem-solving, as opposed to the problem-avoiding, process.

☞ Explicitly Teach More Adaptive Ways
of Coping with Academic Stress and Anxiety

Among the several benefits of demystification is that it tends to help students under-stand how their maladaptive coping strategies — such as avoidance, aggression, and carelessly rushing through work — only compound their academic difficulties. Once Ricky was helped to grasp the nature of his neurodevelopmental profile and establish realistic goals, the next step was to teach him ways of coping with academic stress and frustration that would allow the achievement of his goals, which in this case cen-tered on the returning to a regular high school and earning strong enough grades to allow him to play sports. The more adaptive strategies in this case were structured around his regular participation in daily executive skills coaching sessions (see Chap-ter 9 for a discussion of this approach) and after-school remedial sessions.

☞ Use Daily Guided Oral Reading Practice and Silent Reading Practice

Given the impact of Ricky's oral and silent reading dysfluency on his engagement with and comprehension of required reading materials, it was essential for his remedial program to include daily guided oral and silent reading practice sessions. Chapter 6 discusses the importance of building the fluency with which children with executive functioning weakness read text to improve their comprehension. Research and clinical experience has shown that among the most effective ways of building fluency is to provide students with frequent guided oral reading practice sessions (National Read-ing Panel report; National Institute of Child Health and Human Development, 2000).

☞ Teach Strategic Reading

Ricky, like many students with his profile, tended to read in a rather passive manner, with whatever cognitive energy he might invest being directed to the act of decoding. While fluency-building techniques like guided oral reading sessions tend to have the added benefit of improving comprehension, many students with executive weakness often struggle with comprehension by virtue of their attention/working memory deficits (Dehn, 2008) and related passive reading style (Brown, 2006). Chapter 6 discusses this phenomenon, as well as the importance of explicitly teaching students like Ricky to approach and execute reading tasks in a strategic manner. Before-reading strate-gies such as goal setting, during-reading techniques such as visualizing and question-ing the author, and after-reading approaches such as summarization can be powerful ways to build the cognitive activation with which students with executive dysfunction engage in the reading process.

☞ *Provide Instructional Scaffolds to Diminish*
the Demands Placed by Writing Assignments

No academic task places greater stress on the brain's executive systems than writing. Good writing is dependent on a host of executive skills, including the ability to structure/plan thoughts, hold writing plans in working memory while they are being followed, and monitor the accuracy and quality of what is placed on paper. (Chapter 7 discusses the relationship between written language and executive function in more detail.) Ricky's written language struggles were typical of many adolescents with marked executive function weakness, making him in clear need of organizational and monitoring scaffolds (see Chapter 7).

☞ *Provide Individualized Executive Skills Coaching*

While it remains common in high schools across the country to structure services for students with executive function weakness around study skills (i.e., academic support classes), secondary students may respond better to more individualized executive skills coaching interventions. Chapter 9 discusses this approach and some best practice methods of implementing it. Ricky's executive skill profile included enough general struggles with task and materials organization, study skills, and assignment completion that he was likely to benefit from the opportunity to meet on a daily basis with a teacher or school-based clinician who would monitor and coach his executive functioning.

☞ *Provide Daily, Systematic Home-School Communication*

Among the factors that contributed to Ricky's worsening tendency to complete assignments in the regular school setting was the lack of communication between his teachers and parents regarding what he had not done. Progress reports were only sent home every few weeks, allowing Ricky to "game the system" by telling his parents that he was keeping up with his work while telling his teachers that he was "almost ready" to turn in assignments (the student equivalent of, "The check is in the mail"). To improve Ricky's work completion and studying upon his return to the regular school setting, it was imperative for his work completion habits and other elements of performance to be funneled by teachers on a weekly (and sometimes daily) basis through the executive skills coach. This communication was bidirectional, allowing his parents to share their impressions and concerns with the teachers, through the coach, just about every day. While such close home–school linkage regarding work completion and test preparation is far from a panacea, it tends to give children with executive deficits far less "wiggle room" in which to practice maladaptive coping strategies. See Chapter 9 for a discussion of the forms and procedures that can be highly effective in supporting the assignment planning and completion of this population across home and school contexts.

Executive Functioning
Semistructured Interview

Parent Version

For each item, the parent should respond with the extent to which the child exhibits the behavior by using the following response choices:

- *not a problem* (the child rarely shows this behavior or does so at levels that seem typical for his or her age)
- *mild problem* (the child shows the behavior more than most children his or her age seem to, but not to such a degree that it has been an obvious problem)
- *moderate problem* (the child clearly shows the behavior, but with parent and/or teacher support the behavior/issue has been generally manageable)
- *definite problem* (the child clearly shows the behavior and it remains a serious problem even with parent and/or teacher support)
- *unsure/don't know*

Goal setting, decision making, and planning

Item	Parent's response	Details
Avoids or has difficulty making decisions about the topic or content of school projects		
Avoids or has difficulty setting personal goals regarding school achievement and/or other important activities (i.e., improvement of athletic or artistic skills)		
Seems to live from "moment to moment," without setting goals or making plans		
Avoids or has difficulty developing clear goals/plans for writing assignments, or fails to follow these plans when writing (tends to just "wing it" and hopes things will turn out okay)		
Avoids or has difficulty developing clear plans for longer-term projects		
Avoids or has difficulty developing plans to manage other fairly complex tasks (e.g., if asked to clean out garage or basement, will just start anywhere and continue to work in a random manner)		

(continued)

Attention, task initiation, self-monitoring

Item	Parent's response	Details
Is easily distracted in non-preferred tasks situations (e.g., homework and chores)		
Needs numerous prompts/cues from adults to remain focused ("on task") in non-preferred task situations		
Struggles with sustaining attention while reading (finds most reading tasks "boring")		
Requires numerous prompts from parent in order to *start* homework and other non-preferred projects		
Requires numerous prompts/cues from parent in order to *complete* homework		
Works in a rushed, seemingly careless manner on homework assignments and chores		
Becomes bogged down during homework and chores by seemingly minor difficulties (just can't seem to solve problems on his or her own)		
Appears to pay little attention to the quality/accuracy of work and is often unaware of errors		
Requires frequent prompts and reminders from parent in order to complete chores		

Materials organization

Item	Parent's response	Details
School backpack and notebooks/binders are poorly organized and generally messy		
Struggles with keeping track of materials needed for school/homework each day		
Desk and/or other homework areas are poorly organized and generally messy		
Bedroom and personal possessions in a state of disarray		

Time management

Item	Parent's response	Details
Does not set aside sufficient time to complete daily home-work assignments		
Does not set aside sufficient time to complete longer-term projects		
Rarely completes daily home-work and longer-term projects in a timely manner		
Rarely arrives on-time for school and other important activities		

Working memory

Item	Parent's response	Details
Frequently unable to follow multiple-step directions (e.g., "Go upstairs, put your dirty clothes in the hamper, take a shower, and then call me when you're done")		
Forgets to do things such as turning off lights after leaving room, closing doors that should closed, wiping feet when coming inside, and so forth.		
Forgets various details of non-preferred tasks (e.g., if cleaning bedroom, forgets to put away all the things he or she was told to put away)		
Forgets the directions for daily homework assignments (or needs frequent reminders of directions)		
Struggles with recalling what he or she is trying to say while talking (frequently "losing train of thought," says "I forgot what I was going to say")		
Struggles with recalling/ keeping track of intended ideas for writing assignments while writing (e.g., frequently complains about forgetting what he or she wanted to say)		

(continued)

Working memory *(continued)*

Item	Parent's response	Details
Struggles with recalling the content of what he or she reads during and after reading (seems to quickly forget essential details and main ideas)		

Impulse and emotional control

Item	Parent's response	Details
Does things impulsively (without stopping and thinking) that he or she quickly comes to regret		
Struggles with waiting turn in conversations and often interrupts others' conversations		
Struggles with waiting turn in games		
Says things impulsively that embarrass or upset others		
Rushes into and through homework assignments and projects without giving adequate consideration to the instructions		
Tends to injure self or others because of impulsive action (failure to think adequately about a situation before acting)		
Becomes very frustrated by events/situations that would not likely frustrate others to the same degree (has a low frustration threshold)		
Overreacts when frustrated, saying or doing things that result in significant difficulty for self or others (low frustration tolerance)		
Becomes easily and significantly angered by the behavior of others		
Lashes out verbally or physically at others when angered		

Set shifting/adaptability

Item	Parent's response	Details
Insists on things being "perfect" or a certain way, and will resist prompts to move on		
Gets "stuck" on certain parts of tasks and resists moving on		
Reacts with significant frustration to changes in routine and unplanned events		
Reacts with significant frustration, sadness, or anger to disappointments		
Requires lots of support and cuing to get ready for school in the morning and bed at night		
Requires significant support and cueing to transition from preferred activities (e.g., playing or TV) to required activities (e.g., mealtimes and homework)		

With what tasks/types of assignments is your child more likely to succeed?	Why?

With what tasks/types of assignments is your child more likely to experience difficulty?	Why?

What strategies/interventions have helped your child?	How much?

Executive Functioning
Semistructured Interview

Student Version

For each of the items read, students should respond that the item is

- *definitely true* about them
- *sort of true* about them
- *usually not true* about them
- *unsure/don't know*

Goal setting, decision making, and planning

Item	Student's response	Details
It's hard for me to make decisions about school assignments (e.g., deciding what to write about or what kind of project to do).		
I usually don't set personal goals for myself about school-work or other important things. I usually just kind of live day-to-day and moment to moment, rather than following goals.		
I don't make plans or follow plans for writing assignments and projects. Instead, I usually just want to get it done as fast as possible and so just sort of begin and hope for the best.		
I usually don't study for tests, or if I do, I study in a fairly random, unplanned manner.		
I usually don't make plans before beginning chores and other tasks at home. Example: *If your Mom or Dad asked you to clean out the garage or rake up all the leaves in the yard, would you first make a plan about how to do it, or would you just start anywhere?*		

Attention, task initiation, self-monitoring

Item	Student's response	Details
I'm easily distracted in class.		
I'm easily distracted when doing homework.		
I need lots of reminders from my teacher(s) to pay attention or stay on-task in class and from my parent(s) to stay on-task during homework.		

Attention, task initiation, self-monitoring *(continued)*

Item	Student's response	Details
I have a hard time getting started on schoolwork, home-work, and studying for tests. It's like I just can't get myself to sit down and do it.		
I need lots of reminders from my teacher(s) and parent(s) to get started on my work.		
I usually find reading to be very boring and my mind wanders a lot when I read.		
I usually begin schoolwork or homework okay but have a hard time finishing.		
I try and rush through things like schoolwork, homework, and chores to get them done as soon as possible.		
I usually don't check the quality of my work as I work. I just try and get it done as quickly as possible.		
I usually have lots of problems with schoolwork and home-work and need someone close by to help me with them (other-wise I usually stop working).		

Materials organization

Item	Student's response	Details
My school backpack and note-books/binders are usually very messy and unorganized.		
I often can't find the things I need for schoolwork and homework.		
My desk at home (or other homework area/materials) is usually really messy and unorganized.		
My bedroom and most of my stuff at home is usually very messy and unorganized.		

(continued)

Time management

Item	Student's response	Details
I usually don't get my work done on time at school.		
I usually don't get my projects done on time for school.		
It takes me a really long time to get homework and chores done.		
I'm often late for school and other important activities.		
It's hard for me to figure out how long it will take to get things done.		

Working memory

Item	Student's response	Details
I usually can't remember and follow more than one direction at a time.		
I usually forget to do parts of the things I'm working on, and adults have to remind me about the things I forgot.		
I forget the directions for school work and have to be reminded a lot of what to do.		
I forget what I want to say a lot when I'm talking (I'll lose track of my thoughts).		
I forget what I want to say when I start to write or when I'm writing (it's like my mind goes blank and I can't think of my ideas).		
I usually can't remember what I'm reading while I read or soon after I read.		
Math can be hard for me because I forget the steps I'm supposed to take to solve the problems when I'm doing them.		

Impulse and emotional control

Item	Student's response	Details
I say or do things a lot without really thinking about them first.		
I interrupt people a lot when they're talking.		
I have a hard time waiting for my turn in games and also in conversations.		
I say things that later on I wish I hadn't said (because I ended up embarrassing myself or someone else).		
I often start assignments the wrong way or do whole assignments wrong because I didn't take the time to really understand the directions.		
I end up accidentally hurting myself or others because I do things without thinking or paying attention.		
I tend to get easily frustrated by things that other people may not find so frustrating.		
I tend to really overreact a lot when I'm angry or frustrated and say or do things I later regret.		
I get angry really easily.		
I hit or do other aggressive things when I'm angry or frustrated.		
I have a really hard time thinking when I'm mad or frustrated. It's like my emotions just take over.		

Set shifting/adaptability

Item	Student's response	Details
I like things to be a certain way when I'm doing schoolwork or other activities and don't like being made to move on until it's right.		

(continued)

Set shifting/adaptability *(continued)*

Item	Student's response	Details
I get stuck a lot on things when I'm working and need help before I can move on.		
I don't like changes in my usual routines and schedules (I get really frustrated when this happens).		
I usually don't handle disappointments well. I get very sad or angry when good things I expect to happen end up not happening.		
I usually need a lot of help from my parents to stop doing what I'm doing and get ready for bed.		
My parent(s) usually have to call me and remind me a lot before I come to dinner and other meals.		
I have a really hard time stopping what I'm doing and then starting something else when someone says I have to.		

Are there types of schoolwork that you like best or tend to do best on?	*Why?*

What types of schoolwork do you like least or tend to give you greatest difficulty?	*Why?*

What kinds of strategies might help you do better in school?	*Why?*

Executive Functioning
Semistructured Interview

Teacher Version

For each item, the teacher should respond with the extent to which the student exhibits the behavior by using the following response choices:

- *not a problem* (the child rarely shows this behavior or does so at levels that seem typical for his or her age)
- *mild problem* (the child shows the behavior more than most kids his or her age seem to, but not to such a degree that it has been an obvious problem)
- *moderate problem* (the child clearly shows the behavior, but with parent and/or teacher support the behavior/issue has been generally manageable)
- *definite problem* (the child clearly shows the behavior and it remains a serious problem even with parent and/or teacher support)
- *unsure/don't know.*

Goal setting, decision making, and planning

Item	Teacher's response	Details
Avoids or has difficulty making decisions about the topic or content of school projects		
Seems indecisive about how to begin assignments and needs help making decisions and formulating plans for assign-ment completion		
Seems to live from "moment to moment," without setting goals or making plans		
Avoids or has difficulty devel-oping clear goals/plans for writing assignments, or fails to follow these plans when writing (tends to just "wing it" and hopes things will turn out okay)		
Avoids or has difficulty devel-oping plans for longer-term projects		
Avoids or has difficulty with breaking assignments down into smaller parts		
Becomes "lost" in assignments or stops working because of a failure to adequately plan beforehand		
Avoids or has difficulty using strategies when beginning or completing assignments		

(continued)

Attention, task initiation, self-monitoring

Item	Teacher's response	Details
Is easily distracted during independent seatwork		
Is easily distracted during larger group activities (e.g., lectures, classroom discussions, "read alouds")		
Needs numerous prompts/cues from classroom staff to remain focused in nonpreferred task situations		
Struggles with sustaining attention while reading (finds most reading tasks "boring")		
Requires numerous prompts/cues in order to *start* assignments		
Requires numerous prompts/cues in order to *complete* assignments		
Particularly resists engaging in writing tasks		
Works in a rushed, seemingly careless manner on assignments		
Becomes bogged down during assignments in class by seemingly minor difficulties (just can't seem to solve problems on his or her own)		
Appears to pay little attention to the quality/accuracy of work and is often unaware of errors		

Materials organization

Item	Teacher's response	Details
School backpack and notebooks/binders are poorly organized and generally messy		
Desk and locker are poorly organized and generally messy		
Struggles with keeping track of materials needed for class work each day		

Materials organization *(continued)*

Item	Teacher's response	Details
Loses track of important personal items (e.g., gloves, hats, money, notes to/from parent)		

Time management

Item	Teacher's response	Details
Does not complete seatwork assignments within allotted time periods		
Does not set aside sufficient time to complete longer-term projects		
Struggles with estimating amount of time needed to complete tasks		
Avoids or has difficulty adhering to project timelines		
Does not complete or submit daily homework in a timely manner		
Arrives late to school and other important activities		

Working memory

Item	Teacher's response	Details
Unable to follow multiple-step directions		
Needs to have directions or other information repeated		
Forgets or confuses details/steps of instructions, resulting in assignments being started or completed incorrectly		
Forgets or appears confused by classroom routines and procedures		
Struggles with recalling what he or she is trying to say while talking (frequently "losing train of thought," says "I forgot what I was going to say")		

(continued)

Working memory *(continued)*

Item	Teacher's response	Details
Struggles with recalling/ keeping track of intended ideas for writing assignments while writing (e.g., frequently complains about forgetting what he or she wanted to say)		
Struggles with recalling the content of what he or she reads during and after reading (seems to quickly forget essential details and main ideas)		
Forgets to bring important items to and from school ("I knew I needed that, but I forgot to bring it")		

Impulse and emotional control

Item	Teacher's response	Details
Does things impulsively (without stopping and thinking)		
Struggles with waiting turn in conversations and often interrupts others' conversations		
Struggles with waiting turn in games		
Calls out in class		
Says things impulsively that embarrass or upset others		
Rushes into and through seatwork and projects without giving adequate consideration to the instructions		
Tends to injure self or others because of impulsive/ unthinking action		
Becomes very frustrated by events/situations that would not likely frustrate others to the same degree (low frustration threshold)		
Overreacts when frustrated, saying or doing things that result in significant difficulty for self or others (low frustration tolerance)		

Impulse and emotional control *(continued)*

Item	Teacher's response	Details
Becomes easily and significantly angered by the behavior of others		
Lashes out verbally or physically at others when angered		
Makes noises of various sorts in random, impulsive ways		
Fidgets with hands and small objects		
Has difficulties sitting still or remaining in one place (appears to need to be in motion)		

Set shifting/adaptability

Item	Teacher's response	Details
Insists on things being "perfect" or a certain way, and resists prompts to move on		
Becomes "stuck" on certain parts of tasks and resists moving on		
Reacts with significant frustration to changes in routine and unplanned events		
Reacts with significant frustration, sadness, or anger to disappointments		
Requires lots of support and cueing to get ready for school in the morning and bed at night		
Requires lots of support and cuing to transition from preferred activities (e.g., playing or TV) to required activities (e.g., mealtimes and homework).		

(continued)

With what tasks/types of assignments is this student more likely to succeed?	Why?
With what tasks/types of assignments is this student more likely to experience difficulty?	Why?
What strategies/interventions have been effective with this student?	How much?

CHAPTER 5

Moving the Frontal Lobe to the Front of the Class

Seven Core Strategies for Helping Students with Executive Function Challenges

---

Upon completing this chapter, the reader will be able to

☞ Discuss the idea of setting dependency as it relates to the expression of executive function difficulties

☞ Discuss the concept of surrogate frontal lobe and its importance in teaching and supporting students with executive dysfunction

☞ List the seven core strategies for helping students with executive function challenges, discuss the examples provided for each core strategy, and consider situations in teaching that relate to these examples

☞ Consider the extent to which one's teaching and classroom structure exemplifies the core strategies

☞ Discuss the steps that might be taken to make one's teaching and classroom structure more aligned with the core strategies

---

Toward Frontal Lobe–Friendly Classrooms

Students with significant learning and behavioral difficulties often perform better in some classes than others, and this is not just referring to the fairly obvious distinction between a student's behavior in regular education settings versus smaller group remedial contexts. For reasons that are not always apparent, elementary school students with severe social and emotional challenges will sometimes have entire years during which their behavior and performance are much better than they typically show. At the secondary level, the phenomenon may take the form of the student doing well in one or two classes while falling apart (or making life an utter misery for everyone else) in all other subjects. Here, for example, are the kinds of comments I often hear when sitting down with a group of middle school teachers to discuss a student's latest behavioral escapades:

Teacher A: This kid's a holy—no, make that unholy—terror in my class on a daily basis. He calls out constantly, interrupts me while I'm trying to teach, mocks the efforts of other kids, refuses to focus on what we're doing in the room, and won't do a lick of work.

Teacher B: Ditto for me, and I have him in two classes! When I call him on the behavior, he just blows up and I've got to take a huge chunk of time to either settle him down again or get him out of the room. I've lost count of the number of times I've sent him to guidance or the office. He knows I'm not putting up with the nonsense anymore.

Teacher C: Wow. I guess I'm the lucky one here. Sometimes he shows the kind of behavior in my room that you guys are talking about (like when I do a pop quiz or something like that), but most of the time he's really been okay. I think part of it is that he likes math and gets to do the homework for my class in the supervised study block he has with me right after. That allows him to be caught up with the work most of the time. Also, he's in the class in which I've really tried to slow things down. I'm picking fewer battles with this group topic-wise, so I can spread the teaching out and give the kids lots of practice time.

An essential truth about executive function is that different profiles of executive dysfunction are not equally problematic in all settings (Brown, 2002). In other words, the functional impact of various executive function weaknesses is setting dependent. It can be expected that students will perform reasonably well in those learning and social environments that are reasonably matched to their executive skills and other abilities. The converse, of course, is also true. In those academic and social contexts that are poorly aligned to a student's executive functioning needs (that demand, for example, far greater cognitive flexibility, goal-directed attention, and working memory capacity than the student possesses), problems will likely result (McCloskey, Perkins, & Diviner, 2009). While it is difficult—indeed, impossible—for teachers to consistently match their classroom structure and instruction to the broad constellation of executive function profiles that they encounter, much can be done to make classrooms and assignments as frontal lobe–friendly as possible.

This chapter discusses some core prevention and intervention strategies. If applied to the degree practical in the context of heavy teaching loads and the blizzard of other responsibilities faced by contemporary educators, these strategies can contribute to classrooms that are reasonably well linked to the needs of children with a host of executive skill weaknesses. Each strategy is illustrated with concrete instructional or social examples, as well as a brief case discussion. The intervention approaches specific to reading, writing, mathematics, planning/organization, and social functioning that are discussed in the remainder of this book flow largely from the foundational strategies discussed here.

The Core Strategies

Strategy 1: Provide Children with Executive Function Weaknesses with the "Surrogate Prefrontal Lobe" Support They Need to Succeed

As discussed in Chapter 3, the prefrontal cortical structures that enable the efficient use of executive skills are not fully developed in most individuals until the early adult years. The upshot of this neurological reality is that school-age children direct their learning and social behavior with brain structures that are still very much works in progress (Giedd et al., 1999). All children therefore require adults to do a fair amount of their thinking for them, with a gradual shift toward greater levels of independent cognition and self-regulation occurring over the course of later childhood and adolescence. To ensure children's daily survival and enable whatever levels of academic and social success their neurological profiles allow, adults extend their own "stop-and-think" and problem-solving skills to children until children reach the age at which their regulatory capacity can take over. In essence, parents and teachers provide developing children with the "surrogate prefrontal cortical capacity" needed to help them make it safely to late adolescence (e.g., "No Michael, you and Robert may not spend today's indoor recess period jumping from desk to desk. Why? You'll get hurt, dear, or you'll fall on someone else and they'll be hurt").

Research has consistently shown that children with developmental executive function weakness generally require far greater levels of adult supervision (surrogate frontal lobe support) across the grade span than do their more typically developing peers (Barkley, 1997, 2006). To quote Martha Denckla, a neurologist at the Kennedy Krieger Institute at the Johns Hopkins University School of Medicine who has written extensively about developmental executive function, "*on your own* is a death knell for these kids" (Saltus, 2003). Efforts to build autonomy in students with executive function weaknesses by insisting they perform certain tasks by themselves or with the same levels of independence as their classmates with stronger executive skills tend to backfire, often because they require children do things that are beyond the reach of their current neuropsychological capacity. Therefore, if we expect students with executive weaknesses to perform and behave adequately in school settings, we must do more than simply insist they do so and then punish them when they fail to meet expectations. We need instead to look carefully for children's areas of executive function need (see Chapter 4 for discussions of the teacher's role in the assessment process) and provide the level and duration of surrogate frontal lobe support (e.g., adult supervision, instructional scaffolds, social mentoring) required for success.

Strategy Examples

- Individualized (one-to-one) support with the brainstorming and thought organization/sequencing aspects of the writing process

- Frequent adult monitoring of a child's attention during reading group activities, with attentional prompts (via an agreed upon nonverbal or verbal signal) whenever a child goes off task

- Individualized social mentoring provided in cafeteria and recess settings to diminish the amount of impulsive/aggressive/embarrassing (socially self-penalizing) things a child says to peers

- Visual reminders posted prominently in a student's immediate learning environment (e.g., laminated and taped to the desktop, tacked to walls of the study carrel) that prompt the use of certain reading comprehension or editing strategies

☞ Case Example

Situation: Jonathan, a third grader diagnosed with both attention-deficit/hyperactivity disorder (ADHD) and Tourette syndrome, wants friends desperately. Although he is a good athlete and excels at most playground games, his classmates refuse to let him into their kickball and four-square games due to his tendency to impulsively tease others about their mistakes and "blow up" when things do not go his way. Increasingly alone and angry at recess, Jonathan has taken to hanging around the edges of others' activities and making what the playground aide describes as "snide and nasty comments."

Recommendation: Although Jonathan has the athletic skills to succeed at most playground games and is clearly socially motivated, he lacks the impulse control, frustration management, empathy, and social skills to play appropriately with peers at recess. Given this profile, a reasonable course of action would be for a school-based clinician to provide Jonathan with targeted social skill training structured around role playing of the types of game situations that trigger his impulsive aggression and to also spend some time with him during recess to provide the individualized social mentoring needed in real time (the "surrogate frontal lobe" element of the strategy). Social mentoring (described in more detail in Chapter 10) works best when a trained adult monitors the child from a discrete distance (without hovering, but within earshot), and provides him or her with the cues necessary to result in appropriate social problem solving and avoid socially self-penalizing blow-ups.

Strategy 2: Teach New Skills and Content Systematically and Explicitly

As Goldberg (2001) pointed out, executive functions tend to be taxed to a far greater extent by the new and unknown than by the familiar. When you are engaged in routine tasks and activities (e.g., brushing teeth, folding laundry), the higher order aspects of your cognition are largely unneeded as you proceed without much conscious thought through a habituated series of actions. Your executive skills come heavily into play in novel task situations as you engage in the impulse control, problem solving, self-monitoring, and adaptability needed to successfully negotiate the unknown (Roberts, 2007). As mastery develops, you no longer need to exert as much prefrontal capacity to engage in the activity since your ability to do so has become at least somewhat routine (Berninger & Winn, 2006).

Take, for example, the driving of a stick-shift car. Anyone who has learned to operate a manual transmission will recall the considerable self-regulation needed during the initial learning phase to coordinate the shifting of the gear lever with the manipulation of both the clutch and gas peddles (while simultaneously paying attention to the instrument panel and road, not to mention the fretting sounds emanating from the passenger seat). Once mastery of the manual transmission is obtained, however, little conscious thought needs to be given to shifting. Gear changing then becomes a largely automatic process requiring little involvement from the brain's higher cognitive centers. The same is true for the amount of executive function required of children in new academic task contexts. For example, when students are initially learning the algorithm for long division, they do a lot of self-directed cueing to recall the computation steps and apply them properly. Once the algorithm is mastered to the point of fluency, the executive function demands associated with its use drop considerably.

Because novel learning tasks place a particular load on students' executive skills, it follows that children with developmental executive function weakness are more apt to struggle in unfamiliar task contexts than their peers. Teachers can minimize the confusion these students experience when confronted by the new and unknown by presenting novel skills and content in highly explicit, step-by-step ways that clearly link the unfamiliar to the familiar (e.g., "You already know X and Y, and now this is exactly how the new bit Z fits in"). Clear and repeated modeling of new skills by the teacher can be a powerful method of making the implicit explicit, particularly if the modeling is followed by extended opportunities for students to practice the skills with frequent (and direct) teacher feedback. Kinesthetic learning opportunities, such as role playing, can also be highly effective in making the abstract or fuzzy more concrete and clear. Participants in my workshops for teachers on the neurodevelopmental aspects of learning, for example, have frequently noted on feedback forms that their understanding of functional and interaction among different brain structures is eased by the "neurological role plays" that I build into the sessions. In these brief "theater of the brain" episodes, I invite several audience members to the stage to serve as different bits of neuroanatomy and the connections between the structures, and then I demonstrate the interactions by moving among them. Individuals with executive dysfunction tend to particularly benefit from such explicit instructional experiences because the highly structured nature of the demonstrations makes the new information plain to see and organizes it in such a way that learners are required to do less organization of it for themselves.

Strategy Examples

- Presenting liberal amounts of teacher and peer modeling of an unfamiliar arithmetic algorithm using a box template that explicitly presents the algorithm and its steps (see Chapter 8 for examples), and then having students use the template at their seats to solve a series of similar problems

- Demonstrating the writing of a type of a sonnet several times on an overhead projector using the same poem construction template each time, and then helping the class to write a few sonnets together using the template

(before students are asked to develop poems on their own with the template)

- Teaching new vocabulary by acting out the words and using student volunteers to "perform" the words for the class, and then dividing the students into small groups and having them act out the words in different ways

- Building students' comprehension of a text being read aloud to the class by stopping every several pages and role playing key plot elements. This strategy helps to turn student thoughts about potentially confusing situations/concepts in text from, "I think I know what what's happening here" or "I think I know what they mean" to "Oh, I see—now I get it."

- Providing students with the comprehension questions to be answered before they read a passage as a class, and then stopping to explicitly discuss the answers to the questions (and their importance) as they are revealed by the text

☞ **Case Example**

Lisa, a seventh-grade student of below-average intelligence whose particular profile of executive function weaknesses centers on organizing and sequencing deficits, continues to lag well behind her classmates with regard to developing coherent paragraphs. A review of her writing samples indicates that although her spelling, punctuation, and sentence formation skills are generally intact, she does not grasp the basics of creating and linking paragraphs in essay writing (most of her essays contain one very long paragraph, with thoughts presented in a seemingly random manner).

Based on her profile of writing errors, Lisa appears to be in need of explicit instruction in paragraph construction, as well as lots of guided practice in its use. Among the most effective of all curricula developed for this purpose is *Step Up to Writing, Second Edition* (Auman, 2002). Wonderfully concrete and readily applied across a range of subjects and grade levels, the program uses the metaphor of a traffic light to teach paragraph construction and linkage (see Figure 7.7 for details). With numerous supported opportunities to apply this program across the curriculum, it is likely that Lisa's ability to develop and sequence paragraphs will improve significantly by the end of the year.

Strategy 3: Teach Strategies and Explicitly Demonstrate the Manner in Which They Should Be Applied in Real-Life Learning Contexts

Arguably the most important of all classroom skills influenced by the executive functions is the ability to survey a problem situation and determine the strategies needed to address it. This is why children with executive function weakness tend to appear so "rudderless" relative to their classmates when it comes to approaching academic activities. Even if they know a fair amount about a particular subject before taking a test or trying to write about it, they are apt to stumble through the task because they approach it in a fairly ran-

dom manner (e.g., "Let's just see what happens"). Thus, as Meltzer, Sales Pollica, and Barzillai (2007) noted, students with executive function difficulties
tend to be defeated more often in academic setting by the *how* of the learning
and production process rather than the *what*. Lacking the ability to arrive at
effective learning and production strategies on their own, they tend to benefit from explicit teaching of strategies that can be applied across a range of
academic situations (Dawson & Guare, 2004), such as systematic note taking,
studying for tests, organizing/sequencing thoughts for writing assignments,
recalling/comprehending reading content, and organizing learning materials.
Although far from a panacea, systematic strategy instruction in these areas can
help to meet the "surrogate frontal lobe" needs of students with executive
function challenges by providing them with concrete methods of organizing
both the input and output aspects of the learning process.

Strategy Teaching Examples

- Explicitly teaching/modeling (via the use of an overhead projector) of
  the use of two different note-taking strategies for a seventh-grade science
  class, with each strategy being taught in the context of a content unit that
  is aligned to it (e.g., the "triple note tote" strategy [Meltzer et al., 2007]
  would be embedded in a unit on cell biology, with the teacher completing
  his or her own set of notes related to the discussion on the overhead projector; see Chapter 9 for a more detailed discussion of this and other executive function–friendly note-taking techniques)

- Explicitly teaching/modeling the use of prereading strategies to build
  comprehension skill (e.g., before having students read an article from the
  latest edition of *Time for Kids*, a fourth-grade teacher would demonstrate
  for her students how to quickly organize/summarize what they already
  know about the topic using the KWLS approach [What I **K**now, What I
  Want to Know, What I **L**earned, What I **S**till Want to Know], and then require them to complete the first two sections of a KWLS sheet on their
  own before reading the passage; see Chapter 6 for details on this and related thought-gathering strategies)

- Explicitly teaching/modeling the use of a structured prewriting (thought
  organization) strategy for a freshman English class and then requiring
  all students to demonstrate their use of the strategy as they complete
  three specific writing assignments over the course of a month (e.g., the
  teacher might model Graham and Harris's [2005] Stop and List strategy to
  organize/sequence his or her thoughts related to the writing prompt, "The
  Best Movie I Saw During Summer Vacation," before requiring that students
  use the strategy on their own to structure a response to the same prompt;
  see Chapter 7 for details on this and similar prewriting approaches)

☞ Case Example

Situation: Mr. Jones, a sixth-grade language arts teacher, has noticed that several
students in one of his classes really struggle with reading comprehension. Upon
checking into the learning histories and profiles of these students, he discovers that

most were formally diagnosed with ADHD in elementary school or had learning difficulties of other kinds, but had never been found eligible for special education services. In discussing the students' comprehension difficulties with the school's literacy specialist, he notes that while they are generally able to pick up some of the more important details of assigned passages, they describe reading as "boring" and have significant difficulty getting the "big picture" elements of text.

Recommendation: Given the comprehension difficulties reported by this teacher, it is likely that a number of students in this class process text at a fairly shallow level. While this reading style allows them to glean some essential facts and details (e.g., who, what, where, when), it is difficult for them to grasp larger, more thematic elements. Based upon this hypothesis, the teacher may try to incorporate (with the help of the school's literacy specialist) elements of *Visualizing and Verbalizing for Language Comprehension and Thinking, Second Edition* (Bell, 2007) into the curriculum to improve the child's ability to form mental pictures ("visual gestalts") from assigned readings. Chapter 6 discusses this and similar instructional models in more detail.

Strategy 4: Minimize Demands on Working Memory (Limit Simultaneous Processing Load)

As discussed in Chapter 1, it is difficult to overestimate or overstate the role of working memory in the learning and production process. In addition to being essential for concrete classroom activities such as following directions and simultaneously "holding onto" the steps of tasks while following them, working memory capacity is also heavily involved in the ability to comprehend and store information, then retrieve it into consciousness as needed (Dehn, 2008). Children whose working memories are limited relative to peer norms may show clear signs of the limitation across a range of academic tasks, with particular vulnerability displayed in the areas of reading comprehension, applied math, and (above all else) written language. Without question, a child's ability to hold information in working memory can have profound influence on the ability to understand and produce in real-world learning settings.

Given the dramatic impact that comparatively weak working memory can have on academic functioning, it is important that instruction be delivered in ways that minimize the amount of information (e.g., directions, content) students with working memory problems must hold at anyone one time on their smallish "cognitive desktops." The essence, then, of this core principle is that efforts must be made to lower the simultaneous processing load placed on students if they show signs of significant working memory impairment. To accomplish this, instruction must become more sequential in form, such that students can process information to a larger degree in a step-by-step, bit-by-bit manner (Reid & Ortiz Lienemann, 2006). How is a teacher to know when the simultaneous processing load of curriculum elements is too much for children with executive function difficulties? Although students' cognitive overload presentations can vary (e.g., some tune out, some walk out, some freak out), many students will tell you when their cognitive workspaces have been maxed out through comments such as the following:

- I can't keep all that in my head at one time.

- Everything you're saying is too much and it's making my head hurt.

- I read it, but I didn't really understand it because I keep forgetting it.

- I know what I want to write, but when I try to write it down it keeps flying out of my head and I can't remember it.

Even if students' executive function profiles are not reflective of obvious working memory deficits, they may still benefit from instructional adjustments that reduce simultaneous processing load (Paas, Renkl, & Sweller, 2003). For example, children with task organization and sequencing difficulties are also likely to benefit from teaching that is highly stepwise in nature because the concrete sequence of the instruction and tasks lessens the amount of ordering/organization they must do on their own. Children with goal-directed attention deficits are also likely to do better on activities with a step-by-step design because they only require focus on one element at a time.

Strategy Examples

- Clearly separating the stages of the writing process, with students only being required to complete one portion of the process each day (e.g., on the first day, they analyze the prompt and choose a topic; on the second day, they brainstorm ideas and jot them down in abbreviated form in any order; on the third day, they sequence the ideas and arrange them into paragraph groupings; on the fourth and fifth days, they write; on the sixth day, they edit; on the seventh day, they "publish")

- Supplementing oral directions for assignments with clearly worded written instructions that divide tasks into a series of discrete steps

- Separating the note-taking and listening comprehension elements of classroom discussions by pausing at regular intervals to allow students to take notes and providing clear indications of what they should be writing during these periods (e.g., using an overhead projector to model the note-taking for the class)

- Minimizing the amount of factual information students must hold in working memory as they write by "downloading" this information into their immediate instructional environments in the form of word walls, punctuation bulletin boards, and sequential graphic organizers that clearly reflect the sequence of ideas

- Minimizing the arithmetic facts that students must hold in working memory while they solve applied problems by "downloading" addition, subtraction, multiplication, and division facts into their immediate instructional environments in the form of "math fact walls"

☞ Case Example

Situation: Robert, a tenth grader with a long history of ADHD diagnosis and related written language disorders, presents as bright and articulate to his teachers in class discussions, but produces very little on paper. His writing samples also include numerous spelling and punctuation errors, even though he always did well on spelling and punctuation tests as a younger student. Although Robert's scores on intelligence tests consistently reflect above-average cognitive ability, he often fails classes because of missing assignments and writing pieces that do not meet even minimal standards. Despite the wealth of ideas he shows in class discussions, Robert often complains about not being able to think of things to say when writing and generally abandons written language assignments after a few sentences (if he does them at all).

Recommendation: Robert's patterns of written language struggle are fairly typical for students with working memory deficits. Although he has little difficulty sequencing and recalling his thoughts in conversations and class discussions, his rather limited working memory makes it difficult for him to hold onto and organize his ideas (and the language he wants to use to express them) in narrative writing contexts. He therefore is likely to benefit from strategies that substantially lessen the amount of information he must simultaneously process across the stages of the writing process. It may be helpful to modify the curriculum so that the student is required to complete fewer narrative writing assignments across all classes and is given more time to complete those that remain. It would also be helpful to clearly separate the creative/organizational elements of the process from mechanical (actual writing) elements, and use highly structured prewriting approaches such as Stop and List (Graham & Harris, 2005) or BOTEC (Brainstorm, Organization, Topic Sentence, Evidence, Conclusions; Meltzer, Sales Pollica, & Barzillai, 2007; Research Institute for Learning and Development and FableVision, Inc., 2002a) that ease brainstorming and thought sequencing. See Chapter 7 for a detailed description of these strategies.

Strategy 5: Provide Many Opportunities for Guided, Extended Practice

While practice may not actually make perfect, it does build fluency. When students are able to use skills with fluency and automatically recall facts and other elements of content, the load on the prefrontal cortex drops considerably. As discussed in Chapter 3, the brain regions associated with executive function work hardest in task situations that are both unfamiliar and challenging (Goldberg, 2001). As students develop some level of mastery over a given content area or skill, the self-directed cognition that had been directed toward it can be devoted to other problems. Take math fact acquisition, for example. Third- and fourth-grade elementary students trying to master the algorithm for triple-digit subtraction with regrouping will find the learning process far easier if they have already mastered all single-digit subtraction facts (Bedard, Martinussen, Ickowicz, & Tannock, 2004; Dehn, 2008). Students who still have to rediscover these basic facts by counting on their fingers each time will have less working memory space to devote to the more complex regrouping task. They will also have to frequently "shift sets" between higher order algorithm work and more mechanical finger subtraction, which can lead to confusion, missed steps, and other problems. The same principle applies to narrative writing. Students with large expressive vocabularies who have also learned such elements of mechanics as spelling and punctuation to the point of fluency will have this factual information at their fingertips as they write (freeing up their self-directed cognition to the more creative, synthetic aspects of writing), whereas children with smaller vocabularies and less mastery of basic rules will need to devote far more cognitive energy to the mechanical aspects of the writing process (McCutchen, Covill, Hoynes, & Mildes, 1994).

Given the clear impact of fluency and automaticity on available executive skill resources, it seems logical to improve the academic function of students with executive function weaknesses by providing them with plenty of time to practice new skills and integrate new content into what they already know. Unfortunately for students whose executive function falls below developmental norms, teachers are often unable to provide the amount of practice and exposure time needed to turn the unfamiliar into the routine. Local and national assessment demands, increasingly complex curriculums, and a host of other things compete for precious instructional and seatwork time. Some research suggests that teachers' assumptions about the amount of time needed to grasp new skills are contributing factors to the lack of practice available to students. Shrager and Siegler (1998), for example, found that teachers tend to underestimate the time it takes students to consistently use newly learned mathematical strategies, and may therefore move onto other topics/skills before many students are ready to do so. Such a hurried instructional pace only compounds the stress levels of children with executive skill weaknesses, leaving them feeling overwhelmed and disinclined to continue to try to keep up.

Strategy Examples

- Using guided oral reading practice (known as "repeated reading" in its more systematic forms). Because many students with executive struggles find reading boring and/or arduous, they tend to avoid it in favor of high-stimulus activities such as TV and video games, which feed directly into their field dependence. By not practicing reading as much as their peers, these students often fail to develop the fluent reading skills necessary for comprehension and later enjoyment of literacy activities. Among the most helpful interventions with this population—particularly in the elementary grades—is to provide them with daily opportunities to real aloud to an adult trained to constructively correct errors over the course of several months, which can build fluency and increase levels of reading enjoyment and stamina

- Explicitly modeling the use of specific writing templates, and then requiring students to use the templates on numerous occasions over the course of the school year in forming and sequencing ideas associated with a range of writing assignments

- Employing math worksheets and workbooks that present new skills/concepts in a spiraling manner, such that material introduced earlier in the year continues to be practiced on a frequent basis

- Explicitly teaching classroom rules/expectations at the start of the school year, and continuing to practice (via role playing and demonstrations) a rule each week through the end of the year to make sure they stay fresh in students' minds

☞ Case Example

Situation: Marilyn, a third grader of average intelligence, exhibits rote-learning struggles and a range of executive skills weaknesses centered on goal-directed

attention and working memory weaknesses. Although her counting and number identification skills were fine in preschool, Marilyn has struggled with number concept and
has had marked difficulties acquiring basic addition and subtraction facts. Her mother
said, "If she didn't have her fingers, forget it. There would be no way she could do
math." A variety of flash-card and manipulative techniques have been tried with little
success by Marilyn's parents, teachers, and tutors.

Recommendation: Given Marilyn's difficulties with both number concept (i.e., a
sense of what numbers mean) and math fact recall, she would likely benefit from an
instructional strategy that explicitly presents the real value of numerals as she works
with them and also scaffolds the fact recall process so that she is not held back from
learning grade-level math concepts. The TouchMath (Innovative Learning Concepts
Inc., n.d.) system can be quite helpful for both of these purposes. The program uses
a mental manipulative strategy that teaches children to perform basic arithmetic by
counting the TouchPoints on each numeral (e.g., *1* has one TouchPoint, *2* has two
TouchPoints). Advocates of the approach contend that it helps children associate
abstract numerals in long-term memory with real values. Given the power of this remedial approach, it seems likely that with lots of guided exposure and practice with
TouchMath over the course of the third-grade year, Marilyn will move beyond her inefficient finger-counting strategies and will also be able to internalize all single-digit
addition and subtraction facts.

Strategy 6: Keep Things as Predictable and Consistent as Possible

To ease the burden of students with executive skills weaknesses, schools and
teachers should adhere to the principle that consistency is good. When schedules play out in the same way every day and when teachers' procedures for
such things as introducing new concepts, assigning work, and collecting work
remain unchanged, all students (even those with comparative executive
function weaknesses) become habituated to the routines and need to allocate
little self-directed cognition to them. Do consistent routines and procedures
guarantee that students with executive skills difficulties will always adhere
to them? Of course not, but consistency and predictability of process may enhance the chances that students with prefrontal lobe weakness will remember
to do what needs to be done. Across the grade span, educators should start
the year by explicitly teaching their students the behavioral expectations and
organizational routines to be followed, then strive to remain consistent with
these expectations and routines. By doing so, teachers create less stress for
students with executive function challenges than teachers whose procedures
vary to a greater extent. Students with ADHD and related diagnoses often
like to know what to expect in their classes and what to do if they have a
problem (e.g., "Mrs. Ryan is really strict, but I do okay in her class most of the
time because she always does stuff in the same way every day and I can deal
with that. Like, I know we'll always have a quiz on Friday and that she'll give
us the study materials on Wednesday and a pre-quiz on Thursday").

Strategy Examples

- See the quote associated with Mrs. Ryan in the previous paragraph. Although teachers who always do things the same way from week to week

might be perceived by their colleagues and some students as a tad rigid, using a predictable routine lessens the prefrontal cortical strain on everyone in the room because students know exactly when to expect study materials, tests, and assignments and then can develop weekly study schedules that align to the never-varying schedule.

- Develop clear classroomwide organizational systems and adhere to them religiously over the course of the school year. Students with executive function difficulties may require additional supports to stick with the systems (see Chapter 9 for several examples), but they are still likely to benefit from using procedures that are required of all students (as opposed to having to use their own, distinct system). As noted earlier in this chapter, classroomwide organizational procedures tend to work best when the teacher not only explicitly demonstrates them at the start of the year and adheres to them consistently over the course of the year, but also when the systems are "re-taught" at regular intervals to help prevent the natural forgetting that can occur among all students as the school year proceeds.

- Requiring students to use the same or similar graphic organizers and templates to complete the prewriting elements of essays/reports across the school year, as the repeated practice of carefully sequenced prewriting activities will benefit children with executive function weaknesses (and by the end of the school year, all students will likely approach writing tasks in more structured ways than they might have previously, including those whose neuropsychological profiles lead them naturally toward "sit down and wing it" writing efforts)

☞ Case Example

Situation: Katie is a sixth grader with a major homework completion problem. She struggled some in elementary school with getting homework done and handed in on time. Now that she is in middle school and the variety and amount of after school assignments has increased, she has really been floundering. When asked when and where she does her homework, Katie replies, "My parents don't care when I do it or where I do it, as long as I get it done, and so I do it at different times every day and in whatever places in the house has what I need — like sometimes I do it in my Dad's study because that's where the paper, stapler, and printer are." Her parents, who are very busy professionals, admit that although they are committed to their daughter's scholastic progress, they tend to leave the homework responsibility to her: "She's in middle school now and really needs to start taking more responsibility for her own work." A review of Katie's assignment book indicates that although she makes entries in it more days than not, her notation system is very inconsistent and varied.

Recommendation: Some sixth graders can consistently complete homework with inconsistent assignment book use, or by doing the work at different times and places in the home. Katie, however, is not one of them. Although reasonably motivated, she lacks the self-regulation, organization, and time-management skills to get assignments done at home in the absence of very consistent structure and support.

Given this executive function profile, the intervention strategy in this case should involve at least the following: 1) structuring of Katie's daily assignment book use around a particular template that requires specific types of entries across all core classes (with daily parent and teacher checking to ensure compliance); and 2) creation of a consistent after-school homework starting time (e.g., right after dinner) and homework completion space (i.e., a space in which Katie keeps all home-based school supplies — including whatever computer equipment she might possess — and at which she always does her homework). In this case, Katie's parents should take a significantly more active role in monitoring her homework organization and completion ("surrogate frontal lobe"). Although it is true that Katie needs to learn to take more responsibility for her own work, her executive profile is such that she is going to require much more explicit task initiation/organization completion teaching from the authority figures in her life and guided practice before she can be expected to show even reasonable ability to do so on her own.

Strategy 7: Anticipate the Aspects of Tasks and Situations Students Might Find Threatening or Frustrating, and Model Strategies to Manage These Challenges When They Occur

If you have ever been late for work in the morning because of difficulties finding an object essential for daily functioning such as glasses, car keys, or your wallet, you know firsthand the impact that anxiety and frustration can have on executive skills. With time running short and the missing object still maddeningly out of sight, negative emotions start to spike and the quality of the search declines precipitously as one dashes with increasing desperation from pillar to post. Even individuals who are capable in calmer moments of a logical and well-regulated search will find themselves casting about in a more random—and therefore less effective—manner when the pressure is really on. Your ability to engage the executive skills you possess is highly dependent upon the amount of fear and frustration you experience from moment to moment.

Children with limited executive skill capacity relative to peer norms will have less self-directed learning and behavior regulation skills at their command in classroom settings when stressed (Barkley, 1997). Children with executive function profiles that make them vulnerable to being swamped by anxiety and anger (recall the amygdala hijack phenomena discussed in Chapter 3) will have a particularly hard time reigning in their emotions once they are triggered, and are likely to engage in a range of maladaptive coping strategies (e.g., shutting down, disrupting, leaving the classroom).

If teachers want to increase all students' abilities to engage the executive skills they possess, it is essential that efforts be made to keep anxiety, frustration, and stress levels as low as possible (Swick, 1987). Consistency and routines help a lot with this, as do explicit teaching and extended practice. Another key strategy to keep negative emotion levels down in the classroom is for instructors to explicitly show students the parts of tasks that might be frustrating and then model ways to manage the difficulty. By doing this, teachers both normalize the negative emotions students might feel in a given academic context (e.g., "The teacher said we might find this part hard to understand, and so I know it's not just me") and provide students with clear directions regarding ways to handle the dicey spots when they occur.

Strategy Examples

- Before asking students to begin working at their seats on a series of workbook pages, read through all the pages with the class and point out the section(s) that students might find confusing, which both clarifies the directions for this section and demonstrates the best way of managing any additional confusion children might have with it (e.g., "If, when you get to this part, you forget what to do or are still confused, do the first problem just like I showed you up here on the board. I'll leave it up here as an example to you. You can also just raise your hand and I'll come over to your desk and help you. This part is pretty new and tricky, so I won't be surprised if a lot of you need some extra help with it.")

- Before asking her fourth grade students to read a *National Geographic* article on global warming, the teacher does an "article walk" with the class to show them its different headings and to clearly define some key words/concepts with which several of the children may be unfamiliar (e.g., "It will be hard to fully understand this first part unless you know the meaning of the words *looming* and *imminent*")

- Tell the class that if they become confused at any point while reading the article, they should place a question mark in the margin next to the sentences they find difficult; then after everyone has finished reading, the article discussion will begin an opportunity for students to ask questions about their "question mark" sentences

☞ Case Example

Situation: Mr. Smith is the lead teacher in a self-contained special education class program for middle school students with severe emotional difficulties. After completing a unit on Dr. Martin Luther King and the American civil rights movement, Mr. Smith decides to assign all students the task of writing a three-page essay on the civil rights figure of their choice and then presenting their reports to the class. Although he feels this assignment is generally matched to his students' literacy levels, Mr. Smith recalls the behavioral escalations that he and the classroom assistants have had to confront whenever narrative writing has been assigned. He wants to present this project in such a way as to minimize the likelihood of disruptive behavior.

Recommendations: Given his students' writing-related anxieties and marked difficulties managing negative emotions, Mr. Smith decides to present the assignment to the class in a way that recognizes their emotional vulnerabilities. He first notes, for example, that some students may be worried about the topic selection process: "Picking a topic for a report like this can be hard." So, Mr. Smith tells the class that he will meet later that day with each student individually to help them choose a civil rights figure: "I will give each of you a choice of three people, and then help you select the one that's best for you." He also tells the students that they will have 3 weeks to complete the project, that portions of each school day will be devoted to it ("So you won't have to do much at home on your own"), and that in the first several days all they will need to do is answer questions about their individual on a sequential graphic organizer (see Chapter 7 for examples of these and similar "frontal lobe–friendly' prewriting devices).

Because Mr. Smith expects that several of his students may feel overwhelmed with the assignment, even with the scaffolds he has put in place, he also elects to have a candid conversation with the class about the strategies they should use if feeling overly anxious or frustrated as they work on their project. As part of this discussion, he role-plays the negative thoughts that might go through students' minds related to the project (e.g., "This stinks! I'm terrible at writing and there's no way I can write three whole pages on anything. I'm going to end up looking stupid") and also demonstrates the more adaptive things they can think and try to keep themselves going (e.g., "This is hard, but we've got lots of time and I only have to do a little bit each day and, besides, the teachers will help me with each part. If I'm stuck, all I need to do is raise my hand for help").

Are Children Today on Executive Function Overload?

As Lynn Meltzer (2007) of Harvard University observed, changes in public education toward high-stakes testing have shifted the curriculum toward highly challenging, developmentally demanding goals that require students to access executive function processes rapidly and efficiently: "Academic success is now increasingly dependent on students' ability to plan their time, organize and prioritize information, distinguish main ideas from details, monitor their progress, and reflect on their work" (p. xi). The complex nature of contemporary school instruction and assignments has heightened the demands placed on students' executive skills. When the abundance of extracurricular activities in which so many children now engage is added to the mix, it seems that the load on children's executive skills is getting heavier all the time.

What do these societal trends portend for students with executive function struggles? In a word, stress. Teachers often have limited control over the array of mandated assessment and curriculum elements they must foist upon their students. They retain, however, some measure of control over the ways they structure their teaching and classrooms. Although the core strategies discussed in this chapter are far from inclusive and, as noted earlier, even farther from a panacea, their consistent application should help to increase the goodness of fit between the needs of students with executive functioning weakness and the academic and social settings in which they must operate.

CHAPTER 6

Keeping Words and Meaning in Mind

The Impact of Executive Skill on Reading

> ❝I took a speed-reading course and read
> *War and Peace* in 20 minutes. It involves Russia.❞
> —WOODY ALLEN

Upon completing this chapter, the reader will be able to

☞ Discuss the reasons why executive skill is among the most essential "nonlinguistic" factors in the development of reading ability

☞ Describe the impact that different executive functions can have on the development of decoding, fluency, and comprehension skill

☞ Indicate the types of error patterns teachers might expect to see in students with varying profiles of executive dysfunction

☞ Discuss the range of strategies that are likely to be effective in building the decoding and fluency skills of students whose reading difficulties relate to executive weakness

☞ Discuss the range of strategies that should be employed across pre-reading, during-reading, and postreading phases to build the comprehension skill of students with executive weakness

Reading: It's Not Just About Language Skill Anymore

Consider for a moment what you believe about reading and the skills that underlie this most essential of academic abilities. What elements of cognition are particularly important to the development of literacy? It is difficult to dispute an answer that centers primarily on proficiency across a range of core language domains. Research conducted over several decades has demonstrated the essential roles played in the acquisition of reading skill by such language elements as phonemic awareness, phonological recoding, rapid automatic naming, vocabulary, and syntax (McCardle & Chhabra, 2004). Indeed, much of the *Report of the National Reading Panel* by the National Institute of Child Health and Human Development (NICHD, 2000) was dedicated to a discussion of these findings and the assertion of the language bases of literacy.

Given the clarity and consistency of these research results, no attempt will be made here to challenge the links between reading skill and various aspects of verbal ability. Rather, the purposes of this chapter are 1) to demonstrate the essential contributions made by the executive functions in the development of decoding, fluency, and text comprehension skills; and 2) to present a series of related intervention strategies for students exhibiting executive dysfunction. To begin, let us take a look at three hypothetical case vignettes (each is an amalgam of several similar students with whom I have worked over the years).

☞ Meet Griffin

Griffin is a first grader with several of the hallmark signs of phonological dyslexia. He struggled greatly with rhyming activities and other elements of phonological processing in preschool and had lots of difficulty grasping letter-sound linkages across his first two elementary school years. Although his ability to recall the visual aspects of words (orthographic memory) is intact, he remains largely unable to sound out even very basic words on his own. Griffin's teachers and parents have also expressed concern about his marked distractibility across all academic contexts and the related difficulties he has focusing on remedial services. For example, his Reading Recovery teacher reported that she needed to remove him from the small-group program in which he started the year and provide him instead with individual instruction. Griffin's first-grade year is nearing completion and he has made very little literacy progress.

☞ Meet Megan

A bright, happy, and highly social third grader, Megan showed no obvious phonological processing problems in her early childhood years. She also had no difficulties mastering letter-sound correspondences in kindergarten and first grade. She continues to display strong phonetic word attack and spelling skills in single-word contexts, but makes numerous errors when reading aloud from books. Teacher reports and running record data reflect Megan's tendency to guess impulsively at multiple-syllable words based upon the first letter sound, omit or add words that are not in the text, and leave off the suffixes of words. She also frequently skips several words at a time and even entire lines of text without seeming to notice that she has done so. Overall, Megan is described as reading in a rather rushed and impulsive manner and as often failing to read for meaning.

🖙 Meet Glen

Now a tenth grader, Glen is the quintessential bright kid who has "never achieved his potential." Identified with both attention-deficit/hyperactivity disorder (ADHD) and an above-average intellect in his middle elementary school years, he had little difficulty learning to read but displayed little interest in any literacy tasks (e.g., "Reading is boring— it's just a bunch of words"). His parents have long reported having to battle with Glen to get him to read any of his assigned texts from school and to get his other homework done. A passionate electronic gamer, Glen spends as many hours a day as he can in front of his computer and game system. He only reads for brief periods when his parents threaten to dramatically curtail his videogame access. Although his vocabulary remains generally strong relative to age norms, Glen now complains about having a hard time understanding many things he is supposed to read for school (e.g., "It's like I read it and the words make sense, but it's all just a blur and I just forget it right after").

Each of these vignettes helps to illustrate the manner in which executive dysfunctions can impede the acquisition of reading skills. In Griffin's case, difficulties with sustained attention compound the impact of his phonological processing weakness by inhibiting his ability to initiate and maintain focus on remedial activities. Megan has no difficulties with individual word reading, but exhibits highly problematic oral reading fluency patterns because of her distractibility, impulsivity, and self-monitoring difficulties. Thus, even though she is able to decode words as well as most peers, her ability to derive meaning from text is impaired. She essentially just rushes headlong along the "orthographic surface," making numerous errors that impede comprehension. Glen, despite his verbal proficiency, may have had a similar fluency style in his elementary school years. As a high school student with generally strong word reading skill and vocabulary, he has a limited ability to grasp and retain the important elements of what he reads. Reading for Glen is a passive, unfocused exercise in which he goes through the motions, but often fails to determine what is important and construct lasting understanding.

Every school district has plenty of students like Griffin, Megan, and Glen—students whose language-based learning disabilities are either amplified by executive function weakness or whose reading struggles stem primarily from executive dysfunction. Research on children with ADHD has clearly shown the relationship between executive function weakness and difficulties with literacy skill acquisition (Loe & Feldman, 2007). A substantial number of students (upward of 40%; Barkley, 2006) struggle to such an extent with reading that they meet diagnostic criteria for a reading disorder. This chapter takes a closer look at the impact of executive skills on the acquisition of the core elements of reading (decoding, fluency, and comprehension), with particular emphasis given to strategies that are most likely to improve the reading of children with executive dysfunction.

Word Reading

Decoding Defined

Decoding is the ability to decipher printed words by determining the spoken words they represent. To do this, children must have fluent letter-recognition skills, as well as mastery of the letter-sound correspondences that underlie written language (the alphabetic principle). Strong decoders also possess strong phonemic awareness in that they clearly grasp the notion that words are composed of component phoneme and morpheme parts. Vocabulary and syntax skills are crucial to the development of decoding skills because word and syntactic knowledge help students to understand unfamiliar/challenging written words. Finally, fluent word decoding requires strong orthographic processing skills—the ability to analyze the visual structure (orthography) of words, store this information in long-term memory, and quickly access it again as needed in reading contexts. In sum, fluent decoders possess the lexical processing skills to figure out exactly what is on the page and the phonological processing and whole-word memory capacity to translate the visual form to spoken form.

Effects of Executive Dysfunction on the Acquisition of Word Reading Skills

As Levine (2001) noted, some children with significant attention and other executive deficits are able to successfully negotiate the steps to strong word reading skills by falling back on their strong language and memory abilities. Children without the language and rote-learning skills needed to compensate for their self-regulatory weaknesses, however, often find the acquisition of decoding skill to be a slow and frustrating process. Children with ADHD may be unable to sustain their attention with sufficient consistency to learn letter names and/or letter-sound correspondences, resulting in an incomplete or erratic knowledge of phonics, even though the language processing elements of their neurocognitive profiles are otherwise intact. These children do not lack the phonological awareness skill needed to grasp and apply phoneme-grapheme linkages, but may lack instead the ability to focus sufficiently on the letter-sound associations and hold this information in memory adequately to use it for word reading (Brady, 1991; Dehn, 2008). Attention deficits, as Levine noted, can also impact students' ability to fully recognize and process the visual elements of words:

> Superficial attention to detail may obscure for them crucial visual features of letters and words, resulting in inconsistency of visual discrimination. Consequently, unpredictable letter reversals, transpositions of letter sequences, and arbitrary insertion and omissions of symbols may characterize their decoding efforts. If they process only one (possibly irrelevant) visual feature of a letter, it may be associated with an incorrect sound. (1998, p. 308)

Studies have demonstrated the inhibiting impact that attention deficits can have on students' processing of the orthographic (visual) elements of words (Thompson et al., 2005), as well as on the rapid automatic naming skill that underlies the fluent identification of letters and sight words (Hale &

Fiorello, 2004). Other elements of executive function that can influence the acquisition of decoding skills include impulse control, sequencing, and (especially) working memory ability. Children with word reading skills that are marked by an impulsive style may guess at entire words based on the first letter or their structural similarity to other words (e.g., misreading *goal* as *goat*). Ordering difficulties can impact word reading by making it difficult for children to sequence word sounds in a consistent left-to-right manner. For some children with adequate letter-sound correspondence skills, the ability to decode multiple syllable words may be confounded by the tendency to blend word sounds and parts in a mixed-up manner (e.g., reading *adventure* as "adturven" or *favorite* as "vorfavite").

Although working memory weaknesses tend to be particularly harmful to a child's ability to comprehend what they read (as will be discussed later in this chapter), marked working memory limitations can also impair the word reading process (Baddeley, 1986). To fully decode a multiple-syllable word, the reader must suspend its initial position sound in working memory while endeavoring to decode the latter portions (Levine, 1998). Students with significant working memory impairment, however, may lose track of earlier-positioned word sounds while they work on ending sounds, resulting in poorly blended or incompletely decoded words (e.g., *necessary* might be read as "sary," *understatement* might be read as "unstatement").

Fluency

Prior to the turn of the 21st century, reading fluency and instructional methods associated with it were given fairly scant attention by most American educators (Rasinski, Blachowicz, & Lems, 2006). Indeed, it was not until the release of the *Report of the National Reading Panel* (NICHD, 2000) that the essential role of fluency in enabling comprehension came heavily to the forefront in the United States. Because the automaticity with which students read narrative print both influences and is influenced by the executive functions, fluency aspects of the reading process deserve special attention here.

Fluency Defined

Oral reading fluency is commonly identified as the ability to read text aloud with sufficient speed, accuracy, and expression (Shanahan, 2006). It is an essential element of the reading process that links decoding (word reading) to comprehension (deriving meaning from text). Children who decipher text in an automatic manner are freed from having to devote much working memory to the decoding process, allowing them to focus their attention and working memory on the act of comprehension (Samuels, 2006). Children whose oral reading tends to be inaccurate and slow, however, focus much of their cognitive effort on the decoding process; therefore, they are far less able to make sense of what they read.

Impact of Executive Dysfunction on Fluency

The fast and accurate reading of connected text is very bound up in the executive skills of purposeful attention, impulse control, and self-monitoring, as noted by Berninger, Abbott, Billingsley, and Nagy (2001). As was suggested in the previous section on decoding, even children with mastery of the alphabetic principle, strong phonetic word attack skills, and orthographic recall are likely to make a range of word recognition errors when reading narrative text if they cannot sustain attention to the accuracy of their decoding.

The oral reading error patterns of inattentive readers may be characterized by numerous omissions of parts of words (most often suffixes) and small words (e.g., *the, is, a, at*), as well as the tendency to disregard punctuation. Students with this executive function profile also seem to become "lost in the text" with some frequency, in that they struggle with keeping track of their place on the page and sometimes skip whole lines without noticing they have done so. Young readers with impulse control problems, on the other hand, tend to charge headlong through text when reading aloud, making "fluency sins of commission" rather than omissions; that is, they insert word parts, whole words, and sometimes even larger ideas that are not on the page.

Set shifting (cognitive flexibility) is another executive skill that can have significant impact on a child's oral and silent reading fluency. As Samuels (2006) noted, young children still in the process of developing decoding automaticity must continually shift attention back and forth between word identification and comprehension. Children who lack the cognitive flexibility and working memory skills to make numerous spontaneous shifts in cognitive focus may become "glued to the print" (Chall, 1967) and remain effectively stalled at the decoding stages of reading skill development. In other words, these children tend to keep their attention locked on the process of word-by-word decoding; they struggle with the shifts to understanding being made by the more fluent readers at their grade level.

The importance of shifting fairly seamlessly between word reading and comprehension while reading connected text also helps us to understand the fluency struggles of many children with learning disabilities. Older students who must continue to devote a substantial percentage of their self-directed cognitive activity to the decoding process when reading need to make many more shifts between decoding and comprehension than their more fluent peers. Automatic decoders, as was noted earlier, already focus most of their attention and working memory on the comprehension process, and therefore do not have to keep shifting sets between word identification and understanding (Samuels, 1976; Graham & Bellert, 2004).

Children who are "glued to the print" will often exhibit the relatively flat and expressionless oral reading that is common among students with goal-directed attention deficits and other executive function weaknesses. Because they remain generally stuck at the orthographic or surface level of text processing, these children are not reading for meaning and are therefore unable to generate the expression that is characteristic of strong fluency. (See Figure 6.1 for an indication as to where the surface level of text processing seems to logically fit into Barrett's taxonomy of reading comprehension [Barrett, 1967].) The expression with which a child reads therefore is not only a key in-

1. Literal Comprehension: *Recognition and recall of explicitly stated information*
2. Reorganization: *Reorganizing/reordering explicit information from text*
3. Inferential Comprehension: *Forming inferences from text, with regard to such things as themes, main ideas, predictions, and conclusions*
4. Evaluation: *Making judgments about text, with regard to fact versus opinion, adequacy, validity, and appropriateness*
5. Appreciation: *Forming emotional and aesthetic (imagery-based) responses to text (appreciating text at emotional and cognitive levels)*

Kaufman's addition: Processing text at a **surface or orthographic level** (*eyes are scanning the words, with little to no meaning being formed*)

Figure 6.1. Barrett's taxonomy of comprehension. (Barrett, T.C. [1967]. Goals of the reading program: The basis for evaluation. In T.C. Barrett [Ed.], *In the evaluation of reading achievement*. Newark, DE: International Reading Association; adapted by permission.)

dicator of oral reading fluency skill (NICHD, 2000), but is also reflective of whether he or she is processing text at the depth necessary for comprehension.

Comprehension

Reading Comprehension Defined

Reading comprehension can be most simply identified as the derivation of meaning from text. It is also the purpose of reading. Among the most helpful definitions of reading comprehension was put forth by the RAND Reading Study Group (2002), who described it as "the process of simultaneously extracting and constructing meaning through integration and involvement." This elegant description has particular relevance to the topic of executive function, as it stresses the significance of readers going beyond the simple absorption of information in text to the self-directed construction of deeper understanding.

Influence of Executive Functions on Reading Comprehension

It is estimated that approximately 10% of all students possess adequate reading decoding skill yet struggle significantly with reading comprehension (Feifer, 2007). To what can we attribute the comprehension difficulties of so many children with intact word reading skill? Receptive language weaknesses certainly play a role, as do an assortment of environmental factors, such as the adequacy of language models in the home and community and whether children are given appropriate instruction on how to understand what they read. If there is a primary nonlinguistic culprit to the reading comprehension difficulties exhibited by so many children, however, the nod would have to be given to executive dysfunction. The construction of meaning from text is very much dependent upon the quality of students' self-directed cognitive abilities (Gaskins, Satlow, & Pressley, 2007; Hale & Fiorello, 2004). A study, for example, demonstrated the link between students' working memory and planning skills and their comprehension skills. If executive capacity is lacking to a significant degree, comprehension may suffer even if all words on the page are being accurately identified (Feifer, 2007).

Among the things that distinguish good readers from their less academically proficient peers is their ability to remain aware of both themselves and the text as they read. Numerous authors, including Tovani (2000, 2005), Levine (1998, 2002), and Daniels and Zemelman (2004) have discussed the importance of self-awareness, self-monitoring, and metacognitive skills to the comprehension process. Tovani's summary of this capacity is especially helpful:

> Good readers monitor their comprehension. They know when the text is making sense and when it isn't. They recognize signals that indicate when they are understanding what they are reading, and when they are confused. Good readers separate themselves from struggling readers when they recognize they are confused and then do something to repair meaning. Good readers use "fix-up" strategies, which can be taught at any age. (2005, p. 5)

Research also tells us that effective readers approach and consume texts in a strategic manner (RAND Reading Study Group, 2002). That is, they develop goals and plans for comprehension even before they pick up a book, and revise their plans as necessary while reading. They then employ a range of effective "thought–holding" strategies during reading, such as notetaking and highlighting, to ensure that they will be able to recall (or at least find) the most salient facts and conceptual elements after reading. Strong readers pose questions to themselves as they progress through text and make mental (or physical) note of instances when information either confirms or conflicts with background knowledge (Beck & McKeown, 2006). They also "read between the lines" as necessary, reasoning and drawing inferences based on information that might not be explicitly stated. Finally, when the actual reading is completed, good readers pause to reflect on the key conceptual and factual elements, integrate this new information into their knowledge set and existing schemas, and extend their thinking by coming up with some new ideas (e.g., "If I was writing this book, rather than having the ship captain go down with his ship when it sank, I'd have him swim to shore instead"). In a word, skilled readers *think* when they read (Harvey & Goudvis, 2007), performing a fluid cognitive dance between the knowledge extraction and meaning construction elements of text processing.

What element of neuropsychological function enables all of the wondrous metacognition performed by skilled readers as they comprehend text? The executive functions, of course. As Gaskins, Satlow, and Pressley noted,

> To assure comprehension is occurring, the reader taps into the power of executive control, a volitional process that allows him to monitor and take charge of the construction of meaning while reading. It is a student's capacity to plan, monitor, and, if necessary, re-plan comprehension strategies in the service of understanding. (2007, p. 194)

Children who are challenged to a significant degree with any of the elements of the metacognitive strand of executive function (see Chapter 1) will likely struggle with comprehension even if their decoding skills are intact. For example, students with planning struggles may approach the consumption of texts (particularly those of the nonpreferred variety) in a random, poorly

Table 6.1. Influence of specific executive skills on reading comprehension

Planning skills: The ability to read with a specific question or purpose in mind when seeking specific information. Planning skills also involve the strategy a reader uses to process information

Organizational skills: The way a reader puts together text in a cohesive manner. Also, when distracted, the ability to return to the text and resume the story flow

Working memory: Temporarily suspending previously read information in the mind while simultaneously linking to new information being read

Cognitive flexibility: Shifting patterns of thoughts processes to the organizational parameters of the text being read, and not continuing to focus on material

Verbal fluency: Speed of processing linguistic information at the word level to facilitate passage comprehension at the text level

Concept formation: Depth of understanding of the text

Response inhibition: Refraining from jumping ahead when reading text and missing salient aspects of the passage

Sustained attention: The ability to focus on a text for prolonged periods of time and resist distractions

planned manner and therefore view most reading activities as acts of passive knowledge acquisition (e.g., "My eyes are open and focused on the book and I'm looking at all the words. Therefore, I'm reading"). Children with self-awareness and self-monitoring issues are apt to have limited recognition of their levels of comprehension as they read and may therefore be unable to sense when they must pause, go back, and engage in fix-up strategies. See Table 6.1 for a list of executive functions and their influence on reading comprehension, as developed by Feifer (2007).

The importance of the working memory system to the reading comprehension process deserves a bit of special attention and is difficult to overstate. As was noted earlier, the extent to which you comprehend what you read is significantly dependent on the capacity to simultaneously process text at both the mechanical (decoding) and meaning construction (comprehension) levels (Beck & McKeown, 2006). Fluency difficulties will by themselves confound comprehension by forcing young learners to devote most of their attention and working memory space to the act of word reading (leaving little room on the "cognitive desktop" for meaning to be built). However, it is important to note that even fluent readers can demonstrate poor comprehension if their working memory capacity is sufficiently small (Cain, Oakhill, & Bryant, 2004).

As discussed in Chapter 1, working memory is the "cognitive stewpot" in which new information is mixed with prior knowledge to allow comprehension to occur (see Figure 6.2). Some students, because of genetics and the environments in which they were raised, enter school with working memory capacities that are large enough to allow all the simultaneous processing needed for grade-level academic tasks (including reading comprehension). Some students, however, have small or "leaky" working memory systems that are unable to contain the various bits and pieces of information needed for comprehension to occur (Levine, 2002). Thus, even if these children have the decoding and vocabulary skills needed to construct effective meaning out of what they read, they often fail to do so with sufficient quality because they

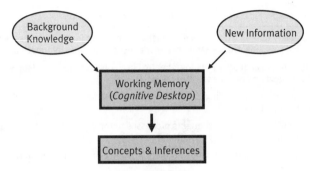

Figure 6.2. The literacy mix in working memory.

cannot manage the simultaneous processing demands. Some students with significantly limited working memories may, for example, forget the content gleaned from the beginning of a paragraph by the time they get to the end of that paragraph (Baddeley, 1997). Other students with a limited working memory profile may find their temporary cognitive storage capacity (working memory) to be so overwhelmed by unfamiliar content entering the brain that they have very limited capacity to actually think about the material or link it to prior knowledge (e.g., "Think? Who can think? I'm just trying to get through this stuff"). Still other children have working memory profiles that are highly fragile in nature and prone to "content dumps" in reading and listening comprehension contexts. These students may actually possess sufficient cognitive desktop space to simultaneously process all they need to think about, but have very limited capacity to protect working memory from distraction. Thus, when reading, they tend to comprehend well if they are in a very quiet place, but frequently lose their task-related thoughts when reading in noisier home and school settings (e.g., "Thanks a lot for burping, dude—now I've got to go back and reread these last two pages").

Strategies to Improve the Word-Reading Skills of Children with Executive Dysfunction

> ❝ The most fundamental responsibility of schools is teaching students to read. Indeed, the future success of all students hinges upon their ability to become proficient readers. ❞
> —LOUISA MOATS (1999)

Consistent with the core strategies outlined in Chapter 5, children whose acquisition of decoding skills is hampered by executive dysfunction require instructional models that are highly explicit, systematic, intensive, and strategy focused (Torgesen, 2004). Because so many students with executive deficits and other learning disabilities struggle with purposeful attention and working memory, their needs seem to be poorly aligned with whole-language instructional methods that largely eschew the systematic teaching and practice of decoding skills. Although literacy models that operate from the whole-language perspective are now on the decline in the United States, their problematic influence continues to linger in some school systems, thus resulting in literacy instruction at the younger grades that is often far too "squishy" and random to benefit students with learning disabilities and executive function challenges (Moats, 2000, 2007). This section provides some instructional strategies that are likely to build the word-reading skills of children whose early literacy struggles can be attributed in whole or part to executive deficits.

Systematic, Synthetic, and Multisensory Phonics Instruction

As was made clear by Jean Chall's 1967 synthesis of the research on the most effective ways of teaching children to decode, and again decades later by the *Report of the National Reading Panel* (NICHD, 2000), most children learn to read words best if their early literacy instruction places emphasis on systematic phonics instruction. Systematic and explicit methods of teaching letter identification and the alphabetic principle are certainly essential for children with phonological processing problems, but they are also very important to developing the decoding skills of children with executive function weakness.

Students with purposeful attention problems and other forms of executive dysfunction can struggle with learning to read words because of difficulties with keeping the names of letters and their corresponding sounds in their cognitive workspace (working memory) long enough to get them into long-term memory. Therefore, these children may demonstrate short-term knowledge of a particular letter sound or word attack strategy one day, but then be completely unable to recall this bit of information the next day (or sometimes even just several minutes later in the same day). Word identification strategies that emphasize systematic, explicit teaching methods and that keep returning to specific skills until they are clearly mastered are far more likely to produce lasting skill development in children with executive function challenges because they make clear what is being taught and include lots of guided repetition.

Word reading curricula such as *Letterland* (Freese & Wendon, 2003) and *Jolly Phonics* (Lloyd, 1998) that are not only systematic and explicit but also multisensory in nature seem particularly well suited for young children with executive dysfunction. *Letterland* (see Figure 6.3) teaches kindergarten and first-grade children the names and corresponding sounds of the letters (and letter combinations) by giving each letter a character name that includes its associated phoneme sound (e.g., *K* is the Kicking King, *S* is Sammy Snake). The program also incorporates a lot of body movement into the learning of letter-sound correspondences by having children do such things as form themselves into the letter *K* and then hop about the room making a kicking motion (while repeating "Kicking King"). The inclusion of this kinesthetic aspect to the phonics instructional model makes it even more explicit, and thus the approach may be that much better suited for children with attention and working memory deficits.

Emphasize Common Orthographic Patterns

The word-family approach to the teaching of decoding is often a helpful supplement to systematic phonics instruction and can be an effective means of

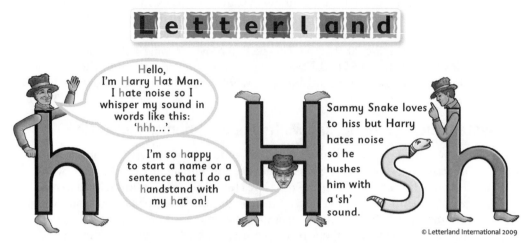

Figure 6.3. *Letterland* teaches kindergarten and first-grade children the names and corresponding sounds of the letters (and letter combinations) by giving each letter a character name that includes its associated phoneme sound. (*Source:* Letterland, http://www.letterland.com).

remediating the decoding difficulties of students with executive function weakness. As Levine (1998) noted, emphasis on common letter patterns (i.e., word families) and structural elements that occur frequently in words (e.g., prefixes , suffixes, root words) can increase the automaticity with which children with attention difficulties decode words; it may make them less susceptible to impulsive guessing at words or failing (because of distractibility) to notice key orthographic components. Some studies (e.g., Willcutt, Pennington, Chhabildas, Olson, & Hulslander, 2005) have suggested that the decoding struggles of children with ADHD can be associated with orthographic coding difficulties (i.e., failing to note key visual features of words). Given this, remedial strategies that systematically target the building of orthographic coding skills may be effective in improving the word reading skills of children with attention deficits and other forms of executive dysfunction.

Explicitly Teach and Have Students Practice Left-To-Right Sound Blending

Children whose profiles of executive function weakness include sequencing and shifting difficulties may struggle with correctly ordering the sounds of words. Therefore, instructional methods that encourage children to focus on the parts of words with which they are most familiar may need to be supplemented with clear instruction to go back and put the whole word together progressively in a left-to-right order. Many instructional models and classroom practice often just assume that children will know to go back and blend the sounds together in the correct sequence. Or, as Beck (2006) noted, teachers may encourage children to blend letter or syllable sounds together, but often neglect to teach an explicit strategy to accomplish the sequential blending (e.g., how to blend them together is the problematic link).

The blending method that Beck (2006) advocated is referred to as *successive* or *cumulative* blending. It tends to place less stress on students' working

/c/   /r/   /cr/   /i/   /cri/   /s/   /cris/   /p/   crisp

Figure 6.4. Example of a successive blending approach. (From Beck, I.L. [2006]. *Making sense of phonics: The how's and why's.* New York: Guilford Press; adapted by permission.)

memory systems than final blending approaches, in which teachers ask children to say each letter-sound contained in a word (e.g., /c/ /a/ /t/) and then finally blend them all together. As Beck reported, such an approach requires children to suspend all previous sounds in working memory while decoding the subsequent ones, and then hold all the sounds in working memory while attempting final blending. Beck's successive approach diminishes working memory load by teaching children to successively blend all previous sounds in the word on which they are working into the position sound they are up to. For example, if the child is blending all the sounds contained in the word *crumb*, the child would say the first two sounds in the word and blend them together (/c/ and /r/ become /cr/). The child would then say the third sound and immediately blend it with the first two sounds (/cru/). This process is followed until all the sounds in the word are cumulatively sequenced. See Figure 6.4 for further illustration of this frontal lobe–friendly blending approach.

Strategies to Improve the Reading Fluency of Children with Executive Dysfunction

The deriving of meaning from text is much less likely to occur in the absence of fluent reading. Unless children with executive skill impairments can process the lower-level aspects of reading such that they can decode with sufficient speed and accuracy, they will need to compensate for their lack of fluency by directing their already limited executive control skills to word identification—leaving precious little attention and working memory space available for comprehension (Klinger, Vaughn, & Boardman, 2007). Thus, if there is a population of learners that is absolutely in need of strong fluency skills, it is children with executive function weaknesses. This section examines a few key strategies that are likely to improve the speed and accuracy with which these students read.

Provide Frequent Opportunities for Guided Oral Reading (Repeated Reading)

The key to building reading fluency is guided oral reading practice (NICHD, 2000). Research has clearly shown that providing children frequent opportunities to read aloud to an adult who is following along with the text and monitoring/correcting the accuracy of the child's reading can build the automaticity of word recognition (Meyer & Felton, 1999) and improve overall oral reading fluency. To help improve the reading fluency of students with executive function challenges, adults can listen to them read aloud every day for 15–20 minutes, gently and consistently correcting the errors they make.

There are a variety of ways to conduct guided oral reading, with some being significantly more formal and structured than others. The least systematic method simply involves listening to a child read every day from a variety of texts that are at or just above the child's comfort level. A somewhat more structured approach is to use a basal text with a set of words that occur repeatedly across several stories so that the child is exposed to specific words to the point of mastery (Berninger & Richards, 2002). Repeated reading in its purest sense is the most structured and systematic form of guided oral reading. It involves the selection of a carefully sequenced series of reading passages and requires students to read each passage with enough speed and accuracy before moving on to the next one. The repeated reading element of the *Great Leaps* curriculum (Campbell, 2008) is structured in this manner.

Preview Unfamiliar Books and Text Passages

Recall the discussion in Chapter 3 about the extent to which new and unfamiliar content taxes the executive functions. Whenever developing readers are asked to read something for the first time (particularly if its structure and vocabulary are somewhat unfamiliar), a significant chunk of the executive control system will be devoted to managing the newness of the activity. Therefore, the demands of novelty are apt to pull children with executive function weakness toward a word-by-word decoding level of text processing ("gluing them to print"), which will slow reading speed and confound comprehension.

To limit the impact of novelty on fluency and comprehension of students with executive dysfunction, it is generally helpful to preview new books (and even shorter passages) to make explicit the structure and sequence, as well as to allow the opportunity to decode new or tricky words in advance. Recognizing the value of text previewing, many teachers of all grade levels take students on "book walks" and "article walks" to review the headings, sequencing, and key vocabulary, and just generally highlight what to expect when the reading starts. This strategy may be particularly suited to the needs of children with executive skills weaknesses, not only because it reduces the newness of unfamiliar readings, but also because it provides an explicit demonstration of the organization and sequence of the text.

Explicitly Cue Students Before They Read

The fluency error patterns often witnessed among children with executive skill weaknesses include the tendency to omit whole words or parts of words, distractedly or impulsively guessing at words based upon whatever orthographic features grab attention (e.g., reading *hotel* as "house"), and skipping whole lines of text without any recognition of having done so. Although the guided oral reading practices discussed earlier should diminish these problematic tendencies over time, the reading fluency of students with executive function difficulties can improve faster if they are explicitly reminded about their disfluency patterns before a guided oral reading session with visual cues (see Figure 6.5) and prompts such as the following:

Figure 6.5. Example of a visual cue to use before a guided oral reading session.

- "Now remember John, today I really want you to focus on reading through each whole word completely and correctly before moving on to the next."

- "Okay, Megan, let's really try to focus today on reading all the words that are on the page. Although you're becoming a better and better reader with all of our practice together, you still have the tendency to skip words when you read. To help you remember to work on these things, I made you this little sign that I'm going to put up here on the desk just above the book. It just reminds you of what you're trying to do when you read."

Using Fingers and Other Place Markers

As Levine (1998) noted, children with attention and other executive weaknesses often lose track of their place on pages and become lost in the text (e.g., "Um . . . I forgot where I was"). By encouraging these students, particularly in the elementary years, to use their finger, a ruler, or index card as a place marker, teachers may be able to improve students' focus on the text and minimize their chances of wandering astray. Meltzer et al. (2006) recommended placing the index card above the line, rather than below, to reduce the maladaptive habit of rereading the same line and to keep students' focus on each subsequent line.

Strategies to Build the Comprehension Skill of Students with Executive Dysfunction

The comprehension skills of children with executive function weaknesses are heavily predicted by their reading fluency. Thus, one of the most important comprehension-building strategies for this population is to increase the accuracy and speed of their reading of connected text; then, as much of their limited attention and working memory space as possible can be devoted to understanding. But does reasonable fluency guarantee comprehension? Alas, no. The construction of meaning from text is also heavily dependent upon a range of language comprehension factors, as well as the extent to which children can read strategically (Klinger et al., 2007). Students with comparatively strong executive skills will more naturally trend in the direction of strategic reading, whereas children with executive function weaknesses will be far less likely to read in a purposeful, self-monitored fashion.

For children with executive function challenges, struggles with the acquisition of purposeful reading skill would not be cause for much concern if it was common practice for all students to be explicitly taught to read strategically. However, as both the National Reading Panel (NICHD, 2000) and the Rand Reading Study Group (2002) have noted, this is far from the case. Particularly in content classes at the middle and high school levels, many educators do not teach students how to best understand required reading materials (Tovani, 2005). Therefore, children's ability to comprehend may be defeated by a combination of neurodevelopmental factors that makes it difficult for them to read in a self-directed, cognitively active manner, as well as by teaching that fails to build strategic comprehension skills. The instructional recommendations in this section center primarily on methods of building the strategic reading abilities of students with executive skill weaknesses before, during, and after reading.

Before Reading: Teach and Model the Importance of Thought Gathering

There is an inherent logic to the notion that we are all likely to better understand reading material or a lecture if we first gather in our minds what we know and think about the topic at hand (i.e., activating prior knowledge; Beers, 2003). Thus, before asking fourth graders with significant executive function challenges to read an article on volcanoes, it is best to first ask them to make a quick list of all the things they may already know about volcanic eruptions (perhaps using a thought-gathering template like Appendix 7.1) and then discuss the topic with the students as a group before they start reading. Such structured activities will have the effect of inserting relevant prior knowledge/beliefs into working memory from the recesses of long-term memory, which should enable the consumption of new information in the text in a more focused, task-related state of mind.

Before Reading: Teach Students to Develop a Plan for Comprehension

Good comprehension does not just happen; it is the result of planning. So how do we get children with executive dysfunction to organize their thoughts and set up a comprehension plan before they read? Teachers should explicitly teach students to do this, and then give them lots of guided practice in the use of this prereading strategy (Gaskins et al., 2007). This approach flows logically from the thought-gathering strategy discussed previously, so they should probably be taught and used together. It makes sense to first teach students to gather up their prior knowledge and beliefs, and then to determine what more they would like to learn from the passages before them. The tried-

What I Know	What I Want to Know	What I Learned	What I Still Want to Know

Figure 6.6. The KWLS (What I **K**now, What I **W**ant to Know, What I **L**earned, What I **S**till Want to Learn) approach to background knowledge activation, comprehension planning, and comprehension review. (From Ogle, D. [1986]. K-W-L: A teaching model that develops active reading of expository text. *The Reading Teacher*, *39*, 654–674. Copyright © 1986 by the International Reading Association [www.reading.org]; reprinted by permission)

and-true KWLS (What I **K**now, What I **W**ant to Know, What I **L**earned, What I **S**till Want to Learn) approach (see Figure 6.6) is one of the most concrete and time-efficient methods of helping children systematically activate prior knowledge, identify what they would like to learn from the current reading, and (after reading) to summarize new information and plan for future learning (Ogle, 1986).

Before Reading: Book Walks and Text Surveys

This strategy, discussed earlier with regard to its potential impact on fluency, is also quite likely to improve students' comprehension (Gaskins et al., 2007), particularly if they have executive function weaknesses of an organizational, working memory, or organizational nature. By "walking" students through a particular book chapter, textbook section, or magazine article and highlighting its organization and key elements, teachers can provide all kinds of advance organizers, diminish the unfamiliar, and explicitly point out the important things that should be given attention. Similar effects can be achieved with older students by having them survey the text before reading for clues about what is likely to happen in the passage and for other essential elements such as main ideas, text structure, and key vocabulary (Gaskins et al., 2007).

Levine (1998, 2002) has written extensively about the difficulties that students with attention/executive function weakness can have with saliency determination (i.e., figuring out what is important during reading). The best way to defeat such difficulties in text processing may be to explicitly show children (in advance of reading) what is important and what is less so.

> " Reading is not a spectator sport. "
> —MARY HELEN PELTON (1993)

During Reading: Teach Students That
Good Readers Are Cognitively Active Readers

One reason that so many children with ADHD (a disorder of executive function) become addicted to video games (Gentile, 2009) and television may be that these stimulating electronic entertainments often require little in the way of active processing. The high-impact content keeps coming at children from the video screens, requiring little more of the viewer than to sit back and lap up the engaging images. Reading, on the other hand, requires children to actively construct meaning and enjoyment from the series of words on the page. Because reading requires such self-directed building of understanding, it is more challenging in many respects than following the pictures on a video screen.

Good readers, by virtue of their natural neurocognitive skills and the teaching they have received, learn early on in their literacy skill development that the more cognitive effort they put into reading, the more they get out of it. Many children with executive function difficulties, however, have a hard time constructing meaning on their own from text and approach the act of reading as if it requires no more self-directed cognitive engagement than watching television. Children who read with their minds set on "watch TV" mode (waiting, in essence, for the enjoyment and information/understanding to leap off the page into their brains) will scan the print before them in a rather passive manner and will likely find the activity to be boring and pointless (e.g., "I read it but I don't get it"). Therefore, it is essential to teach all children (particularly those with executive function weaknesses) to think actively about what they are reading while they are reading it (Harvey & Goudvis, 2007).

To help get this point across to students, teachers may want to use the metaphor of an electronic magnet. Specifically, just as an electronic magnet can only attract metal objects if it is both "turned on" and focused in the right direction, so too can children's brains only pull enjoyment and information from texts if they are focused and turned on by thinking.

During Reading: Stress the Importance of Visualization

Some research suggests that students with visual working memory weaknesses may struggle with reading comprehension because they have a harder time than most peers with forming and maintaining visual images from what they read (Goff, Prat, & Ong, 2005). Because many children with executive function challenges have limited working memory capacity, they are apt to have difficulty holding text content in their minds long enough and well enough to form mental pictures associated with it. Therefore, teachers may want to train these students to pause every several seconds while they read to try and picture the content in their minds and then talk to themselves about what they imagine.

The model developed by Bell (2007) emphasizes the importance of helping children form gestalts (i.e., whole concepts and broader understandings) by forming structured mental images from the pieces and details of what they read. The verbalizing aspect that stresses the importance of the description of the images and related gestalts that are formed supplements the visualizing element. The verbalizing/visualizing model relies heavily in the initial train-ing stages on teacher-directed questions that help students form the needed images from text, making use of a series of cue words (e.g., *what, size, color, shape*) that provide a structure around which the mental pictures are formed and discussed. This program and similar visualization approaches (e.g., Hib-bing & Rankin-Erickson, 2003) may help students with executive dysfunction to overcome their otherwise superficial text processing tendencies. By com-pelling children to pause and think deeply enough about what they are read-ing to form mental images about it, visualization methods create opportunities for rich elaboration of text content in working memory.

During Reading: Monitor Comprehension

Comprehension, even among strong student readers and highly literate adults, tends to wax and wane. Good readers recognize that the quality of under-standing goes up and down over the course of any reading activity. They pay attention to how well they are absorbing the content and take whatever cor-rective action is necessary to repair understanding when it fails to occur (To-vani, 2005). Students with executive skills weaknesses, however, often lack the self-awareness, self-monitoring skills, and working memory skills to gauge the quality of their comprehension. Such students may not realize that they have failed to comprehend until they are required to demonstrate that they have done so. These children therefore need lots of explicit teaching and practice in comprehension monitoring and repair (Gaskins et al., 2007).

The most effective way of conveying these skills to children with execu-tive function difficulties may be through a combination of teacher modeling in think-aloud contexts and questioning in individualized guided oral read-ing settings. "Think alouds" (in which the teacher reads out loud to the class from an assigned text and models active thinking related to comprehension) are becoming common occurrences in classrooms of all grade levels. In addi-tion to using this method to highlight particular passages, it can also be used to demonstrate comprehension difficulties and strategies to repair them. For example, a teacher can purposefully stop at a section of text that includes an awkward bit of phrasing or an unusual turn of phrase, noting to the class his or her confusion as to what the author was trying to convey. The teacher may then quickly demonstrate a method or two to fix comprehension, such as rereading the sentences above the challenging section, repeating the chal-lenging section slowly and aloud to oneself to see if that helps to clarify things (often it does), or stopping for a moment to look up unfamiliar words (McCardle, Chhabra, & Kapinus, 2008).

During Reading: Teach Holding Strategies

Although students should definitely be taught to attempt to fix their com-prehension as they read, there are times when comprehension cannot be repaired and the reader must keep going. Metacognitive, self-aware readers adaptively manage these situations by keeping a record of their irresolvable points of confusion, as well as their other questions, comments, and flashes

An effective way of 'coding' one's thoughts
about text

✓   Confirms what kid already thought

X   Contradicts what kid thought

??   Puzzling—huh?

*   Important

☺   New or interesting—cool!

Figure 6.7.   Coding text. (From *Strategies That Work: Teaching
Comprehension for Understanding and Engagement* [2nd ed.],
by Stephanie Harvey and Anne Goudvis, © 2007, reprinted with
permission of Stenhouse Publishers.)

of brilliant insight by jotting them quickly down in the margins of text or
on small sticky notes that get pasted right into the relevant text section (Tovani, 2005). These comprehension "holding" strategies are terrific methods
of downloading important elements of comprehension out of previous working memory space and into the immediate environment where they can be
looked at again and addressed after reading.

Harvey and Goudvis (2007) emphasized the importance of teaching students a concrete coding approach to placing their thoughts into text (see Figure 6.7). This quick and elegant method of thought holding seems to be particularly frontal lobe–friendly, as it is easily remembered and involves little
writing. (Too much writing during reading might cause children with executive function challenges to lose their train of thought, forcing them to go back
and reread large sections to get back on track.) If one plans to use such thought-
holding methods with students with executive function weaknesses in classroom settings, the strategies should be explicitly demonstrated first by the
teacher, with all students being required to use them in structured ways over
time to ensure adequate opportunities for guided practice (Tovani, 2005).

After Reading: Teach the Art of Summarization

As Levine noted, regular practice in summarization "helps children engage
in reading and process meaning, select what is most salient, and practice their
organizational skills" (1998, p. 336). In other words, summarizing the essential elements of a text may help to crystallize children's comprehension of key
elements, while also requiring them to flex some important executive function muscles. Students with executive skills weaknesses may struggle with
summarization because of their difficulties with saliency determination, organization, and working memory. Therefore, they may require more explicit
instruction with regard to the "how" of creating useful summaries before they
can do so on their own.

As with other recommendations in this chapter, teachers should explicitly demonstrate effective summarizing strategies for students several times
and across a range of text contexts (Klinger et al., 2007; McCardle & Chhabra,
2004). Teachers may take a second postreading book walk (for younger children) or passage survey (for older students) after the reading has been com-

pleted and highlight the essential points of the text. Just as a prereading book walk or text survey will likely aid fluency and comprehension by providing a sense of the text structure and what readers can expect as they move along (Gaskins et al., 2007), a postreading review of the text will help students with limited working memory and saliency determination skills to focus once again on essential elements. Once these elements have been noted, the teacher should form them into a succinct (yet complete) summary for the students and then ask the students to develop their own summary (using their own words). As Schenck (2003) pointed out with regard to the comprehension and recall of verbal material, students generally cannot remember what they cannot say. Having students rephrase the teacher's summary in their own words and eventually state their own summaries of text passages may help to move key learning points from working memory into long-term memory.

After Reading: Use Structured Reading Response Logs

As the next chapter discusses in some detail, students with executive skills difficulty often find the prospect of writing to be somewhat less appealing than, say, a trip to the dentist for a 2-hour root canal. Abhorrence for putting pen to paper consistently defeats the reading log/journal response of children with executive function weakness (and the learning associated with it). Shallow text processing, difficulties with text organization, and set-shifting problems (shifting from text consumption to text production) also contribute to the minimal response problem. Because the knowledge and understanding that students acquire from text are often extended through writing about reading (Fisher & Frey, 2007; Graham & Harris, 2005), children who lack writing skills and/or resist written language tasks are afforded fewer opportunities to embellish their comprehension of academic reading material.

Many teachers across the middle elementary to high school grades, in my experience, use rather vaguely structured response journal formats that do little more than ask students to write their impressions of what they just read. Such limited assignment structure usually links poorly to the profiles of students with executive dysfunction, as it places heavy responsibility for decision making, initiation, and response organization squarely on them. Children with executive dysfunction may respond more effectively and productively to a highly structured reading-response format that limits a lot of the guesswork, decision making, and thought organization elements of the response process. Tovani (2000, 2005) developed one such response-log template (see Appendix 6.1). Naturally, for students with executive function struggles to approach the use of even well-structured response templates like this, it is first necessary for the classroom teacher or special educator to demonstrate its use a number of times (e.g., on an overhead projector, after the class as a group has read the same passage, after the class has listened to the teacher read aloud from a book).

After Reading: Use Dramatic Role Play

Few things get key points and concepts from text into children's heads better than the chance to act out these elements in role plays or to watch others act them out (Phenix, 2002). The literal demonstration of important scenes or interactions makes them more real to students of all grade levels, particularly those whose neuropsychological profiles make it hard for them to formulate mental images associated with what they read. Dramatic role playing of scenes from books and other readings has the added benefit of stimulating everyone's interest (even the most "tuned out" will usually perk up when a role play starts), which means that key learning content may find its way into many more brains. Readers' Theater, a structured form of dramatic role play in which students read from scripts adapted from books they are reading in class, provides participants with a repeated reading activity that has the added benefit of building fluency (Worthy, 2005).

Reading Response Log Template

Title: _____

Author: _____

Page: _____ to _____ = _____ (total number of pages read)

What were three main ideas, points, or parts from the reading you did today?

1. _____

2. _____

3. _____

*Restate the three ideas, points, or parts into a **summary** in the space below. You can add more ideas, points, or parts from the reading into the summary.*

Write a response to what you read in the space below and on the back of this page that tells about a connection you made to all or part of the text. It needs to be at least 7 sentences long. If you need more room, finish your response on a separate sheet of paper and <u>staple it to this one</u>. Be sure to start your response with one of these sentence starters:

- *This connects to my life because . . .*
- *I wonder . . .*
- *This is important because . . .*
- *This made me think about . . .*
- *I didn't understand _____ because _____*
- *I really liked this because . . .*

_____

_____

_____

_____

_____

_____

_____

_____

_____

In *Executive Function in the Classroom: Practical Strategies for
Improving Performance and Enhancing Skills for All Students* by C. Kaufman.
(2010, Paul H. Brookes Publishing Co., Inc.)

CHAPTER 7

From Brain to Paper

The Executive Foundations of Writing

" I love being a writer. What I can't stand is the paperwork. **"**
— PETER DE VRIES

" My writing speed is akin to headstone carving. **"**
— GLORIA STEINEM

" Writing is easy; all you do is sit staring at a blank
sheet of paper until drops of blood form on your forehead. **"**
— GENE FOWLER (AS CITED BY TROIA, 2006)

Upon completing this chapter, the reader will be able to

☞ Indicate why written language generally places far greater stress on most students' cognitive capacity than oral language

☞ Discuss the impact of various executive function weaknesses on student performance across the prewriting, drafting, revising, and editing stages of the writing process

☞ Indicate which of the stages of the writing process should be given greatest emphasis when attempting to build the writing skill of students with executive weakness

☞ Discuss the range of strategies that may be effective in developing the prewriting, drafting, revising, and editing/proofreading skills of students with executive weaknesses

☞ Discuss the accommodations that can be effective in lessening the writing-related stress experienced by students with executive dysfunction

The Writing Process

Anyone who has put pen to paper or fingers to keyboard is familiar with the acute frustration that often accompanies the act of composition. Even the most gifted authors have noted the struggles associated with the writing process, as the quotes at the beginning of the chapter attest.

Research on the writing skills of American students provides further testament of the difficulties associated with mastering this essential communication skill. A report from the National Assessment of Educational Progress (Persky, Daane, & Jin, 2003) found that only 25% of children could be classified as competent writers for their developmental stage. The same assessment showed that a mere 2% of American high school students graduate with what can be considered advanced writing skills (Dingfelder, 2006). Given these rather gloomy written language proficiency rates and the struggles accomplished writers continue to face as they churn out text, there seems little reason to doubt that writing can be very hard indeed.

Why does the generation and transcription of thoughts prove so difficult for the human mind? Spoken language, after all, is produced with relative ease beyond the early childhood years. Isn't written language simply a printed extension of speaking? As I hope to make clear in this chapter, the answer to this question is an unequivocal *no*. While speaking and writing are both elements of expressive language and therefore heavily related, they place very different loads on the brain's information processing capacity. Oral expression, as Feifer and DeFina (2002) and Berninger and Richards (2002) have noted, does not require the speaker to focus much on the "exactness" of language because the listener, via the conversational turn-taking process, is able to fill in understanding by asking questions and making comments. Speaking is also a generally rapid and transitory medium (Feifer & DeFina, 2002) that requires far less simultaneous processing than writing.

The vast majority of the things you say across the day simply tumble out of your mouth with little serious planning and structuring. Unless you or someone else records it, your speech vanishes instantly into the ether, leaving behind no permanent record. Writing, on the other hand, requires not just the expression of language, but also its careful transcription into the seeable realm. Because it involves the construction of thought on a visual level, there are a host of mechanical elements associated with it—spelling, letter size, word spacing, punctuation, capitalization, and syntax to name a few—that must be appropriately delivered for the reader to make sense of what is being said. The encoding of language into its visual form—particularly for younger and challenged learners—takes both thought and time, which substantially ramps up the simultaneous processing demands on the brain.

Writing therefore compels the producer to focus not just on the content of language (which is all speech requires), but also on the many mechanical things that must be correct for language to be legible and understandable in print. Because society dictates that written expression be correct in both form and content, the writer is bound to engage in a fairly elaborate, multidimensional process that involves seamless travel among its well-known phases: prewriting, writing, revising, editing, and publishing (Dehn, 2008). It is the very nature of writing, with all its simultaneous processing demands and phases that must be fluently shifted among, that makes it such a burden on students' cognitive capacity in general (Flower & Hayes, 1980; McCutchen, 2006; Torrance & Galbraith, 2006) and executive skills in particular. Indeed, one would be hard pressed to conceive of a task that places greater stress on executive skills than written language. This chapter explores the executive/self-regulatory requirements of the writing process, then offers a series of recommendations designed to reduce the fear and loathing students with executive function weakness experience when compelled to put pen to paper.

Executive Function and Writing

As most teachers discover early in their careers, many students with significant executive function difficulties "hate" to write. I have interviewed hundreds of these children over the course of my years in the school psychology trenches and have found that while a percentage have what might be portrayed as mixed emotions about reading and math, most describe writing, or their ability to write, with words such as "hate," "bad," "stupid," and "terrible." Research on these students has substantiated these comments, with studies showing that writing difficulties are without question the most common academic difficulty experienced by students with attention-deficit/hyperactivity disorder (ADHD) diagnoses (Mayes & Calhoun, 2005). Moving beyond diagnostic labels, other studies have demonstrated that executive function weaknesses are common among children with a range of written language difficulties (Hooper, Schwartz, Wakely, deKruif, & Montgomery, 2002).

What is it about writing that puts so many of these children over the edge? Of course, tasks that are cognitively challenging for students in general will likely be experienced as particularly difficult and tedious by students with executive dysfunction. But the main reason that so many students with executive function weakness struggle to a marked degree with writing may be that the expression of language on paper is bound up in the *generation of output*. Recall from Chapter 3 that the prefrontal cortex and its various efferent connections are associated with cognitive and motor output (Hale & Fiorello, 2004). As Goldberg (2001) indicated, the frontal lobes are the brain's primary initiators and maintainers of action. Therefore, relative processing weaknesses in the prefrontal cortical regions or its numerous connections are most likely to impact those aspects of academic functioning related to production, leading to what Levine (2003) referred to as *high output production failures*—working hard, but producing little (Bashir, 2008). Before moving on to the range of strategies to improve the writing skills of students with executive dysfunction, the following sections take a closer look at the specific ways in which executive function weakness can impact written output by examining its influence across the stages of the writing process.

Prewriting

Research has shown that while prewriting planning and thought organization take on major importance in the middle and high school years, children in early elementary school generally do not plan before they write (Bereiter & Scardamalia, 1987; Graham & Harris, 2005; McCutchen, 2006). When given an assignment, young children tend to jump right into their written response, using a *knowledge telling* approach (Bereiter & Scardamalia, 1987) that is limited to a statement of whatever is known about the topic at hand (with each subsequent sentence being influenced primarily by the one that came before it, as opposed to a larger planning process). This reliance on what might be called the "wing-it-and-hope-for-the-best" approach to writing is largely functional at the younger elementary school level, given the development expectations of the curriculum and the amount of individualized writing support provided by classroom staff through the conferencing process.

To write successfully at the upper elementary, middle, and secondary levels, students must make the shift to a more planned and reflective writing approach that devotes increasing time and effort to the prewriting elements of task analysis, brainstorming, and thought sequencing/organization (McCutchen, 2006). Students who fail to make this transition in response to the intensifying curriculum demands generally produce immature and very brief written pieces that compare poorly to the work of their more goal-directed peers.

Which students end up planning to fail by failing to plan? Many of them may have executive function difficulties. Lacking the self-directed cognitive ability needed to sufficiently reflect on what assignments require, set goals/establish plans for their completion, and then sequentially execute writing plans, these students continue to rely on the knowledge-telling approach to writing well beyond the grades at which this method is successful (Graham, Harris, & Olinghouse, 2007). In other words, these students get stuck at an immature phase of writing skill development, largely because the knowledge-telling approach requires less effort overall (Graham et al., 2007) and places less initial load on the executive skills (e.g., "Brainstorming and planning? Ugh, I hate that stuff—I'm just gonna start and get this lame assignment over with").

I say less "initial load" on the executive system, because what soon becomes apparent to anyone watching a student with executive function difficulties attempt to write for any length of the time with the wing-and-a-prayer approach is that by failing to establish at least a basic plan to follow at the outset, these students may end up writing themselves into all kinds of corners and dead ends (see Figure 7.1). Trapped by whatever half-baked bits and pieces they were able to get onto paper, many students with executive dysfunction become frustrated with what they see before them and lack any clear sense of how to improve the situation. This may lead to either a quick baling out of the writing assignment (e.g., "I'm done . . . I guess") or major frustration ("This assignment is so lame. It totally sucks!").

Working memory weaknesses are a key contributor to the prewriting aversion of many students with executive dysfunction. Chapter 1 introduced Elkhonon Goldberg's (2001) concept of *memory of the future* and the role it plays in the goal-setting, planning, and work completion process. In case you are having difficulty summoning this discussion back into your own working memory, here is a quick refresher. Working memory serves, in essence, as your cognitive desktop or workspace. Working memory capacity is predictive of goal-setting and planning skill, as one can only establish goals and plans to achieve them (memories of an intended future) if they can be held in the cognitive workspace long enough to be developed and realized. There-

Figure 7.1. This Peanuts cartoon is a great illustration of this "Now what do I do?" phenomenon. (Peanuts: © United Feature Syndicate, Inc.; reprinted by permission.)

fore, students with working memory weaknesses would be expected to have difficulties creating and following plans for their writing because they lack the cognitive workspace to focus on these higher-order elements of text generation while simultaneously attending to lower-order mechanical elements (McCutchen, 2006). This leads to what one might label as the tendency to "write in the moment" (and from moment to moment) rather than developing and following self-developed written language roadmaps. Significant working memory limitations can also dramatically hinder the work of students with executive weakness during the writing phase of the process, as discussed in the following section.

Writing and Drafting

Picture a juggler managing to keep several balls in the air. This is a very apt metaphor for the simultaneous processing demands required by text production. The act of writing is challenging for many people because it requires the mind to deal with many things at one time (see Figure 7.2), including (but not limited to) the following:

1.   Task demands (i.e., directions)

2.   Audience expectations

3.   Goals and purpose

4.   Ideas (i.e., what the writer hopes to convey)

5.   Sequence of ideas

6.   Spelling rules

7.   Grammar rules

8.   Punctuation rules

9.   Capitalization rules

10. Syntax rules

11. Vocabulary

12. Letter formation (for younger children and older students with handwriting challenges)

13. Word spacing (for younger children and older students with handwriting and spatial processing challenges)

Literacy specialists could likely add more items to this list without much difficulty. Hopefully, though, the essential point has been made regarding the intense simultaneous processing demands of writing. Because students have to simultaneously focus on all these conceptual and mechanical aspects of language production as they endeavor to get their thoughts on paper, students with working memory constraints as compared with developmental norms are compelled to either work at a snail's pace (e.g., "John, it's been 20 minutes and you've only written one sentence") or disregard several elements of writing to retain focus on a few ("Megan, what you've said here is nice, but it is full of spelling, punctuation, and capitalization errors").

Working memory difficulties are not the only element of executive dysfunction that can substantially impact the writing phase of the larger writing process. Significant deficiencies in any of the executive skills discussed in

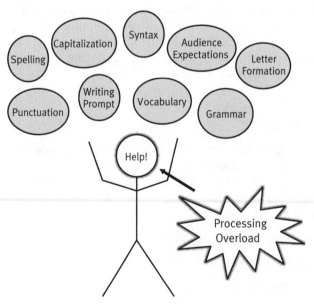

Figure 7.2.   Processing overload.

Chapter 1 can result in a student producing text that is either very brief or poor in quality. Weak impulse control, for example, may result in children rushing through the act of writing, leading to numerous errors, poorly sequenced thoughts, and text that wanders far afield from what the assignment directed. Sustained attention deficits can be reflected in writing samples that include numerous stray thoughts, omitted words, and sentences that link poorly together (Feifer & DeFina, 2002). Attention difficulties paired with working memory deficits are also a likely contributor to the processing speed and word retrieval struggles that many children with executive dysfunction experience as they try to write. As Hale and Fiorello (2004) suggested, students who lack the self-directed ability to search their long-term memories for the words/phrases needed while writing will likely find the act of text production to be slow and laborious:

Teacher: You're going to need to really speed up, Brandon, if you expect to finish that journal entry in time for recess.

Brandon: I'm trying to go faster, but my brain keeps forgetting the words I want to say and I have to think of them all over again!

Revision

The revision stage of the writing process centers on improvement of the content elements of writing. Children are generally taught that after they write a first draft, they should carefully reread their writing with an eye toward improving both the quality and clarity of the narrative (Gardner & Johnson, 1997). Defined in this manner, text revision is an indisputable act of self-regulation. To examine your own writing from a critical perspective, you must have both the self-awareness and self-regulatory skills to allow at least reasonable scrutiny of the sentences you have labored to express in print (Graham et al., 2007). Because one of the core features of executive function weakness is difficulty with stopping and thinking about oneself and one's actions (Barkley, 1997), it is often very difficult for students with executive dysfunction to engage in revising. Just as their neuropsychological profiles tend to inhibit deep text processing when reading others' writing (see Chapter 6), these students' working memory, attention, cognitive flexibility, and impulse control difficulties limit the ability to effectively examine their own text. Thus, when told to go back and reread their work in a careful, critical manner, they tend to lack the self-regulatory capacity to do so. These students may employ a rather superficial form of revision, resulting in teacher–student dialogues that sound a lot like this:

Teacher: Jacob, why are you just sitting there? Aren't you supposed to be revising your business letter draft?

Jacob: Yeah, um . . . I guess. I mean . . . I did. I'm done.

Teacher: How can that be? You just finished the draft 2 minutes ago.

Jacob: Well, I read through it again and it seems okay to me [shrugs].

The emotional and motivational aspects of executive function can also dramatically impact a student's ability to engage in revision. As noted earlier, the simultaneous demands of the act of writing are often so overwhelming for students with executive function weaknesses that they tend to become quickly exhausted by their efforts in the drafting phrase of the process. Once "done" with a draft, therefore, they consider their mighty efforts to have sufficiently fulfilled the assignment demands and want nothing more to do with the narrative they produce (e.g., "I'm done—finally. Take it away, I never want to see it again"). Getting these students to reengage with their writing samples often requires Herculean efforts on the part of teachers, who must endeavor to build the writing skills of kids with executive dysfunction without pushing them to the point of diminishing returns—or no return.

While most students are taught to revise their writing in a distinct revision stage, skilled writers learn that text production is actually a highly recursive (back-and-forth) process that rarely follows the linear five- to six-step process emphasized in writer's workshop models (Kaufer, Hayes, & Flower, 1986; Fisher & Fray, 2007; Graham et al., 2007). That is, strong writers not only carefully revise their work after completing a draft, but also engage in lots of "on the fly" revision while they write. Research by Kaufer et al. (1986) found that skilled writers tend to pause and consider what they produce after every several words, making changes as needed before moving on. Revision in the authentic writing process therefore requires high levels of set-shifting ability to move fluidly between text generation and text revision. Lacking this cognitive flexibility and often just wanting to complete writing assignments as quickly as possible, many students with executive weaknesses write in a rather rushed, nonreflective manner; they are often more concerned with task completion (e.g., "Am I done? When can I be done?") than with the production of quality work.

Editing/Proofreading

While there is substantial overlap between revising and editing—given that both are bound up in the improvement/correction of text based on careful review—traditional writing instruction draws a distinction between these elements of the writing process (Speck, Hinnen, & Hinnen, 2003). Revision, as noted earlier, relates primarily to the enhancing of text content, while editing is more often associated with the noting and fixing of mechanical problems, such as spelling, punctuation, capitalization, and syntax errors. Although a range of executive skills (including working memory, purposeful attention, impulse control, and set-shifting ability) can impact the accuracy and consistency of a student's editing, the aspect of executive function most often discussed in the context of this stage of the writing process is self-monitoring (Troia, 2006). To be reasonably competent editors/proofreaders of their own work, children must have sufficient self-awareness to recognize the types of mechanical errors they are prone to make and the self-directed monitoring skill to completely scan the page for the broader range of errors that may be present. Because not all teachers instruct their students in the use of highly structured and sequential editing systems, students can experience working memory overload by trying to find and correct several different kinds of errors at one time (e.g., "Carlos, you did a pretty nice job correcting your spelling errors here, but what about the other errors? A lot of sentences are missing capital letters at the start, and where are the commas we talked about?").

Summary of the Impact of Executive Function on Writing

Figures 7.3 and 7.4 summarize the essential differences between the recursive writing processes employed by students with and without developmental executive function weakness. Better writers—those who are presumably without substantial executive struggles—are able to employ appropriate self-regulation across all phases of text production, shifting smoothly among phases of writing as they crank out text (Zimmerman & Risemberg, 1997). As a function of their previous writing successes, they tend to approach each new writing assignment with at least reasonable levels of self-confidence and motivation. These self-efficacy expectations and intact executive skills allow these students to persist with effective writing process strategies even when the going gets tough.

In contrast, students with significant executive dysfunction relative to peer norms are apt to view their writing skills as quite limited and writing tasks as highly laborious—to be avoided whenever possible. Lacking the executive skills needed to tolerate and engage in prewriting activities, they generally just leap into writing assignments and stick with the knowledge-telling approach (i.e., one somewhat random thought after another), which is common among young children and students with learning disabilities (Bereiter & Scardamalia, 1987; Graham & Harris, 2005; Graham et al., 2007). By virtue of their limited working memory capacity, they struggle greatly with the

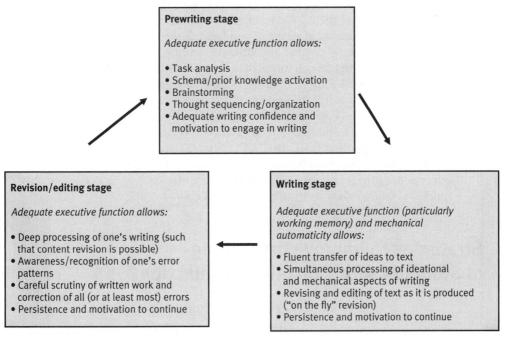

Figure 7.3. Recursive writing stages.

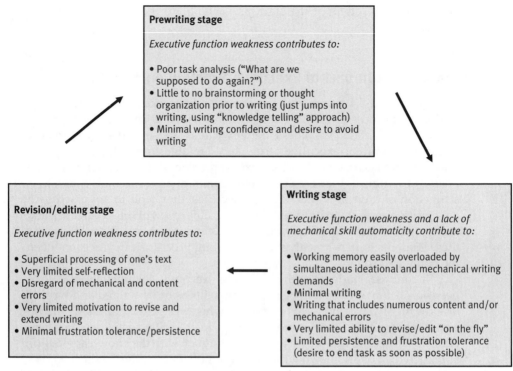

Figure 7.4. Recursive writing stages as affected by executive dysfunction.

simultaneous processing requirements of the drafting phases (Dehn, 2008; McCutchen, 2006). Thus, these students may produce very little on paper ("I keep forgetting what I want to say" or "I can't think of anything to write") and/or writing that includes numerous mechanical errors.

Fatigued by the act of drafting and lacking the deep text-processing and self-monitoring skills needed for effective editing, children with executive dysfunction tend to view all forms of revision as tedious, loathsome activities ("I said I'm done!"). Finally, because of their limited cognitive flexibility and self-regulatory capacity, students with executive weaknesses often struggle with the numerous cognitive shifts among the forethought (planning), performance (writing), and self-reflection (revision/editing) phases necessitated by the writing process (McCloskey, Perkins, & Van Divner, 2009). Given the comparatively poor fit between their cognitive profiles and the demands of academic writing, is it any wonder so many students with executive dysfunction come to view writing as a frightful chore?

Strategies to Improve the Writing of Students with Executive Dysfunction

"Opportunity favors the prepared mind."

–LOUIS PASTEUR

Prewriting: The Essential Intervention
Stage for Students with Executive Dysfunction

The phase of the writing process that is most crucial to the success of students with executive dysfunction may be prewriting. Given their goal-setting, planning, working memory, and self-monitoring limitations, these students tend to have great difficulty structuring their writing "on the fly" during the drafting phase, and therefore must organize their thoughts in advance if they are to have a chance of producing narrative that is reasonably substantial, coherent, and error free. Research has shown that when students with learning disabilities are explicitly taught prewriting planning strategies, the quality and length of their writing improves considerably (Troia, 2006). However, many children with executive function weaknesses have a rather dim view of prewriting tasks because these activities forestall the desired goal of getting writing assignments over with as quickly as possible (e.g., "You want me to do all that and then write the essay? That will take forever").

How do we get students with executive function difficulties to cooperatively engage in the systematic forethought activities needed for most forms of academic writing? Here are a few suggestions:

1. *Build systematic prewriting processes into the curricula so that all students (not just those with individualized education programs [IEPs] and Section 504 plans) are required to use them on a regular basis.* When only students with learning disabilities have to engage in detailed prewriting activities ("John, your IEP requires that we give you a linear graphic organizer like this before you write, so here it is—let's do it together now") is that these children feel all the more overwhelmed and angered by the writing process (e.g., "What? Why do I have to do this extra graphic organizer if nobody else has to? It's not fair"). By making systematic prewriting a nonnegotiable aspect of a class's standard writing requirements, it becomes part of the production process in which everyone must engage, not an onerous extra task for students with writing difficulties.

2. *Explicitly demonstrate how the use of systematic prewriting activities ultimately makes writing easier.* Because the perceived difficulty and tedium of writing tasks is the major reason most students—not just those with executive function weakness—want to be done with them as soon as possible, it makes sense that the prewriting instructional process should give explicit emphasis to the ways in which planning before writing makes the writing process itself faster and easier. During the discussion and modeling phases of the explicit teaching process, therefore, it is important to unambiguously show students how the time and effort devoted to prewriting are likely to save them time and effort while they write. To do this, teachers may first demonstrate using a "think-aloud" technique about how failing to plan in advance leads to writing oneself into a corner (e.g., "Oops, class . . . look what's happened. I'm sort of stuck now and will have to go back and rewrite these last few sentences because they really don't go with the top part—it's not going to make a lot of sense. Ugh, that's going to take some time"). Once students have been concretely shown the writing struggles that tend to occur in the absence of adequate

planning, their willingness to use structured planning processes is likely to increase.

3. *Stress the idea that "thought gathering" (i.e., prewriting thought organization and planning) is simply a standard part of writing.* One way to overcome the natural "knowledge telling" writing style of younger children and older students with learning struggles is to explicitly teach in the early elementary school years the idea that a gathering of one's thoughts should almost always precede the mechanical act of writing. Thus, children should be taught as early as second grade that before they make an entry in their daily journal or write a brief story, they need to first give some thought to both the content and order of what they want to say (e.g., "First I think, then I write"). The first planning/organizational strategy discussed in the next section seems particularly suited to this task.

Planning/Organizational Strategies

Thought Gathering

In thought gathering, one first conjures up and organizes ideas before they are effectively put on paper. To explicitly teach the notion that thought development and organization should precede writing to younger children, as well as older children with executive skill weaknesses, it may be helpful to start off "low tech," using a basket, sticky notes, and a whiteboard (see Figure 7.5).

After explaining the importance of thought gathering to the larger writing process and establishing a related writing prompt (e.g., writing a thank-you letter as a class to the town's fire chief for the chance to tour a fire engine and learn about fire safety), the teacher provides all students with a couple of sticky notes and directs that students write down a thought or two that could be included in the letter. Once everyone has jotted down their ideas, the teacher holds up a basket and directs the group to come up and put their sticky notes inside as a way to concretely represent the thought-gathering

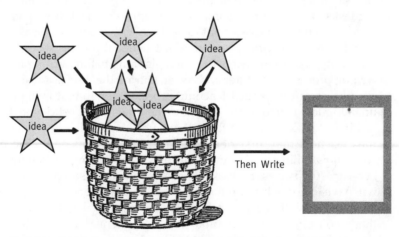

Figure 7.5. Helpful metaphor to teach the prewriting strategy of thought gathering.

aspect of the writing process. When the ideas are all in the basket, the teacher transfers them to the whiteboard, sticking them up in whatever order they are retrieved.

Calling the entire class to the front of the room, the teacher then initiates a thought organization discussion, with the various sticky-noted ideas being grouped together into categories (e.g., favorite parts of the field trip, important fire safety tips, different ways of saying thank you) and then sequenced. When the thoughts have been grouped and ordered, the students are sent back to their seats. The teacher then leads the actual writing of the thank-you note on an overhead projector using the sequenced sticky-note thought map on the whiteboard as a guide.

After this technique has been lead by the teacher a few times across a range of writing modalities, responsibility for the management of the strategy is gradually transferred to the students. Students may use it first in small groups to gather and sequence thoughts for writing assignments. The last phase of the thought-gathering strategy involves doing away with the baskets and sticky notes entirely and replacing them with a related graphic organizer (see Appendix 7.1). Adhering to the gradual release of responsibility framework (Fisher & Fray, 2007), it would be helpful to use the organizer at least once or twice in small groups before students are required to use it on their own as a prewriting strategy.

Graphic Organizers

Graphic organizers have become a staple of the teaching profession across curricula and grade spans. They are, in short, everywhere, and this is far from a bad thing. Many students benefit from graphical representations of knowledge, and teachers often find it helpful to lead conceptual discussions by embedding content into a visual frame that reflects the linkages and differences among various types of information (Bromley, Irwin-DeVitis, & Modlo, 1995; Hyerle, 2009). The power of graphic organizers as planning/organizational tools for writing has become so widely accepted in the educational community that there is a seemingly endless supply of graphic prewriting templates available on the Internet and from academic publishing companies.

Clearly, the development and dissemination of graphic organizers for both learning and production has become a big business. However, are all the webs, maps, charts, and diagrams in today's classrooms well aligned to the writing needs of students with executive function weaknesses? The answer to this question is a resounding *no,* as any teacher who has ever tried to get a student with ADHD or Asperger syndrome to write a narrative from a complex circular story web will tell you. Although story maps have their value in helping children to analyze the key elements of a book or develop the pieces needed for their own stories, organizers that lack any obvious sequential flow of ideas (see Figure 7.6) can be poorly suited to the needs of students with sequencing and organizational needs. Even if these graphics display the important elements that must be included in a written piece, they do not present the would-be writer with a clear sense of where to begin and how to continue. Thus, many students with executive function struggles may complete this type of organizer, generally with teacher assistance, only to find it fairly useless with regard to getting their writing started and completed:

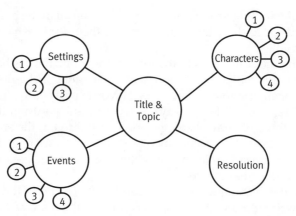

Figure 7.6. Story map example.

Teacher: Danny, why haven't you started writing yet? I helped you finish your story map 15 minutes ago.

Danny: I don't really know what to do. I mean, I have this thing, but now what do I do? I don't know how to start and where to put things and stuff.

Teacher: Danny, isn't it obvious? It's all right there in your map. You have all the details you need right there. Just write them now into your story.

Danny: Um . . . okay, but I still don't really get what you mean. How do you do it?

The types of graphic organizers that are most likely to help students with executive function weaknesses to both organize/sequence their thoughts before writing and then confidently transfer the thoughts to narrative are those with an obvious sequential, step-by-step, flow—linear graphic organizers (see Appendixes 7.2 and 7.3). Upon completing either of these organizers, a student should at least possess a fairly clear roadmap to follow with regard to starting, continuing with, and completing a writing assignment. The next strategy can also be structured around a linear/sequential graphic organizer, but has the added benefit of being embedded in a larger, systematic prewriting process that includes goal setting and brainstorming.

Stop and List

The Stop-and-List approach was developed originally by Troia, Graham, and Harris (1999) and described in some detail by Graham and Harris (2005). It was expressly designed to build the goal-setting, planning, and organizational skills of children with executive function and other written language difficulties. Highly structured by the *stop* and *list* mnemonics, the strategy requires students to develop an overarching goal for writing and then systematically brainstorm, select, and sequence their ideas before engaging in the drafting phase of the writing process (Graham & Harris, 2005).

There are three core steps to this approach. The first step (*stop*) reminds students to inhibit the impulse to jump blithely into their writing and to instead first develop a goal for the piece they will ultimately create. As Graham and Harris (2005) noted, each letter of the *stop* mnemonic represents a word in the guiding phrase: *s*top and *t*hink *o*f a *p*urpose. Once students have established their writing goals, the *list* stage of the prewriting process kicks in: list *i*deas and *s*equence *t*hem. During the *list* step, students simply brainstorm as many ideas as they can think of related to the writing prompt at hand and their specific writing goals. The next step requires selecting from the several brainstormed ideas those that will be included in the written piece. Once the selection process has been completed, students then order their ideas and reflect this sequence by placing a number next to each one.

Appendix 7.4 contains the Stop-and-List template that I adapted from the methods described by Graham and Harris (2005) to help address the prewriting needs of a group of middle school students with Asperger syndrome (all of whom were particularly writing averse). It requires the student (with a teacher's support) to specify a writing goal at the top, and to then list brainstormed ideas in the left-hand column in bulleted form. The middle column provides space for the ideas that will actually be included in the writing piece to be checked, and the third column is where the sequence of checked ideas is reflected. A fourth step has been added at the bottom of the page that directs students, before writing, to anticipate the likely paragraph structure of their written piece by marking each selected/sequenced idea with a specific highlighter color to reflect the paragraph to which it will belong.

Brainstorm-Organize-Topic Sentence-Examples-Conclusion (BOTEC)

The BOTEC method, published originally in *Essay Express* (Research Institute for Learning and Development and FableVision, Inc., 2002b) and presented by Meltzer, Sales Pollica, and Barzillai (2007), is another prewriting organizer that is well suited to the needs of students with executive skills weaknesses. My adaptation of the original BOTEC organizer is shown in Appendix 7.5. Although it produces a somewhat less elaborate and detailed writing plan than other sequential prewriting graphics (note that the plan portion is limited to the bottom third of the page), the fact that it contains all the essential prewriting steps in a single-page format may make it less overwhelming and therefore more acceptable to students with executive weaknesses than more lengthy prewriting organizational systems. Although the task demands of this and similar planning templates are straightforward, teachers should still introduce them to students via an explicit teaching and guided practice model. Teachers can show it initially via an overhead projector, model its completion using teacher ideas and those from students, and then write an essay or story with students using the template as a guide.

Somebody-Wanted-But-So

Developed originally by Macon, Bewell, and Vogt (1991) as a "during and after" reading strategy to improve students' comprehension of plot elements such as conflict and resolution, the somebody-wanted-but-so approach can also be a highly effective means of helping students brainstorm and organize their own ideas for stories prior to writing (Foster & Marasco, 2007). The model—whether used for story analysis or story production—operates from the assumption that just about every bit of fiction developed since the dawn of time contains four essential elements:

1. A lead character (*somebody*)

2. Who desires something (*wanted*)

Somebody	Wanted	But	So
(Character/protagonist)	(Goal/motivation)	(Conflict/challenge)	(Resolution)
Cinderella	Out of the rags; a handsome prince; to go to the royal ball	Initially prevented from going to ball by the scheming of a nefarious stepmother and two socially challenged stepsisters	The mother of all happy endings, initiated by the wonderful wand waving fairy godmother
ET	To go home	Captured by government scientists; poked and probed like a lab rat	Escapes, phones home, makes assorted kids and bikes fly, and is picked up by a spaceship

Figure 7.7. Example of a traditional *somebody-wanted-but-so* organizer. (Adapted from Macon, J.M., Bewell, D., & Vogt, M. [1991]. Plot relationship chart, from Responses to Literature: Grades K–8 [p. 8]. Copyright 1991 by the International Reading Association [www.reading.org])

3. Whose goals are thwarted in some way (*but*)

4. Who achieves/receives some kind of resolution—good or bad (*so*)

Figure 7.7 shows an example of a graphic organizer that is commonly used for character and plot analysis with this method. Although this tried-and-true organizer will likely be effective in helping children understand and retell essential story elements, it may not be a good basis from which to develop original stories, particularly for students with executive weakness who generally need more detailed and sequential story maps before they can shift to the drafting process with reasonable confidence. Appendix 7.6 contains a modified version, which is considerably more structured and designed to encourage the production of a more detail-rich story.

Paragraph Writing Strategies

A popular complaint among secondary-level English teachers is that many students leave elementary school without understanding even the basics of paragraph construction (Persky et al., 2003). To what can we attribute a student's inability to write a decent paragraph by the secondary school years? Learning difficulties such as executive dysfunction certainly underlie a portion of writing skill weaknesses, but another factor may be the ambiguous writing instruction that children sometimes receive (Troia, 2006).

Although an increasing number of elementary schools have developed sequential writing curricula and standards mandating that students exhibit specific written language skills from kindergarten to fifth grade, it remains common practice for elementary-school children to receive writing instruction that is highly eclectic, variable, and generally "squishy" in nature. I refer to this discontinuous writing curricula sequence as the "a little of this, a little of that" instructional approach, in that it tends to rely on incidental/casual teaching of narrative writing rather than explicit instructional procedures that build systematically and sequentially from year to year (Troia, 2006).

Children with executive function difficulties may be challenged by nonsystematic writing instruction, as their neuropsychological profiles can make it difficult to pick up the mechanical aspects of narrative generation in the absence of the explicit teaching and practice of strategies (Graham et al., 2007). Thus, they require explicit instruction in paragraph construction, and then guided extended practice in the systematic development and sequencing of paragraphs. The two methodologies discussed in the following sections are particularly structured and clearcut (and therefore frontal lobe–friendly).

Step Up to Writing

Developed by Maureen Auman (2002), *Step Up to Writing* employs a traffic-light metaphor (i.e., green means *go*, yellow means *slow down*, red means *stop*) to teach students the essential structural elements of paragraph construction (see Figure 7.8). Although sometimes criticized for being overly rigid and as tending to encourage students to produce paragraphs in an overly formulaic manner, it is exactly this high degree of structure and consistency that makes the method so well aligned to the needs of students with executive weaknesses.

Although a detailed presentation of this method is beyond the scope of this book, here is a quick summary of how it works. Using the traffic-light metaphor, the *Step Up to Writing* model of teaching paragraph construction stresses the importance of a logical flow from topic sentence, main ideas (with supporting details/examples), and concluding sentence. Using a green marker on an overhead projector or a whiteboard, the teacher demonstrates that a paragraph starts with a topic sentence that introduces the larger theme (or

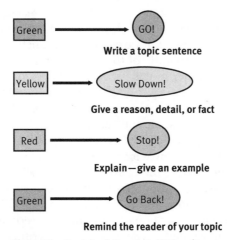

Figure 7.8. Example of *Step Up to Writing*. (*Source:* http://www.sopriswest.com/)

general statement) of a paragraph (green is used for its association with the "green for go" element of a traffic light). A yellow marker is then used to reflect the need to slow down and write an idea, reason, or fact. The teacher next uses a red marker to reflect the more definite stop that occurs in paragraph writing when an example related to the idea, reason, or fact is provided. Finally, the green marker is used again to write the concluding sentence because the writer is restating the topic sentence to some degree, thus reminding the reader of the paragraph's main theme or statement.

Once children become familiar with this essential paragraph flow, they are taught to add additional main ideas and supporting examples before offering the concluding sentence. Here is an example of a third-grade child's response to the prompt, "What makes a good teacher?" using the Auman's three-color approach (text that had been green is now presented in bold print, text that had been yellow is now in italics, and text that had been red is now underlined):

> **A good teacher does two things.** *She makes the classroom nice.* <u>A good teacher has lots of books for us to look at and posters on the wall.</u> *A good teacher also teaches us new things.* <u>She lets us learn about other countries and experiments in science.</u> **Teachers are the most important part of school.**

Unlike the standard hamburger- and sandwich-themed graphic organizers that are commonly used in elementary schools to demonstrate paragraph structure—in which the top piece of bread is the topic sentence, the bottom piece of bread is the concluding sentence, and the various ingredients in the middle are the main ideas and details—Auman's (2002) traffic light model provides some structure to the "filler" or middle elements of the paragraph by demonstrating how main ideas should precede smaller examples. By so doing, the *Step Up to Writing* method makes the paragraph-development process more explicit to children with learning difficulties and is apt to cut down on frustrated comments such as, "I don't know what my ingredients should be!"

Modified Sandwich Graphic Organizer

Because many regular and special education teachers are fond of the "sandwich-type" graphic organizers as means of teaching paragraph organization, a more structured example is provided in Appendix 7.7, which seems more suitable for students with executive dysfunction. Like the *Step Up to Writing* model, this adaptation of the classic sandwich organizer endeavors to make clear the manner in which ideas/reasons follow the topic sentence and are followed by more specific examples. Also inspired by the *Step Up to Writing* model is the presentation of possible transition statements to help students state their main ideas and conclusions.

Although this adapted organizer (and the *Step Up to Writing* method, for that matter) will not be suitable for the full range of paragraphs that students need to learn to write over the course of their school years, practice with it still conveys the essential point that all paragraphs should have logical flow and should transition logically from one to the next. Teachers with word-processing experience and about 20 minutes of preparation time can adapt this template to suit whatever type of paragraph writing they are endeavoring to teach to students whose writing difficulties relate to significant planning/ organizational weaknesses.

Systematic Editing Strategies

Many students with executive skill weaknesses have a marked aversion to revision and editing. Once they have completed their first draft, they act as if it has been either chiseled in stone or written in blood, and may resist all prompts to even proofread their work. The basis of their refusal often lies in the view of writing as a lengthy, complicated, and often agonizing process that is best gotten through with all possible dispatch (e.g., "I'm done! Phew . . . glad that's over!").

Given these perceptions, how do teachers get these students to accept and practice the idea that writing almost always requires some degree of editing and fixing? One answer to this question is the same one used to address the question of how to get students with executive weakness to participate in systematic prewriting activities: Structure writing instruction so that everyone in the class is following the same set of procedures. For prewriting, all students—not just those with IEPs and Section 504 plans—should use identical templates and related activities to plan their work before drafting. The same principle should apply to the editing phase of the writing process: All students should be required to follow the same structured series of editing procedures before moving on to the publishing stage.

Because many students, not just those with executive dysfunction, struggle with tasks that require them to focus on several things at one time, there is logic to making the proofreading processes as sequential and as easy to access as possible. This is likely why a range of acronym-driven editing strategies, including COPS (Ellis & Lenz, 1987), SCOPE (Bos & Vaughn, 1988), and COLA (Singer & Bashir, 2004), have received increasing acceptance in the educational community in recent years. Table 7.1 summarizes the essential elements of each of these methods.

Although the particular editing emphasis and order varies to some extent from model to model, they all share the underlying philosophy that the policing of one's text is best conducted in a stepwise manner. Students taught to use the SCOPE strategy, for example, learn to reread their draft five separate times, looking for a different error type each time (e.g., spelling, capitalization, word order). Consistent with the explicit teaching message repeated throughout this chapter, teachers planning to implement one of these strategies would be well advised to model its use and then provide opportunities for students to practice with it in small groups before requiring independent application. It may also be helpful to dedicate a bulletin board to this strategy and/or laminate small versions of it for all students to tape to the top of their desks or writing folders. To further benefit the students with executive function weakness, the strategy can be even more tightly structured by requiring students to check off each step on a strategy rubric before moving on to the next step.

Table 7.1.   Acronym-driven editing strategies

SCOPE (Bos & Vaughn, 1988)	COPS (Ellis & Lenz, 1987; described by Graham & Harris, 2005)	COLA (Singer & Bashir, 2004)
Check:	Check:	Check:
1. **S**pelling	1. **C**apitalization (Have I capitalized the first words of sentences and proper nouns?)	1. **C**ontent (Are all parts of the assignment covered? Is there a definite beginning, middle, and ending? Is any information unrelated to the topic or not needed?)
2. **C**apitalization		
3. Word **o**rder[a]	2. **O**verall appearance (How neat and organized is my writing?)	
4. **P**unctuation		2. **O**rganization (Do the ideas follow each other in a logical order? Do all paragraphs have topic sentences and supporting details?)
5. **E**xpress a complete thought (Does each sentence express a complete thought?)	3. **P**unctuation (Do I have periods at the end of all sentences, and have I inserted commas, semicolons, and apostrophes where necessary?)	
	4. **S**pelling (Do all my words look like they're spelled correctly? Use a spell checker or dictionary to check on the ones I'm not sure of.)	3. **L**anguage (Will each sentence make sense to my reader? Is each sentence well built? Do I use unusual words that make my writing interest?)
		4. **A**ppearance (Does each sentence start with a capital and end with correct punctuation? Have I capitalized names, specific places, or titles in my paper? Are all words spelled correctly?)

[a]Given the marked tendency among children with executive function weakness to omit small words when writing, it is important to explicitly teach that this step also includes looking for words that have been left out.

Writing Accommodations for Students with Executive Dysfunction

Strategic writing instruction, particularly when embedded in the context of explicit teaching methods that gradually release responsibility for task direction to individual students, can be highly effective in helping children with executive difficulties engage in the writing process (Graham & Harris, 2005; Graham et al., 2007). There are students, however, whose executive weaknesses are either so pronounced or so poorly aligned to certain narrative writing assignments that no amount of scaffolded writing instruction can convince them to put pen to paper. To get these individuals to write with something even approaching confidence and cooperation, accommodations generally need to be in place to further reduce the self-direction and simultaneous processing demands of written language. This section discusses bypass strategies that are apt to be most successful with children whose executive skills fall below developmental norms.

Dictation (Scribing)

Children receiving the dictation accommodation are generally allowed to dictate the first drafts of narrative writing assignments to an adult or fluent-writing peer, who then transcribes the thoughts onto paper. Although the actual dictation procedures can vary widely from child to child and assignment to assignment, in its most common form the student dictates first drafts of assignments and then is responsible for working with greater levels of independence through the revision/editing and publishing aspects of the writing process. Because oral language does not require the producer to fret about such writing mechanics as spelling, punctuation, capitalization, and other elements of printed grammar, working memory capacity can be devoted entirely to the language and ideational elements of writing.

Many children with pronounced executive deficits who tend to become overwhelmed by the simultaneous processing demands of independent narrative writing find it easier to develop their thoughts if they can speak them and leave the tedious mechanical elements to someone else. Although some research has demonstrated the power of dictation approaches in building the length and quality of the writing of students with learning disabilities (MacArthur & Graham, 1987; Tindal & Fuchs, 2000), a potential downside of this approach relates to its somewhat addictive nature; that is, a percentage of students become so accustomed to writing in collaboration with a scribe that they become greatly resistant to writing much of anything on their own. Thus, if dictation is provided to a student as an accommodation, it is essential that its role in his or her writing plan be clearly defined, as well as the steps that will be taken over time to gradually fade its use in favor of scaffolds that encourage more independent text production.

Sentence Starters

In my experience, regular and special educators have long used the accommodation of sentence starters to provide some explicit structure to the dreaded blank page. In its most traditional form, the teacher places a series of starter phrases on a page (e.g., *Once upon a time . . . , The part I liked best . . . , Next . . . , At the end . . .*) that the student must finish and then follow with additional sentences. This approach can also be structured around a series of specific question prompts, turning a more complex assignment that requires lots of self-direction and planning/sequencing skill to organize and answer into a list of specific questions to be answered (see Figure 7.9).

Original assignment:

Pick your favorite fairy tale and develop a "fractured" version of it. Make sure you also make at least three illustrations and show in your writing how the main characters resolve an essential conflict.

Modified assignment:

List the five main characters in Cinderella.

Where does the story take place?

What was Cinderella's main problem? What was she doing to cope with it?

What might be some funny ways to change the story?

How would one of those changes change the ending?

Figure 7.9. Defeating the dreaded "blank page" phenomenon by providing students with question prompts or sentence starters.

Dividing Larger Assignments into Smaller Chunks

Commonly included in the IEPs of students with executive dysfunction, this approach limits the simultaneous processing and organizational demands of larger writing projects by dividing them into a series of smaller tasks to be accomplished one bit at a time. This strategy, like the sentence starter approach, operates from the "surrogate frontal lobe" perspective in that it places much of the onus for structuring assignment completion on the teacher. As Berninger and Richards (2002) noted, one of the most important roles played by the teacher in developing the skills of novice writers is to serve as their frontal executive functions. When used most effectively, these accommodations are slowly faded over time using liberal amounts of guided practice once students show sufficient success with the most teacher-directed forms.

Extended Time for Assignment Completion

Because of their processing speed and simultaneous processing limitations, many students with executive weaknesses benefit from additional time to get their written language assignments done. However, this accommodation by itself in the absence of strategic supports often just prolongs the agony students experience when required to write. To truly benefit from longer periods to complete their work, individuals with executive dysfunction often require instructional scaffolds of the kind discussed previously in this chapter, as well as lots of "checking in" with teachers during the drafting phase.

Keyboard Access

Although the acquisition of reasonably fluid typing skills can be an arduous chore for many students regardless of their neuropsychological profile, the benefits of writing on a computer or portable keyboard device, such as *AlphaSmart*, often make the work needed to move beyond the "hunt-and-peck" stage worthwhile. Among the many helpful things about writing with contemporary word-processing software is that immediate feedback is given about the accuracy of one's spelling and grammar. Because the computer assumes a portion of the responsibility for these mechanical elements, the writer is able to devote more precious working memory space to the language and ideational aspects of narrative generation. Revising and editing also tend to be easier with digitized than handwritten text, which can contribute to higher levels of engagement in these phases of writing process by students who are otherwise adverse to editing.

Thought-Gathering Template

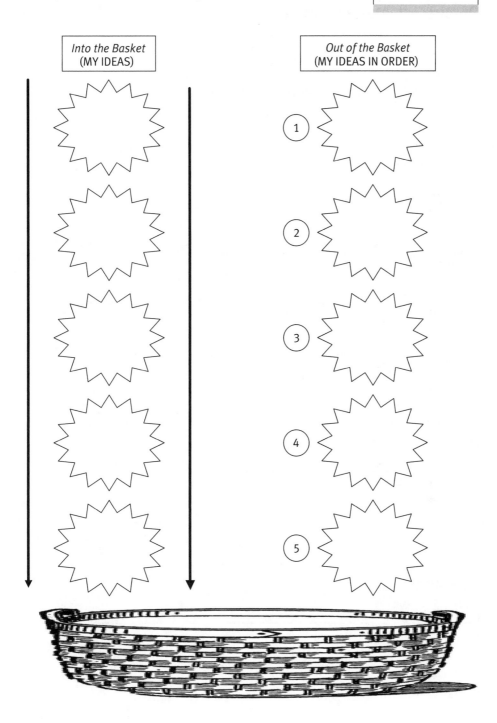

Into the Basket
(MY IDEAS)

Out of the Basket
(MY IDEAS IN ORDER)

1

2

3

4

5

Linear/Sequential
Persuasion Map Example

Goal

To persuade my readers that . . .

First major reason:

> Fact/example

> Fact/example

Second major reason:

> Fact/example

> Fact/example

Third major reason:

> Fact/example

> Fact/example

Conclusion:

Linear/Sequential Story Map Example

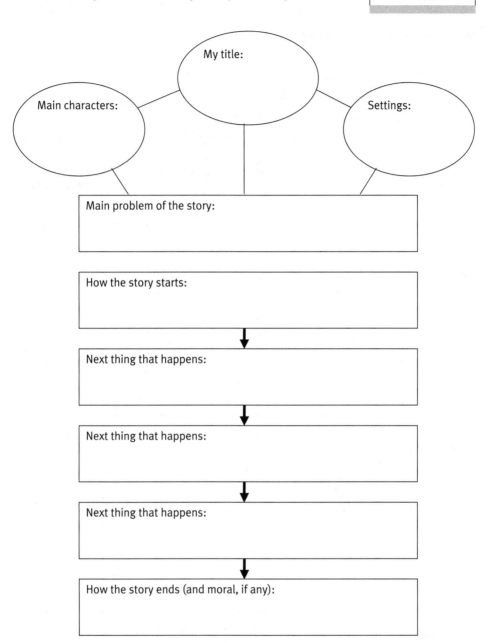

My title:

Main characters:

Settings:

Main problem of the story:

How the story starts:

Next thing that happens:

Next thing that happens:

Next thing that happens:

How the story ends (and moral, if any):

STOP and LIST Template

My goal for this writing assignment is to . . .

_____

_____

_____

List ideas	Which ideas will I use? (use a *)	Sequence of ideas (use a #)
_____	_____	_____
_____	_____	_____
_____	_____	_____
_____	_____	_____
_____	_____	_____
_____	_____	_____
_____	_____	_____
_____	_____	_____
_____	_____	_____
_____	_____	_____
_____	_____	_____

Last step: Once you've got your ideas sequenced, use different highlighter colors to show the paragraphs they will go into (for example, all ideas for first paragraph can be marked with yellow, those for second paragraph can be marked with blue, and so forth).

From Graham, S., & Harris, K.R. (2005). STOP and LIST: Goal setting, brainstorming, and organizing. In _Writing better: Effective strategies for teaching students with learning difficulties_ (p. 56). Baltimore: Paul H. Brookes Publishing Co.; adapted by permission. Copyright © 2005 Paul H. Brookes Publishing Co., Inc. All rights reserved.

In _Executive Function in the Classroom: Practical Strategies for Improving Performance and Enhancing Skills for All Students_ by C. Kaufman.
(2010, Paul H. Brookes Publishing Co., Inc.)

144

BOTEC Example

Brainstorm **O**rganize **T**opic Sentence **E**xamples **C**onclusion

Assignment (*what you're supposed to write about*): _____

_____

_____

Brainstorming (*list some possible ideas for your writing here—use only a few words for each and don't worry about the order for now*):

1. _____
2. _____
3. _____
4. _____
5. _____
6. _____

Organize and Order (*Pick at least 3 of the ideas you've just listed and then write them on the lines below in the order that would make the most sense. Which should come 1st, 2nd, 3rd, and so forth?*)

1. _____
2. _____
3. _____
4. _____

Topic Sentence (*Get the ball rolling! Write a topic sentence that introduces your whole essay or story*):

_____

_____

_____

Examples and Details (*List all of your chosen ideas and add at least one detail or fact for each*):

Idea #1: _____

        Detail: _____

        Detail: _____

Idea #2: _____

        Detail: _____

        Detail: _____

Idea #3: _____

        Detail: _____

        Detail: _____

Conclusion (*Write one sentence that summarizes all the major points in your essay/story*):

_____

_____

From *Essay Express*, Research Institute for Learning and Development and FableVision, Inc., © 2005; adapted by permission.

In *Executive Function in the Classroom: Practical Strategies for Improving Performance and Enhancing Skills for All Students* by C. Kaufman.
(2010, Paul H. Brookes Publishing Co., Inc.)

Modified SOMEBODY-WANTED-BUT-SO Template

Directions: Answer the questions in the boxes below. This will help you brainstorm and organize some of the most important parts of your story.

(1)

Somebody: Who is the main character in your story?	
Wanted: What is the main thing your character wants in the story? What are his/her primary goals or desires?	
But: What conflicts develop or other things happen that make it difficult for the main character to achieve his/her goals?	
So: How is the conflict resolved? Does the main character get what he/she wants?	

(2)

Who are the other characters in your story?	
In what settings does your story take place?	

(3)

How does your story start?	
What happens next?	
Then what happens?	
What happens after that?	
How does your story end?	

From Macon, J.M., Bewell, D., & Vogt, M. (1991). Plot relationship chart, from *Responses to Literature: Grades K–8* (p. 8). Copyright © 1991 by the International Reading Association (www.reading.org); adapted by permission.

In *Executive Function in the Classroom: Practical Strategies for Improving Performance and Enhancing Skills for All Students* by C. Kaufman. (2010, Paul H. Brookes Publishing Co., Inc.)

Modified "Sandwich"
Organizer for Paragraph Construction

The purpose of my paragraph is to: _____

_____

Topic Sentence

_____
_____
_____

Idea, Reason, or Fact
(Possible transitions: "First of all . . ." "First . . ." "The first thing that happened . . .")

_____
_____
_____

Example

_____
_____
_____

Idea, Reason, or Fact
Possible transitions: "Second of all . . ." "Another reason why . . ." "The next thing that happened was . . .")

_____
_____
_____

Example

_____
_____
_____

Concluding Sentence
(Possible transitions: "In conclusion . . ." "So, this is why . . ." "All in all . . .")

_____
_____
_____

CHAPTER 8

Bringing Numbers into Focus

Executive Function and Mathematics

“I never did very well in math — I could never seem to persuade the teacher that I hadn't meant my answers literally.”

— CALVIN TRILLIN

Upon completing this chapter, the reader will be able to

☞ Discuss the challenges that the new constructivist math curricula can pose for students with executive weaknesses

☞ Discuss the impact of various executive functions on the acquisition and application of math skills

☞ Describe the essential features of the procedural (or algorithmic) type of math disability

☞ List and discuss the essential principles that should guide the development and implementation of math instruction for students with executive function weaknesses

☞ Discuss the range of strategies that can be effective in building math fact fluency, algorithm acquisition/application, and word problem-solving skills of students with executive weaknesses

Math's Changing Face: From Memorization to the Construction of Meaning

Math is new again. If you are a classroom teacher or special educator, particularly at the elementary level, you may already be familiar with the seismic shift that has taken place in mathematics education over the last several years. Based on new standards for instruction developed in 1989 and again in 2000 by the National Council of Teachers of Mathematics, school districts across the country have been jettisoning curricula centered on the memorization of basic facts and the drill and practice of standard algorithms; instead, they have embraced new models of instruction that emphasize discovery learning and meaningful problem solving (Roditi & Steinberg, 2007). Owing much of their structure to constructivist theories of learning (i.e., learning is an active process that occurs most effectively when self-constructed), curricula such as *Everyday Math* (University of Chicago School Mathematics Project, 2007), *Investigations of Number, Data, and Space* (TERC 2006) and *Math Trailblazers (Teaching Integrated Mathematics and Science Project, 2008)* are touted by their proponents as effective means of moving students beyond rote learning of teacher-directed procedures toward a deeper (self-constructed) understanding of math concepts and the ways they can be applied to the solving of authentic problems (Murray, 1998). These new programs are designed to produce children who are not only proficient in core calculation skills, but also are able to think mathematically when confronted by an array of life's challenges.

A constructivist math curriculum such as *Everyday Math* (University of Chicago School Mathematics Project, 2007), requires some substantial changes in traditional teacher–student roles. In the conventional math classroom, the teacher and text materials serve as the fonts of knowledge, with students dutifully learning and practicing the facts, procedures, and concepts presented. As Russell (1996, 1999) noted, such old-style instruction generally requires students to

- Work alone

- Adhere to the standard procedures handed down by the teacher

- Focus on the accuracy of responses

- Complete as many problems as possible within set time frames using standard algorithms

Classrooms adopting the discovery/problem-solving methods, on the other hand, require students to engage and display a different skill set during math periods. These include the ability of students to

- Work collaboratively with others (Russell, 1996)

- Discover and work through their own methods of solving math problems

- Reflect on their own reasoning and that of other students (Russell, 1996)

- Employ a range of strategies to address problems (i.e., there is no "one right way")

- Demonstrate/communicate mathematical understanding via a range of modalities including writing and pictures (Russell, 1996)

The "new" math places far greater demands on students' executive function skills than more traditional instructional methods. As Roditi and Steinberg discussed, conventional mathematics teaching practices allow the teacher to serve as the lead executive and provide instruction "in a structured, systematic way within highly organized classroom environments" (2007, p. 238). Therefore, in these "old-school" curriculum models, the teacher bears virtually all responsibility for strategy instruction and strategy selection; the teacher must make sure that students understand and practice the "right way" to solve the range of problems they encounter in the classroom. This heavily mechanistic and teacher-directed learning model may not be particularly stimulating for students with executive function weaknesses, but it is reasonably aligned to their needs since required strategies are explicitly taught and practiced in a structured, repetitive manner. On the other hand, the new constructivist curriculum trends, as Roditi and Steinberg noted, may prove quite challenging for children with executive dysfunction "who cannot independently generate the structures, templates, and self-regulation strategies they need to learn effectively in the math classroom" (2007, p. 238).

My purpose here is neither to condemn nor even substantially criticize the constructivist math curriculum trends. Programs like *Everyday Math* have a fairly broad research basis and have been adopted in regular education contexts with reasonable satisfaction by districts around the country (Carroll & Isaacs, 2003). Although somewhat controversial and potentially problematic for students with learning disabilities, it seems likely that their popularity and influence will continue to spread in the years to come. The challenge for teachers, as Roditi and Steinberg suggested, is to implement these authentic/meaningful problem-solving instructional practices while also providing "the systematic scaffolds necessary for children with executive function problems who struggle to learn in the math classroom" (2007, p. 239). To help classroom staff meet these challenges, this chapter will first detail the relationship between executive skills and mathematics, then present a range of strategies that can effectively build the math skilla of students with executive function weaknesses.

The Impact of Executive Function on the Acquisition and Performance of Math Skills

Regardless of whether one is learning math via traditional instructional methods or a new constructivist curriculum, the nature of mathematics skills is such that its acquisition and demonstration tends to heavily involve the brain's executive systems. After all, math is about the solving of problems; whenever the human mind is consciously engaged in the act of problem solving, the executive functions take a lead role in cognitive processing. As Blair and Razza noted,

> The relation of executive function to mathematics ability is particularly apparent when considered from the standpoint of what it is that children are expected to do, cognitively speaking, when solving mathematical problems. Proficiency in mathematics at all levels requires the individual to reason actively about problem elements when arriving at possible solutions. The problem-solving

process requires the individual to represent information in working memory, to shift attention appropriately between problem elements, and to inhibit the tendency to respond to only the most salient or most recent aspect of a given problem. (2007, pp. 658–659)

Math skills are also clearly bound up in strategy selection and execution. Recent curriculum trends place a great burden on students to select among a range of possible strategies and, at times, to even develop and reflect on their own to solve problems. However, even conventional instructional paradigms present problem situations (e.g., word problems) in which the operation/strategy needed for the solution must first be determined before being applied.

Executive processing is required for strategy identification, and also serves as the cognitive foundation of strategy implementation (Roditi & Steinberg, 2007). To accurately operate a given algorithm or other problem-solving method, students must sustain the strategy (including its various steps in appropriate order) in working memory as it is executed while also monitoring the accuracy of the implementation. Overall, math in its variety of forms requires children to engage in a great deal of self-directed and self-regulated cognition as they move through the stages of problem review, strategy identification, and strategy application. The executive skills drive and manage this problem-solving process, and are therefore arguably the element of cognition most important for effective math processing (Feifer & De Fina, 2005).

Neuroimaging research on the brain has substantiated the essential roles played by the executive systems as individuals learn and apply math skills. As Blair and Raza (2007) pointed out, findings in the developmental literature reflecting a relationship between executive function and math skill are consistent with the overlap found by neuroscientific studies among the neural regions supporting executive function and those enabling numerical ability and quantitative reasoning. Interactive circuitry among the frontal and parietal lobes that plays an important role in executive function has also been shown to support elements of numerosity and calculation skill (Blair & Raza, 2007). The functional interaction between these brain regions is logical when one considers that the parietal lobe plays key roles in both the spatial and calculation ("number crunching") elements of math functioning, and that the prefrontal cortex takes the role of the analyzer, director, and monitor of problem solving. The extent to which the executive systems need to come online during mathematical tasks is largely dependent upon the degree of ambiguity and complexity of the problems at hand. The routine application of math skills, such as applying the standard long-division algorithm for the five-hundredth time, would place a much lesser load on a student's executive capacity than the learning and initial application of skills. As Hale and Fiorello noted, the automaticity with which students can solve math problems has a clear impact on frontal lobe involvement in problem solving:

Think of the problem 8 x 7, and you easily rely on your ventral stream/temporal lobe to come up with 56. Now think of 16 x 7. Most of us do not know the multiplication tables beyond the 12 or 13 level, so this now becomes a computation task—one that will require both parietal and frontal lobe functioning to carry it out. (2004, p. 217)

Children who have not learned basic math facts to the point of automatic recall will have less executive skill capacity to direct toward the strategic/problem-solving levels of math processing because they have to frequently pause and fill their attention and working memories with lower order skills, such as counting (Berninger & Richards, 2002). Most experienced teachers have witnessed this phenomenon firsthand; they are therefore well acquainted with what can happen to students' problem-solving skills when they lose their place within an algorithm because of the need to stop with some frequency to rediscover basic facts, such as as $8 + 5$, $11 - 3$, and 7×7. Thus, students lacking the math fact mastery of their classmates will often need to possess greater executive capacity than their peers with greater fact fluency to make the numerous shifts necessary between fact computation and problem solving.

Now that we have considered the contribution of executive skills to the math problem-solving process, let's take a closer look at the influence executive dysfunction can have on the acquisition and performance of math skill.

Failing to Compute: Executive Dysfunction and Math Skill Application

A working memory lapse in Wonderland:

> ❝ 'Can you do addition?' the White Queen asked. 'What's one and one and one and one and one and one and one and one and one and one?' 'I don't know,' said Alice, 'I lost count.' ❞
>
> –LEWIS CARROLL, *ALICE'S ADVENTURES IN WONDERLAND* (1865)

Because math problem-solving skills are inextricably linked to executive skills, children with executive function weaknesses likely struggle to a greater extent with math than their peers who have stronger self-directed cognitive capacities. Bull and Scerif (2001) found that mathematical ability was significantly related to a range of executive function measures, with greatest correlation shown between math skill, impulse control, and working memory. These findings prompted the authors to conclude that executive functioning difficulties—particularly those of a self-regulatory nature—lead to problems with switching among strategies and evaluating strategy effectiveness in problem-solving contexts.

Blair and Raza (2007) also found a strong correlation between impulse control and the acquisition of early childhood math competency, noting that the ability to inhibit potentially erroneous response tendencies when confronted by irrelevant or distracting information appeared essential to the development of initial academic skills. Other studies (Keeler & Swanson, 2001; Swanson & Beebe-Frankenburger, 2007, as cited by Dehn, 2008) have highlighted the relationship between working memory capacity and math skill, with emphasis given to the impact of limited working memory on strategy selection and implementation. Research by Geary and Brown (1991) has suggested that a variety of executive skills can impact strategy choice, whereas the work of Swanson and Sachse-Lee (2001) has indicated that executive processing influences students' knowledge of algorithms (Keeler & Swanson, 2001). Based on the findings of these and related studies, it seems safe to conclude that children with executive deficits are more likely to struggle with math than peers with stronger executive capacity. Research on students with attention-deficit/hyperactivity disorder has confirmed that math weakness occurs frequently in individuals with executive function weaknesses (Barkley, 2006; Zentall & Ferkis, 1993).

The specific struggles that children with executive deficits show in math contexts will be largely determined by the specific nature of their executive function profiles. Children with purposeful attention deficits, for example, may display several key gaps in their math skills because of inconsistent attention to instruction and practice. Chronically inattentive students also tend to misread signs and problems with some frequency (e.g., "We were supposed to divide for all these? I thought they were all takeaways!") and can be prone to omitting key information from word problems when problem solving. Students with planning weaknesses, on the other hand, often approach math problems in a fairly random or passive manner, resulting in a failure to access/apply the strategies needed for problem solving. Significant difficulties with impulse control often manifest in a fairly reckless attacking of math problems (e.g., "Directions? Who reads directions?"), whereas frustration management problems will typically show themselves in quick abandonment of problems and rather limited academic coping skills. Table 8.1 lists several of the more commonly cited executive skills and the math weaknesses that may be associated with them.

As discussed in Chapter 4, close scrutiny of students' work samples and observations of their behavior while problem solving can offer helpful clues to the nature of their executive function profiles and related math difficulties. Hale and Fiorello (2004) discussed the value of asking children to verbalize their problem-solving approaches to allow for examination of their math fact and algorithm knowledge. To illustrate this diagnostic method, they offered the example of Lucy, who verbalized the following while endeavoring to solve a double-digit addition problem, 64 + 13:

> First I look and see if is addition or subtraction. OK, addition, so you always go top to bottom, and left to right. So I add 6 + 4, and that equals 10, and the 1 + 3 equals 4, and then I add them together, top to bottom, 10 + 4 equals 14. (2004, p. 211)

If one only looked at Lucy's answer to this problem, as Hale and Fiorello (2004) noted, it would be difficult to determine how she arrived at such a whopper of an erroneous response. The error could be a factor of many things, including carelessness, misreading of the sign (subtracting instead of adding and then getting the subtraction wrong), or a very problematic knowledge/execution of the double-digit addition algorithm. The verbalization provides a fairly clear indication that her breakdown is occurring at the level of place value and algorithm knowledge (Hale & Fiorello, 2004). Lucy's single-digit addition is adequate and she used an algorithm while problem solving, but the algorithm she employed was so flawed that she was unable to even come close to the correct answer. This is suggestive of attention weakness during the instructional phase—she was likely tuning out with some frequency while the algorithm was being taught, leading to her rather sketchy grasp of the

Table 8.1. Math difficulties linked to areas of executive dysfunction

Executive dysfunction	Possible manifestations in math contexts
Purposeful attention deficits	Ignored or misread signs
	Misread word problems
	Skill gaps associated with failure to adequately attend to instruction (Lerew, 2005)
	Inconsistent performance
	Place value misaligned (Feifer & De Fina, 2005)
	Decimals incorrectly placed
Working memory deficits	Failure to follow multiple step directions
	Incorrect responses to words problems associated with difficulties holding all the elements of the problems online in working memory (e.g., "Oh, I forgot that the trains were heading in opposite directions!")
	Incorrect responses to calculation problems associated with difficulties holding necessary algorithm steps in working memory (e.g., "John, you got all these long division problems wrong because you excluded the *compare* step. See?")
Planning deficits	Failing to approach problems in a planned, strategic manner (random or passive problem-solving style)
	Selecting the wrong algorithm and/or problem-solving strategy
	Allowing too little space on page in which to problem solve (e.g., "I can't finish this—there's no room!")
Organization deficits	Difficulties setting problems (Feifer & De Fina, 2005)
	Inconsistent lining up of columns and equations (Feifer & De Fina, 2005)
	Frequent erasers (Feifer & De Fina, 2005) and restarts (e.g., "Robbie, your paper is a mess. I can't even tell what you've done here.").
Shifting/cognitive flexibility deficits	Difficulties shifting among algorithm steps and other elements of problem solving (e.g., "Tonya, you've written all the problems down really nicely and all your columns look great, but you haven't solved any of them. It's really time to start.")
	Becoming stuck on one type of algorithm on worksheets or timed tests include a variety of problem types (e.g., "Michael, you added for all of these problems, but some of them required subtraction and others multiplication. What happened?")
	Difficulties shifting to alternative problem-solving strategies (e.g., "That's not how I do it and so I don't even want to hear about it!").
Self-monitoring deficits	Failing to check work before submitting
	Failing to note "careless" errors and impossible responses while problem solving (e.g., "Jennifer, for this one you said that 25 + 19 = 205. Does that make any sense to you?")
	Erratic performance (some days many errors, some days few to no errors)
	Numerous errors when copying problems from book to paper or from whiteboard to paper
Sequencing deficits	Performing algorithm/problem solving steps out of order
	Lining up elements of problems in incorrect sequence
Retrieval fluency deficits	Slower retrieval of learned facts (Feifer & De Fina, 2005)
	Inconsistent recall of learned facts in problem-solving contexts (Feifer & De Fina, 2005)
Impulse control deficits	Leaps too quickly into solving word problems and other applied problems before having fully processed all the elements
	Calculation errors associated with a failure to pause and process long enough (results in numerous "careless" errors)
Frustration tolerance deficits	Tends to quickly abandon challenging problems (e.g., "No way, this is way too hard for me!")
	Shows poor coping skills when confronted by challenging problems (e.g., "The teacher says to do it this way, but I just don't understand it, and so I just sit there and don't do it and then she gets all mad at me!")

steps to take when adding two-digit numbers—as well as difficulties with self-monitoring and number sense. Students at this developmental level who had greater self-scrutiny of the quality of their work and a more solidly established sense of number value would have quickly dismissed the answer Lucy obtained because 13 more than 64 could not possibly be 14.

The Procedural Subtype of Math Disability

Known also as *anarithmetria* (easily the most gracefully poetic of all neuropsychological terms), the procedural subtype of math disability is characterized by marked difficulties recalling and applying strategic algorithms when problem solving (Feifer & De Fina, 2005). Students exhibiting this form of math disability struggle not with recalling the basic facts of math (as do students with verbal subtypes of dyscalculia) or with comprehending the visual-spatial concepts, but rather with processing the stepwise procedures needed for accurate mathematical problem solving. The breakdown for children with the procedural subtype therefore occurs at the syntactical (step-ordering) level of processing (Feifer & De Fina, 2005). Recall Lucy, the procedurally challenged youngster whose problem-solving verbalization was discussed in the previous section (Hale & Fiorello, 2004). The steps she recalled and followed in attempting to solve a double-digit addition problem reflect the algorithmic breakdown one would expect to see in students with this subtype of math disability.

While a range of executive dysfunctions could potentially become manifest in the procedural form of dyscalculia, the cognitive skill most commonly associated with algorithmic processing deficits is working memory (Geary, Hoard, & Hamson,1999; Hitch & McCauley, 1991). Students with substantially limited working memory capacity relative to peer norms often lack the conscious processing space needed to hold and manipulate the steps of algorithms in consciousness while attempting to apply them in problem-solving situations (Dehn, 2008). Thus, they tend to forget or confuse the sequence of steps that must be followed to arrive at the correct answer, often falling back on immature counting strategies to solve problems (Hale & Fiorello, 2004).

If you have ever worked with an older elementary school or middle school student who attempted to solve problems such as 17×4 or $45 + 36$ by making and then counting elaborate series of tally marks, you have witnessed fallback to an inefficient counting strategy following algorithm meltdown (or avoidance). The important point to remember about the error patterns shown by students with this math disability subtype is that, regardless of whether they try to count their way through math problems or rely on their faulty recall/application of algorithms, they struggle at the *how* level of math processing. They might frequently forget, for example, how to divide a three-digit number by a one-digit number, how to bisect an angle, or how to reduce a fraction to its simplest form. If not also encumbered by language processing difficulties, students are unlikely to struggle with recalling basic facts. Lucy, for example, had no apparent difficulty recalling and applying single-digit math facts. Where she broke down, as noted, was with accurate recall of the algorithm steps in which to apply the facts.

Principles and Strategies to Improve the Math Performance of Students with Executive Function Weaknesses

Because, as Roditi and Steinberg (2007) noted, students with executive function difficulties struggle with both the acquisition (input) and performance (output) of math skills, the methods used to teach them matter a great deal. Before presenting the range of concrete strategies that can be helpful in building the mathematics skill of students with executive dysfunction, this section discusses the manner in which some of the core intervention principles introduced in Chapter 5 apply to the teaching of arithmetic and math concepts.

Children with Executive Function Weakness Require Math Instruction that Is Highly Explicit, Direct, and Strategic

How should math be taught to students whose neurodevelopmental profiles make it difficult to grasp and recall the procedural elements of problem solving? By using instruction that strives to make strategies and the types of problems they are linked to as clear as possible. Although constructionist critics of traditional math curriculum approaches note that the mechanical linkage of algorithms to math problem types tends to prevent students from grasping and applying the concepts that underlie the strategies (Kamali & Dominick, 1998; Schoenfeld, 1987), I would argue that there is no reason that the math concepts themselves, such as multiplication and division, cannot be taught in a highly concrete manner before the problem-solving algorithms associated with them are explicitly presented and repetitively practiced.

Many readers may have been inspired by Jaime Escalante, the gifted teacher celebrated in the 1988 movie *Stand and Deliver*. Confronted by a classroom full of bright but poorly educated and poorly motivated teens from East Los Angeles whose math skills were well below grade expectancy, he began teaching fractions by demonstrating how apples, when chopped with an impressively sized cleaver, form quantities of less than one. Once the students grasped this concept of portions of a whole, Escalante explicitly taught them how to compute with fractions before using his wonderful combination of concrete (prop-based, real-world) instruction and strategic algorithm practice to turn his students into advanced-placement math achievers over a relatively short period of time.

If there has ever been a model of the idealized math instructional environment for students with executive function weaknesses, Escalante's classroom would have to be it. He took the mystery and abstractness out of math by showing an initially uninterested student population how math really mattered in their daily lives; and then directly, in a highly scaffolded manner, helped them master the computational tools needed to apply the concepts in academic contexts. Children with executive function difficulties may like math more when they experience a consistent sense of "getting it"—that is, when they know exactly what to do (or at least how to start) when presented with the problems that constitute the math curriculum. Teachers can provide them with that sense of math mastery by teaching math concepts in a demystified, concrete manner, and by teaching the problem-solving algorithms to which they relate in an explicit, step-by-step fashion.

Minimize the Number of Algorithms Taught and Scaffold the Strategy Selection Process Until Students Become Confident in Self-Directing Their Own Strategic Problem Solving

Among the complaints most frequently voiced by teachers and students about the new constructionist math curriculums is that they require the teaching of too many (and sometimes inefficient) problem-solving options and place inordinate responsibility for strategy selection on students (Freedman, 2005). For children with executive function weaknesses, the presentation of numerous strategic algorithms for a particular problem type puts them at risk for strategy processing overload (Roditi & Steinberg, 2007). Because they struggle with self-directed problem solving relative to peer norms, students may shut down or experience fairly high levels of stress if they must sort through a diverse range of applicable algorithms on their own before computing. In light of the difficulties this population has with such executive skills as decision making and strategy selection, it may be important to keep the number of strategies they are taught for the various math problem types to a relative minimum and to scaffold strategy identification by providing explicit cues regarding the specific algorithms that should be used to solve specific problems.

Minimize Demands on Working Memory by Building Math Fact Retrieval Fluency and by Explicitly Embedding Strategic Algorithms into Worksheet Materials

Few things defeat strategic problem solving quite as effectively as overloaded working memory. When students must devote a substantial portion of their cognitive workspace to the rediscovery of basic facts (e.g., $10 - 7$, 6×6) or the effortful recall of algorithm steps, they have precious little working memory capacity left for higher order elements of math problem solving (Dehn, 2008; Delazer et al., 2004). For this reason, fluent knowledge of math facts and algorithm steps—or, failing that, ready access to math facts and algorithm steps—is essential for many students with limited working memory capacity and attention deficits. Subsequent sections of this chapter address methods of building math fact fluency in students with executive function weaknesses, as well as scaffolding the algorithm learning/application process by embedding algorithm steps (in visual and/or verbal form) right into teacher-constructed worksheet materials.

Children with Executive Function Weakness Need to Be Encouraged to Approach the Solving of Math Problems in a Careful, Methodical Manner

As Levine (1998) and Blair and Peters Raza (2007) have noted, the math-error patterns often associated with executive dysfunction relate to an overly hurried work tempo and an impulsive/superficial processing of information on the page. To become more successful math students, these individuals need to be shown how to talk to themselves as they work about the strategies they are using and the accuracy of their responses. Teachers who not only explicitly demonstrate problem-solving strategies, but who also show how they make decisions regarding strategy use and monitor the correctness of their work in real time, are modeling the internal dialogues children with executive weakness need to master to become more methodical math students.

Strategies to Build Math Fact Fluency

Among the factors that can dramatically impede the math performance of students with executive function weakness is slow or erratic recall of basic math facts. Children who continue to use counting strategies to rediscover the facts they need when working on more elaborate problems end up with little working memory space left to devote to the higher order strategic elements of problem solving (Hasselbring & Bryan, 2005). Thus, their math work tends to be slow, labored, and replete with errors associated with both poor fact recall and poor algorithm execution. Meltzer et al. (2006) differentiated math fact mastery into three distinct categories:

1. *Autofacts:* Math facts a student has mastered to the point of automatic recall

2. *Stratofacts:* Math facts a student can slowly figure out using idiosyncratic strategies, such as counting

3. *Clueless facts:* Math facts a student cannot recall at all on their own

Clearly, the more autofacts students have at their disposal when addressing math problems, the more space they will have on their cognitive desktop (working memory) for the thinking elements of problem solving (e.g., problem analysis, strategy selection, and strategy implementation). Stratofacts are certainly more helpful and adaptive than clueless facts, but will need to be transformed as quickly as possible into autofacts to minimize the space they consume in working memory. Figure 8.1 contains a math fact grid developed by Meltzer et al. (2006) that can be used to assess students' levels of fact mastery across the various single-digit fact domains. The strategies discussed in the following sections may be well suited to building fact acquisition and the automaticity of fact retrieval in children with executive function weaknesses.

Child's Name: _____ Class: _____

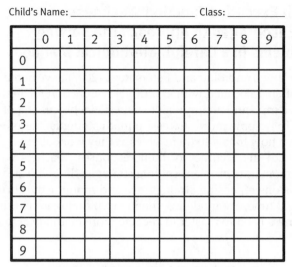

A – Autofact   S – Stratofact   U – Unknown Fact

Figure 8.1. Multiplication fact grid. (From *Strategies for Success: Classroom Teaching Techniques for Students with Learning Differences, 2nd Ed.* [p. 103], by L.J. Meltzer, B.N. Roditi, J.L. Steinberg, K.R. Biddle, S.E. Tauber, K.B. Caron, & L. Kniffin, 2006, Austin, TX: PRO-ED. Copyright 2006 by PRO-ED, Inc.; adapted by permission.)

Strategy 1: Build Number Sense by Working with Number Lines

The speed and accuracy of fact mastery can be predicted by the extent to which students grasp and internalize the number line in the early grades (Gersten & Chard, 1999; Schneider, Grabner, & Paetsch, 2009). First- and second-grade students who clearly understand that 6 is 4 more than 2, and can see this in their mind's eye in the form of an internal number line, are in a far better position to remember the addition fact 4 + 2 = 6 than children who must rely solely on rote memorization. Internalization of the number line also aids the acquisition of multiplication and division facts, as it helps students understand that 3 × 7 means the same thing as *7 three times.* Students with working memory weaknesses may be better able to grasp addition, subtraction, multiplication, and division facts if their instruction allows the manipulation of the facts on a 0–100 number line using strips of paper or cardboard that represent quantitative units (see Figure 8.2). Overall, teachers who suspect that a deficient number sense is contributing to a student's math fact acquisition struggles may be well advised to consider taking a step back and building the child's number sense through concrete number-line work to bolster conceptual understanding of number value.

Strategy 2: Less Is More — Teach Only a Few Facts at a Time

Some children have neurodevelopmental profiles that enable them to be terrific fact gatherers. Because of their strong attention spans, working memories, sequential processing abilities, and long-term memory skills, they seem to readily absorb the mountain of factual information upon which literacy and math skill is predicated. For students with various types of attention and

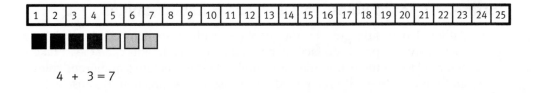

4 + 3 = 7

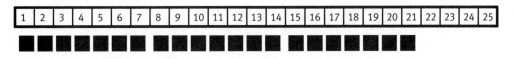

7 x 3 is the same thing as '7 three times'

7   +   7   +   7   =   21

Figure 8.2. Using number lines to build number concept and fact acquisition.

other executive weaknesses, however, the acquisition and retrieval of math facts can prove quite challenging (Marshall & Hynd, 1997). It is not unusual for these children to know facts one day and then be unable to recall them the next (causing no small amount of aggravation for both themselves and their teachers).

To minimize the fact-acquisition stress that these students may experience in school, it is important to dole out math facts in bite-size units. Bley and Thornton (2001), specialists in the math needs of students with learning difficulties, recommended the teaching of math facts through a tracking approach that involves presenting struggling learners with only a few carefully chosen facts at a time. Rather than asking students to memorize the multiplication table by proceeding in the traditional progression (i.e., from the ones to the twos to the threes), the tracking method advocates for the clustering of facts into smaller groups and then proceeding to additional groupings only after children show consistent mastery of the initial facts.

Strategy 3: Use FASTT Math

Fluency and Automaticity Through Systematic Teaching with Technology (FASTT Math; Hasselbring, Goin, & Bransford, 1988) is an individualized instructional program designed to develop automatic recall of basic math facts from numbers 0–9 and 0–12. This computer-based program has a credible research base and may be potentially well suited to the needs of many children with executive skill weaknesses. The software uses an "expanding recall" method to help students to shift newly learned math facts from working to longer-term memory. The program presents only three facts at a time in any given 10-minute session, and provides a range of practice activities (including worksheets) that are designed to enable the holding of the facts in working memory for increasingly longer periods of time until they become mastered (i.e., stored and reliably accessed in long-term memory).

Strategy 4: Teach Rules, Patterns, and Number Families

Although one of the great headaches about math for so many children relates
to its heavy emphasis on fact memorization, math students can at least take
some solace in the reality that our number system includes numerous rules
and patterns that—if understood—can ease fact acquisition. Because rules
and patterns, by their very nature, help organize larger groups of information, their use with students with executive function difficulties as part of the
fact-teaching process may be helpful. Meltzer et al. (2006) presented the following range of rule- and pattern-based strategies that may be well aligned
to the needs of children with working memory and other executive function
struggles:

- *Direct teaching of the "terrific tens" pattern.* Younger elementary school students are impeded from acquiring basic addition and subtraction facts
  simply because they fail to grasp the range of single-digit number pairs
  that, when added together, equal 10. In the absence of this crucial realiza-
  tion, they are compelled to use a counting strategy to determine that 7 +
  3 = 10, rather than just remembering the relationship that 7 and 3 have
  with regard to the number 10: When you add them together you get 10,
  and when you subtract one from 10 you get the other. Many students pick
  up all of these "ten-ness" relationships among single-digit numbers over
  the course of the first few years of formal education. However, for students with learning struggles (including executive function weakness),
  the relationships are only acquired after being carefully taught. To accomplish this direct instruction, Meltzer et al. (2006) recommended embedding the "terrific tens" pattern into a strategy card or worksheet (see
  Figure 8.3).

- *Directly teach all of the multiplication table rules.* If these rules are mastered,
  they can make the otherwise tedious and grinding rote memorization
  of the multiplication table substantially easier. They are also helpful for
  strengthening number concepts, as most highlight important patterns and
  relationships among numbers. All of the rules noted below were adapted
  from statements in Meltzer et al. (2006, pp. 105–108), unless otherwise
  indicated.

  0 rule: Zero multiplied by any number equals 0.

  1s rule: Any number multiplied by 1 equals itself.

  2s rule: Skip count by 2, keeping track with fingers or tally marks the number of times you have counted.

  5s and 10s rule: Skip count by 5 or 10, keeping track with fingers or tally
  marks of the number of times you have counted.

  9s rule: Subtract 1 from whatever number you are to multiply by 9 to get
  the first number of your answer. You get the second number by determining what number added to the first number equals 9. For example,
  you can figure out that the first digit in the answer to the problem 6 x 9
  would be 5 by subtracting 1 from 6. You can get the second digit (4) by
  remembering that 5 + 4 = 9.

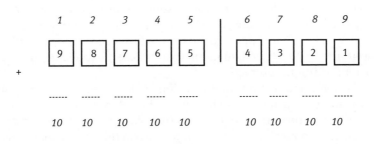

Figure 8.3. Terrific Ten's Strategy. (From *Strategies for Success: Classroom Teaching Techniques for Students with Learning Differences, 2nd Ed.* [p. 104], by L.J. Meltzer, B.N. Roditi, J.L. Steinberg, K.R. Biddle, S.E. Tauber, K.B. Caron, & L. Kniffin, 2006, Austin, TX: PRO-ED. Copyright 2006 by PRO-ED, Inc.; adapted with permission.)

Alternative 9s rule—the finger-cue method (Bley & Thornton, 2001): Have students hold both hands in front of them with palms facing outward, and demonstrate that one can easily determine the product of 9 multiplied by any other single-digit number by counting, left to right, the number of fingers associated with the digit and then bending that finger. The number of fingers to the left of the bent finger determines the first digit of the product and the number of fingers to the right of the bent finger determines the second number. For example, suppose that a student was trying to figure out the answer to 9×7. Using this method, she would count her fingers left to right until reaching the seventh finger—the index finger on her right hand. After bending that finger, she would simply count the number of fingers to its left across the two hands, and that would give her 6. The number of fingers to the right of the bent finger would be 3, giving her the answer (63).

Strategies to Build Algorithm Learning and Recall Mnemonics

Because students with various forms of executive function weaknesses often struggle with retrieving algorithm steps while problem solving, there is clear logic to structuring algorithm instruction for these students such that the sequence of steps is linked to an easily remembered verbal device (Roditi & Steinberg, 2007). You may recall a variety of situations from your own school years in which the learning and recall of information was eased by the use of teacher- or student-crafted mnemonic devices (e.g., *Every Good Boy Does Fine* for the notes on the lines of the treble clef; *My Very Educated Mother Just Sent Us Nine Pizzas* for the names/order of the planets in the solar system— although the latter is consigned to the dust bin of history now that Pluto has lost its planetary status). Math, because of its heavy emphasis on fact and algorithm recall, has long been a source for inventive mnemonic strategies, including *MiDAS* for the "golden rule" or order with which mathematical operations (multiplication, division, addition, and subtraction) must be applied and *Does McDonald's Sell Burgers Done Rare?* for the steps of the standard long-division algorithm (divide, multiply, subtract, bring down, repeat as necessary). Roditi and Steinberg (2007) cited the well worn but ever-catchy *Please Excuse My Dear Aunt Sally* acrostic for the sequence of steps involved in the simplifying of algebraic equations (parentheses, exponents, multiplication, division, addition, subtraction).

The reason these formulaic learning devices continue to enjoy such popularity among teachers and students is that they work. Research over the years has demonstrated that associative learning strategies improve both acquisition and recall of academic information (Ehren, 2000). For teachers of children with significant executive function weaknesses, the time and effort they devote to the development of algorithm- and content-specific mnemonic devices is likely to be rewarded with improved student performance. Naturally, as with any strategies attempted with individuals with executive function challenges, structured verbal memory approaches will prove most effective if taught explicitly (e.g., "Let me show you an easy way to remember all the steps we just went over") and cued in a scaffolded manner several times before students are expected to use them on their own (e.g., "Before we all work on these two problems, let's just quickly remind ourselves of the mnemonic strategy we came up with to remember the order of the problem-solving steps").

Visual Cuing Strategies

Many people have had the experience of staring at a math problem and having only the dimmest recollection of how to begin solving it. Thoughts such as "I used to know how to do this" or "Rats—why can't I remember how to do this? Was I there when this was taught?" tend to dominate consciousness in these situations, further diminishing the amount of working memory available to the problem-solving process. What did we wish for in those moments of math-related anxiety and frustration? The most honest answer would probably be escape, but failing the opportunity to bolt, we wanted someone or something to come along and remind us of how to start—and, ideally, of the next couple of steps. Verbal memory strategies, such as the mnemonic devices discussed above, can often serve as that crucial long-term memory jog. However, for many children with significant executive dysfunction, the algorithm learning and practice process needs to be even more explicit and supported. This is where explicit visual cues come in. They can take an abundance of forms, but all provide at least a relatively clear indication of the steps that need to be followed for accurate problem solving.

Bley and Thornton (2001) emphasized the power of these teaching devices, showing how seemingly simple graphic elements such as arrows, circles, squares, and color coding can provide students who are algorithmically challenged with a roadmap to follow in starting and completing math problems. Figures 8.4 through 8.8 present color-coded algorithm templates adapted from models from Bley and Thornton (2001)—what I refer to as *box templates*. Because they explicitly embed—via graphic structure and color coding—the algorithm steps necessary for accurate problem solving, they are likely

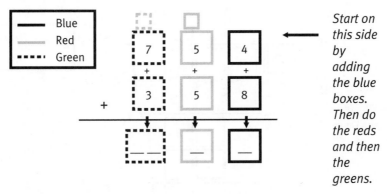

Start on this side by adding the blue boxes. Then do the reds and then the greens.

Write your answer again here: ____, ____ ____ ____

Figure 8.4. Three-digit by three-digit addition box template. (From *Teaching Mathematics to Students with Learning Disabilities,* 4th Ed. [pp. 24–27], by N.S. Bley & C.A. Thornton, 2001, Austin, TX: PRO-ED. Copyright 2001 by PRO-ED, Inc.; adapted with permission.)

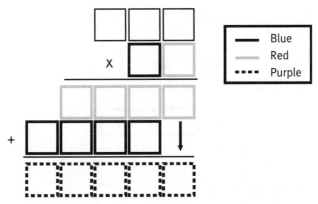

Figure 8.5. Two-digit by three-digit multiplication box template. (From *Teaching Mathematics to Students with Learning Disabilities,* 4th Ed. [pp. 24–27], by N.S. Bley & C.A. Thornton, 2001, Austin, TX: PRO-ED. Copyright 2001 by PRO-ED, Inc.; adapted with permission.)

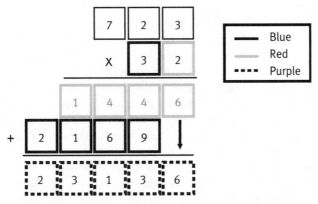

Figure 8.6. Two-digit by three-digit multiplication box template (completed). (From *Teaching Mathematics to Students with Learning Disabilities,* 4th Ed. [pp. 24–27], by N.S. Bley & C.A. Thornton, 2001, Austin, TX: PRO-ED. Copyright 2001 by PRO-ED, Inc.; adapted with permission.)

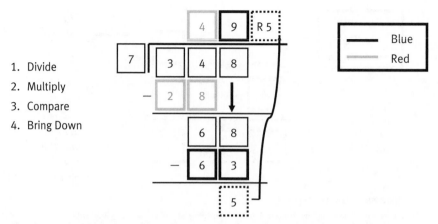

1. Divide
2. Multiply
3. Compare
4. Bring Down

Figure 8.7. Standard long-division algorithm box template. (From *Teaching Mathematics to Students with Learning Disabilities*, 4th Ed. [pp. 24–27], by N.S. Bley & C.A. Thornton, 2001, Austin, TX: PRO-ED. Copyright 2001 by PRO-ED, Inc.; adapted with permission.)

$$4^3 = ?$$

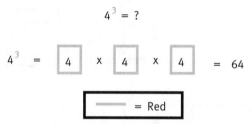

Figure 8.8. Exponent multiplication algorithm box template. (From *Teaching Mathematics to Students with Learning Disabilities*, 4th Ed. [pp. 24–27], by N.S. Bley & C.A. Thornton, 2001, Austin, TX: PRO-ED. Copyright 2001 by PRO-ED, Inc.; adapted with permission.)

to benefit children with executive function weaknesses and other students whose learning profiles make it difficult to recall and follow problem-solving procedures.

Bley and Thornton (2001) recommended using colors that are easily distinguishable in the color-coded templates to help set off each algorithm step from the others. They preferred red and green, although I used red and blue in the two-digit by three-digit multiplication template presented in Figures 8.4 and 8.5, as this allows the combining of these two colors into purple (red + blue = purple) to reflect the addition required in the last algorithm step. Ideally, box templates will also include verbal reminders of the algorithm steps to follow (as in Figures 8.4 and 8.7). Although color-coded box templates like these can be easily created by any teacher with colored markers and a steady hand, the ready availability in most schools of software like PowerPoint, Publisher, and PageMaker makes things even simpler. Once developed and saved in digital form, they can be readily adapted and color printed in whatever quantity might be needed. Once digitized, the templates could also be color printed onto transparency film to allow their adaptation for overhead projector use.

Strategies to Improve the Solving of Word Problems

Word problems may present particular difficulty for students with executive skills weaknesses (Bley & Thorton, 2001; Roditi & Steinberg, 2007), with issues ranging from attention problems that impact the accuracy with which the problems are read, working memory struggles that limit ability to hold all the various bits and pieces online during problem solving, and planning/ organizational difficulties that throw off problem setup. These executive dysfunctions can dramatically impair a child's ability to solve math problems embedded in narrative. To help improve the word-problem work of children with executive function weaknesses, teaching methods should be focused on breaking down the steps of the problem-solving process so that it becomes a rather deliberate implementation of George Polya's (1957) now famous mathematics problem-solving model:

1. Understand the problem being posed (i.e., what the problem is about)

2. Select a strategy (i.e., the best way to solve the problem)

3. Execute the strategy (i.e., carefully implementing the problem-solving plan)

4. Check the solution (i.e., reviewing the answer for reasonableness and accuracy)

Given the power of acronyms to help students remember important problem-solving elements, the teaching of Polya's steps may be eased through the use of the *STAR* mnemonic (see Figure 8.9), adapted in the following sections with permission from the Access Center (www.k8accesscenter.org) to better align with Polya's model.

Search the Word Problem

Because students with executive functioning weaknesses may be prone to misreading the operational demands of word problems due to inattention, planning deficits (Feifer & De Fina, 2005), or impulsivity (resulting, for example, in adding when they should have subtracted or multiplying when division was required), it is crucial that they be trained to scan and circle (or highlight or underline) the words and phrases that provide indication of the

---

STAR Strategy for Problem Solving

S earch the word problem for operation terms.

T ranslate the words into a simple picture and then pick a strategy to solve the problem.

A nswer the problem by executing the strategy.

R eview the solution.

Figure 8.9. STAR strategy for problem solving.

Table 8.2.   Lists of math operation terms

Addition	Subtraction	Multiplication	Division
Sum	Take away	Product	Quotient
Add	How many did not have	Multiplied by	Per
Altogether	Remaining	By	A (as in gas is $3 *a* gallon)
Plus	Have left	Times	Percent (divide by 100)
Combine	Less than	Of	Divided by
Increased by	Fewer than	Each group	Parts
How many	Decreased by	If each	Split
More than	Reduced by	How many	Same number
Total	Difference of		Half
In all	How many are not		Quarter
Both			Share

operations required. As with most of the strategies discussed in this book, it would be best to teach this scanning process in an explicit manner using an overhead projector, with the teacher modeling the problem-solving self-speech that he or she would use when reviewing a word problem. Table 8.2 presents the range of terms that students should be taught to look for in word problems that are associated with the four core arithmetic operations.

Translate the Words into a Simple Picture and Then Pick a Strategy

Pictures and other graphics, such as diagrams, can be quite helpful in translating the myriad words and phrases that make word problems into more concrete and therefore understandable visual images (van Garderen, 2007). The better students understand the true nature of the problem before them, the easier it becomes to select the required problem-solving strategy. Let us use the following example to help illustrate the power of illustration:

> Michael and Lisa both drive to the airport from their homes on the same day. Michael's house is 70 miles from the airport and Lisa's is 60 miles from it. Michael drove at an average rate of 50 miles per hour, while Lisa drove at an average rate of 40 miles per hour. If they both left home at 1:00 in the afternoon, who got to the airport first?

By summarizing all the pertinent information from the problem in simple pictorial form (see Figure 8.10), it becomes easier to see the specific nature of the problem and the speed and distance operations required.

The selection of a problem-solving strategy is further eased if students have the range of algorithms and other strategies they might need at hand. Roditi and Steinberg (2007) recommended gathering all math strategies that students with executive function weakness have been taught into a "strategy notebook" that is organized by strategy type and can be readily accessed in math problem-solving situations. They also recommended having students compile much of the information in their notebook on their own through the process of structured notetaking.

Students with more severe executive dysfunction may require greater levels of adult support in assembling and adding to the strategy storage/access

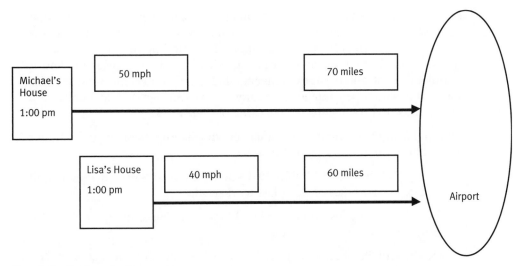

Figure 8.10.   Simple word problem graphic.

system. These students may do better if the strategies and other important information are placed onto laminated cards organized by strategy type and maintained either in a small box or on a binder ring. If this approach is used, it is important for each card (or notebook page) to clearly spell out the algorithm steps, with an example provided for further clarity. It may also be helpful to include other important bits of information in the strategy notebook or binder ring, such as the list of operational words in Table 8.2.

Answer the Problem by Executing the Strategy

Although the presentation of algorithm steps in a strategy notebook page or binder ring card may be sufficient for some students, others (as was noted earlier) require more explicit visual cueing of the steps that need to be taken for accurate problem solving. The execution of operations required by word problems, therefore, is another math problem-solving situation in which algorithm box templates and similar visual cueing systems may come into play.

Review the Solution

The next section of this chapter addresses structured methods that students can use to check the reasonableness and accuracy of the calculations they have made.

Self-Monitoring ("Checking") Strategies

Recall the discussion about the relationship between executive function weakness and editing in Chapter 7 and you will have a sense of the math-checking difficulties of students with executive skill deficits. Just as these students struggle with monitoring the quality of their written output and revising/

editing it as necessary, they tend to avoid the self-directed review of their math work and are therefore prone to "careless" errors. Because the review of one's own math performance is inherently bound up in a range of executive skills (including self-monitoring, sustained attention, working memory, impulse control, and frustration management), it should come as no surprise that a substantial percentage of children with executive dysfunction exhibit very limited to no self-directed checking of their work:

Phillip (hastily handing in his worksheet while simultaneously grabbing for the bathroom pass):   Here, I'm done.

Teacher: Wait a second, Phillip. Did you check your work? Remember all the careless mistakes on your last worksheet.

Phillip: Um . . . I guess. Sure. I mean, I looked it over. Can I go to the bathroom? I really have to . . . you know.

Roditi and Steinberg noted that because these students struggle with "reflecting back" on the quality and the accuracy of their work in general, they often "lack the strategies to first identify and then self-correct their work" in math contexts (2007, p. 252). Thus, the direction to correct their work feels tedious and frustrating, and is largely ignored. In light of the strategic self-checking limitations of individuals with executive function challenges, Roditi and Steinberg stressed that these students require explicit instruction in the use of systematic checking strategies. The following sections present two strategies they recommend, as well as an acronym strategy by Meltzer et al. (2006).

Error Analysis

The first logical step in learning to more successfully note and correct one's math errors is to become familiar with the patterns of errors one makes. Roditi and Steinberg (2007) recommended teaching children with executive skills struggles about the types of errors they most commonly make so that they become less likely to make these mistakes while working and are better able to recognize the errors when checking.

Top Three Hits

Akin to the systematic editing strategies discussed in Chapter 7 (see Table 7.1), this strategy flows from the recommendation to teach error patterns (Roditi & Steinberg, 2007). Once students have been helped to recognize the math mistakes most commonly make with regard to specific types of problems, these error types are listed on a "top three hits" card. The card is meant to be pulled out whenever the student works on a given type of math problem, hopefully acting as both a reminder to avoid the errors while working and a cue to systematically check for the top three mistake types before handing in math tests and worksheets. See Figure 8.11 for an example of a card that might be made for a fourth-grade student practicing the standard long-division algorithm.

Derek's Top Three Hits for
Long Division

1. Forgetting to keep columns straight

2. Multiplying incorrectly

3. 'Bringing down' the wrong number

Figure 8.11. Sample top-three hits card. (From Roditi, B.N., & Steinberg, J. [2007]. The strategic math classroom: Executive functioning processes and mathematics learning. In L. Meltzer [Ed.], *Executive functioning in education: From theory to practice* [pp. 237–260]. New York: Guilford Press; adapted by permission.)

Pounce

Meltzer et al. (2006) developed this strategy as a way of providing a concrete acronym for students to follow when doing systematic self-checking of math performance. The strategy involves encouraging students to visualize a cat pouncing on a math problem to check it:

P: Change to a different color **pen** or **pencil** to change your mindset from that of a student (test taker) to teacher (test checker).

O: Check **operations.**

U: **Underline** the question (in a word problem) or the directions. Did you answer the question? Did you follow directions?

N: Check the **numbers.** Did you copy them down correctly? In the right order?

C: Check your **calculations.** Check for the type of calculation errors you tend to make.

E: Does your answer agree with your **estimate?** Does your answer make sense?

CHAPTER 9

Surviving
the Paper Chase

Organization, Study
Skills, and Time Management

> **"**Organizing is what you do before you do
> something, so that when you do it, it is not all mixed up.**"**
> —CHRISTOPHER ROBIN IN *WINNIE-THE-POOH* (MILNE, 1926)

Upon completing this chapter, the reader should be able to

☞ Describe the myth of laziness and discuss its relevance to students with executive dysfunction

☞ Discuss strategies to build students' skills across a range of executive function domains, including materials organization, homework completion, time management, notetaking, and study skills

☞ Describe executive skills coaching methods and the variables that can impact the success of this intervention model

---

Introduction

This chapter addresses the issues that often spring first to teachers' minds when they think about executive function; that is, for many educators, executive skill is largely synonymous with organizational capacity and study skill. When I ask school personnel to discuss a student's executive function, they tend to focus initially on such functioning elements as workspace and materials organization (e.g., "His backpack resembles a black hole and his locker is a disgrace"), task planning and completion, and preparing for tests

("Carol says that she never studies for tests because she can never find her study materials, which is probably true—she loses everything").

While the planning and organizational elements of executive skill are certainly major determinants of a student's scholastic success, I hope the previous three chapters have made clear the impact that self-directed cognition can have on the acquisition and performance of core academic skills. Executive function is clearly about so much more than just organizing academic materials and getting work done on time. Still, no book on this subject would be complete without a section on what many consider the traditional executive function topics.

Most of this chapter is dedicated to a presentation of the range of strategies that are often effective in helping these students keep track of their materials, complete work on time, and perform better in testing contexts. Before jumping into the intervention discussion, however, it is important to dispel a punitive and still widely accepted myth about the study skill and productivity difficulties of children exhibiting some level of executive dysfunction: the myth of laziness.

Putting Aside the Myth of Laziness

" Probably the greatest value in recognizing the neurodevelopmental/neurocognitive domain called executive functioning is to protect a sizable minority of children from being traumatized by what amounts to adult name-calling. "
—MARTHA DENCKLA (2007, p. 15)

Beware the "myth of laziness." In his book of the same name, Mel Levine (2003) coined this phrase to describe the widespread belief among parents and teachers that most students with organization and production deficits are essentially choosing these difficulties—that they are electing to be indolent and idle as opposed to effortful and productive. I have heard the word *lazy* applied by educators to students countless times over the course of my career, and expect that most experienced educators have as well, even if only because students' workspaces and materials were frequently messy or their work was often late or poorly rendered:

> "He's clearly intelligent, but the laziness thing really gets in the way of his achieving up to his potential. It's a shame, really."

> "If she'd only apply herself and put the effort in, we might see her work up to the level we all think she can achieve. It's so frustrating."

Comments like these are often spoken by teachers of students with executive function weakness, but are almost always well intended, to whip up the achievement motivation that is thought to lie dormant somewhere in the child's subconscious (e.g., "We're just trying to light a fire under this kid to get him going").

Is there a factual basis to the myth of laziness? In the vast majority of cases, the answer is a resounding *no.* Very few children's learning and/or production difficulties (e.g., low grades, "slipshod" work, messy desk and materials, missed deadlines) can be attributed primarily to achievement motivation deficits. This is not to say that achievement motivation deficits do not exist—they certainly do (Bruns, 1992). However, in most cases in which motivation becomes a problem with regard to academic performance, it is not because of a character flaw; rather, the student may have come to believe that he or she lacks the ability to succeed (Covington, 1992; Marzano, 2003). Therefore, motivation deficiency—"laziness"—is far more likely to be a by-product of actual or perceived academic struggles rather than the primary cause of underachievement.

This discussion brings us to the important distinction between deficits of skill versus deficits of will. Whenever we form opinions about a student's academic underachievement as stemming primarily from motivation deficiencies, we are framing the poor test scores and limited production around deficits of will. We're saying, essentially, that the child possesses the necessary skill set to achieve at levels commensurate with his or her intelligence, but lacks the will (i.e., desire, motivation) to do so. When students' scholastic difficulties are characterized in this manner, the fault for the struggles is laid solely at their feet and little regard is given to developing support plans to improve performance. For example, the teacher may say, "Corbin doesn't need accommodations or specialized instruction in my class. He just needs to get his little rear in gear, work harder at keeping his stuff together, study for the tests, get things done on time, and do what I know he's capable of doing."

Because many executive function weaknesses often resemble primary motivational difficulties in academic settings, it is easy to misread a child's persistent struggles with things such as task initiation, materials organization, task planning, and homework completion as stemming largely from laziness (Gioia, Isquith, & Guy, 2001). In other words, it is common for executive function challenges to manifest in academic contexts in ways that society tends to attribute to a lack of caring and drive to achieve. However, most children genuinely want to succeed in school—the hassles for "underachieving" children from parents and teachers are many, and the related self-esteem hits are far from pleasant. Therefore, these students will typically demonstrate better achievement motivation if they achieve a sense of mastery over the type of work they are expected to do (Covington, 1992). Once students are helped past the executive skill weaknesses that can make the organization of materials and tasks such a challenge, their academic self-image tends to surge upward, resulting in internal cognitions such as, "Maybe I'm not such a bad student after all. I can actually do this stuff."

Deficiencies of will are almost always preceded by deficiencies of skill (often executive skill); these skill weaknesses must be systematically addressed for the motivational deficits to diminish. Reliance on browbeating with pejorative labels such *lazy* or *underachiever* almost always fails, as it essentially makes students feel misunderstood and only further drags down their academic self-image.

Strategies

The range of strategies discussed in this section are all designed to build the organizational, planning, and study skills of students with executive function weaknesses. If taught explicitly and implemented with integrity over time, these methods are likely to engender feelings of greater academic mastery and control in students whose neurodevelopmental profiles make it difficult for them to generate and follow organizational systems.

Workspace and Materials Organization

Many students struggle at times with keeping their things and work areas neat, to various degrees. Most parents and teachers accept this basic fact of life, and therefore establish designated areas and related systems to help children keep track of the numerous items needed for academics. For many students with executive function weaknesses, however, the process of maintaining functional workspaces and possession of even the most essential learning materials is a daily exercise of frustration that defies the most tightly structured organizational systems. Books, pencils, folders, and even entire backpacks can be lost, found (or more typically, replaced), and lost again in a matter days (or sometimes, hours or minutes), leaving the student (or often, the student's caregivers) in a constant state of worry over whether the needed items will be in place when work needs to be done.

Although no system or method can guarantee elimination of the calamitous workspace clutter and Dumpster-like backpacks that drag down the productivity of students with executive function challenges, the following strategies—if consistently implemented—may result in fewer frantic searches for needed items as deadlines loom.

Dedicate a Homework Space

Parents should be encouraged to establish one (and only one) homework space and to design a materials management system for the space, which can increase the chances of it remaining generally neat and free of clutter. Just as too many cooks spoil the broth, too many home-based workspaces destroy organizational systems and homework productivity. If students are allowed to do their homework across a range of settings (e.g., bedroom, kitchen table, family room, sibling's room), the likelihood of essential materials being misplaced and/or destroyed increases exponentially.

Students with executive function weaknesses should have one clearly designated workspace in the home, with simple materials organization systems developed and consistently followed regarding its use. Whether it is the bedroom desk or the kitchen table, the child should be required to *always* do homework in this designated space and—most importantly—keep all academic supplies in their designated places in the workspace. If a child's workspace is the kitchen table, the materials can be kept in carefully marked plastic tubs or shoeboxes that are stored nearby and returned to the same location every evening when homework is completed.

Because students with executive function struggles are often easily distracted by extraneous stimuli, every effort should be made early in the school year to habituate them to the use of the materials organization and storage systems. For example, it should not be okay for pens to be left strewn across the desktop after homework has been completed, or the glue stick lent to a younger sibling for a play activity. If students with executive skill difficulties are to develop effective habits of materials management, then adults have to be prepared to strictly enforce the organizational systems put in place in the home at the start of the school year regarding homework.

Encourage Parents to Supervise

As stated, it is essential for students with executive function weakness to have clearcut materials organization systems across home and school settings. However, as Dawson and Guare (2004) noted, the problems that these students have regarding the day-to-day organization of essential school supplies and the ability to get important papers back and forth to school often relates to a lack of adult supervision:

Mom: Jeremy, I don't know what else to do! Your father and I have bought you this expensive desk with a computer stand and put every single school supply you needed inside of it in labeled boxes, and still you've lost nearly everything in only a few days! It's amazing! How do you do it?

Jeremy: I don't know. I use the stuff and I guess I mean to put it back where it goes, but then something happens and I forget and then I can't find it again.

Here, we return once again to the concept of the surrogate frontal lobe. Because students with executive skill challenges may struggle with following even the most meticulously crafted organizational systems, systems and strategies alone will not solve the problem. Instead, parents and teachers of these children need to be prepared to provide the levels of individualized supervision of organizational strategy use needed for habituation to occur. Thus, before a homework session begins, a parent should directly supervise the child's retrieval and return of needed materials to their designated places.

Dad: Okay, Michael. Really nice job on your math homework today. I particularly liked the way you checked all your answers before you showed them to me. Now, let's go up to your room and you're going to show me . . . what?"

Michael (sighing):   How I put everything back where it goes. Yeah, I know, I know . . . .

The same principle of materials organization management should apply in the classroom, to the extent to which teachers' case loads and the immutable laws of physics allow. If a child has substantial materials organization needs, it is incumbent upon school personnel to provide the student with both the organizational systems and individualized support needed to run the systems on a daily basis. Rather than just designing and teaching students the organizational strategies to be used in a given class, therefore, the teacher should directly monitor the implementation of the system by those students whose neurodevelopmental profiles make them in need of such overseeing. No child should be allowed to have a desk, locker, or backpack that is excessively messy. When this occurs, it is because the child's organizational needs are poorly aligned to the materials management and supervision systems used in a classroom.

Use Checklists and Inspections

Students and teachers should use a daily school-to-home checklist, then inspect the backpack to make sure all needed materials are onboard before a student leaves school.

"I forgot my _____ at school" is the phrase that can almost certainly cause eye twitch in the parents of students with executive function challenges. Without the needed item(s), some key bit of homework or studying cannot be done, resulting in the usual family havoc wrought by a mad dash back to the school before it is locked up tight for the night. Among the strategies that can be most helpful in avoiding this stressful state of affairs is the consistent (and supervised) use of a daily school-to-home checklist.

The checklist provided in Appendix 9.1 focuses exclusively on the materials that need to make it into the backpack before the child leaves the classroom, and should be completed by the student in the first several weeks of use under the direct supervision of a classroom staff member. Once a youngster demonstrates sufficient mastery of the form in this supervised setting, responsibility for its use can be gradually released from the teacher in the form of once- or twice-weekly spot checks. Ideally, parents or caregivers should review the form (as well as assignments) every afternoon as soon as the student walks in the door to provide clear oversight of the system on the receiving end.

Daily Homework

In addition to homework difficulties associated with hopelessly cluttered workspaces, lost materials, and essential academic items left at school, the homework completion problems of students with executive function weakness are often associated with the following:

- Forgotten or only partially recalled assignment directions (e.g., "Oh my gosh! Mom, I know it's already past my bedtime and all, but I just remembered that we're supposed to write a book reflection for Language Arts tomorrow!")

- Poor prioritization of homework tasks and time (e.g., "Martin, do you mean to tell me you just spent over an hour cruising around the Internet looking for a picture for the cover of your report, rather than getting started on the writing? Isn't this whole thing due tomorrow?")

- Weak task persistence (e.g., "Melissa, you've still only gotten 2 of the 20 problems done! That's where you were a half-hour ago. What have you been doing up here?")

- Fatigue (e.g., "I'm so wiped right now, Mom, that there's no way I can even think about getting all this done. I'm totally fried, so please don't push me.")

Given the array of factors that can impede the homework productivity of students with executive struggles, it is not surprising that a lack of homework completion is the primary cause of their often problematic grades. Even if these students possess the intellectual might to do well on tests without studying much and have sufficient wherewithal (or teacher support) to get in-class assignments done, their quarter and semester grades are often well below their presumed ability levels because of late or missing homework assignments. Although there are clearly no quick fixes to the homework production problems of most students with executive needs, the following strategies may help them to get assignments done and turned in on time.

Less Is More

Homework undoubtedly serves a number of important purposes with regard to the building of students' academic skills and work habits. It is equally true, however, that homework assignments that are poorly aligned to students' learning profiles tend to cause more harm than good (e.g., poor grades related to missing or incomplete work, family stress/havoc, skipped classes). To develop productive homework assignments for students with executive function weaknesses, teachers must bear in mind the cognitive/emotional fatigue levels these students tend to experience relative to peer norms by the end of the average school day. Their tendencies to view academic molehills as mountains also bears serious consideration, as do their difficulties with managing homework tasks and time in the context of the usual array of after-school activities in which children are generally involved. Therefore, teachers should be highly selective in framing homework requirements for students with executive function difficulties. The well-worn phrase *less is more* definitely applies here.

Because executive deficits tend to particularly impact academic tasks that have strong output requirements, it is often helpful to cut back on the production aspects of homework assignments. For example, teachers can emphasize reading and note-review tasks over activities that stress narrative writing and the self-directed organization of numerous details into new ideas. When considering specific modifications of homework for students with executive needs, the teacher should focus on the instructional intent of assignment given to the larger class. Often, the intent (i.e., the core instructional objective) can be effectively achieved by students with executive function weaknesses, even with the production demands ratcheted down quite a bit.

Establish Consistent Schedules and Routines

Among the best ways of getting anyone to do anything in a consistent, productive manner is to establish a consistent schedule for the activity. When things happen at the same time and for about the same duration every day, our bodies and brains become accustomed to the mustering and spending of cognitive energy during these periods. A random homework schedule is generally more difficult for students to accommodate to, often leading to distractibility, avoidance, and fatigue. Although the nature of many students' after-school activities schedule tends to confound parents' attempts at structuring homework around consistent times, it is still essential for children with executive weaknesses to have regularly scheduled homework periods that should be used for reading, personal journal writing, or some other quiet, cognitive activity on those days in which no homework has been assigned.

Use Highly Structured and Signed Assignment Books

They are known by many different names—assignment books, agenda books, daily homework planners, assignment sheets—but most teachers know them well, regardless of their label and style. When used as intended, these tools have many benefits, including the building of a student's organization, time management, memory, and work completion skills. Given their explicit focus on executive function enhancement, one would expect these books and sheets to go a long way toward reducing the impact of executive function weakness on academic learning and production. However, assignment books are like parachutes and minds—they only work when open. Far too many children with executive function weaknesses use them as little more than backpack ballast:

Mom: Tim, do you have any homework tonight? Remember, you told us you'd start doing a better job keeping on top it.

Tim: Nope . . . Well, at least I don't think I do.

Mom (sighing):   Where's your assignment book? Let's give it a look.

Tim: It might be in my backpack, but I think I left in my locker. Wait, maybe it's in the car. I haven't written anything in it for the last few days, so it's probably not going to help much anyway.

For assignment books to actually help children with executive function weaknesses, their use has to be highly structured and supervised on daily basis. Student compliance often jumps markedly when systems are in place to ensure that the teacher initials the books every day at school (vetting the accuracy of what has been written down) and a parent initials the books at home (acknowledging receipt and review of what has been written down). These compliance monitoring systems across home and school settings tend to work best if required of all students, but can still be effective if implemented consistently for only students with significant executive function weaknesses.

Just as important as daily school and home supervision of assignment book use is explicit teacher direction of what to write down. Even at the middle and high school levels, it tends to be far more helpful to students with executive skill deficits to have school staff tell them exactly what to write in assignment recording tools rather than asking them to rely too much on their own summarization of assignment details. If students with executive function needs are required to develop their own assignment book statements, it is essential that the teacher check them before the school day ends to ensure the accuracy/completeness of what has been recorded.

The structure of the assignment book can also matter a great deal. Although there is often strong temptation on the part of educators and school-based clinicians to include numerous elements into these forms (e.g., self-reinforcement plans, break schedules), one must remember that many students with executive function weaknesses are significantly adverse to writing tasks and are therefore apt to resist daily homework recording systems that involve a lot of writing. An example of a daily homework sheet and assignment book model is presented in Appendix 9.2. In addition to the usual assignment recording spaces, the forms on pages 1 and 2 include sections in which the student indicates the school materials (e.g., textbooks, notebooks) that must be taken home for each assignment. The places for parent and teacher initials are also clearly indicated.

Time Management and Project Planning

Among the clichés about students with executive function weaknesses is that they often wait until the lamentable "last minute" before getting to work on larger assignments. Like many clichés, this one has some basis in logic and fact. Because so many executive skills are needed to manage the time and planning aspects of research papers and class presentations, a variety of problematic executive function profiles can contribute to projects being put off until the due date is just around the corner and panic/chaos ensues.

Although problems developing and following an organizational schema for projects are a major cause of their avoidance for lengthy periods, a contributing factor to the last-minute panic-and-scramble approach exhibited by lots of students with executive function weaknesses is what some psychologists refer to as *limited temporal sense*—that is, difficulty sensing with the accuracy of most peers the passing of time and/or predicting the amount of time different tasks will require. Some research, including a study by Barkley, Edwards, Laneri, Fletcher, and Metevia (2001), has shown that students with attentional and working memory difficulties can exhibit temporal sense difficulties relative to developmental norms. I have observed this limited sense of time in individuals with executive function challenges on many occasions over the years and have noted in particular its impact on project planning and completion. The phenomenon most often takes the form of significant underestimation of the time needed to complete larger academic tasks, as well as genuine surprise that a project's due date or a scheduled test is far closer than expected.

Given the impact that temporal sense limitations have on project completion, it is important for interventions targeting longer-term assignments for students with executive dysfunction to address time-management difficulties in addition to planning struggles. Here are a few project-level strategy recommendations to improve functioning across both of these domains.

Limit or Carefully Structure Topic Choices

As was discussed in Chapter 1, the ability to make decisions is an executive skill. When faced with a potentially endless series of topics for a research paper or construction project, many students with executive needs become so bogged down in the decision-making process that several days or even sometimes weeks go by before they are able to choose the one on which they will focus. To minimize the time and energy these students devote to topic selection, it is almost always helpful to either limit the topic choices available to them (e.g., "You must do your biography paper on one of these three people") or carefully structure/support the topic selection process so that it does not stymie them from moving on to subsequent project elements.

Turn Potential Mountains into a Series of Molehills

Students with executive function weaknesses may see tasks as insurmountable obstacles when most peers view them as essentially manageable. Therefore, these students are apt to be overwhelmed by long-term project demands. When a child's neurodevelopmental profile includes both limited academic coping skills and the tendency to view manageable tasks as unmanageable, the likelihood of project abandonment increases. To keep students with this package of self-regulatory struggles engaged in larger assignments, it is essential to keep their task-related frustration and anxiety to a minimum as they move through the work. The best way to do this is to structure the assignment steps in such a way that each element is experienced as small and doable. This method allows the student to keep checking steps off as completed and, in so doing, to build a sense of project mastery (e.g., "Hey, I thought this research paper was going to be horrible, but I'm already halfway done. Maybe I'll get this finished on time after all").

Be Specific About Project Steps and Deadlines

To mitigate the impact of limited temporal sense on project organization and completion, teachers can take the time-management aspects of longer-term assignments out of students' hands. Rather than issuing somewhat vague spoken reminders about where students should be in the project process (e.g., "And don't forget to keep working on your Africa projects. I hope everyone has the materials together by now and is starting to put together the question-and-answer note cards we talked about last week"), it is far more helpful for students with executive needs to be given very specific project-step instructions linked to specific deadlines. The teacher might say, "Michael, the note-card step of the Africa project should take you about a week. That's it. To make sure you're making good progress, though, let's get started on it today, you and me, during independent work time at the end of the period. Then I want you to bring me five more completed note cards on your topic this Wednesday and five more the following Monday. Come on, let's get that written down in your assignment book. I'll also send your Mom a quick e-mail to let her know the plan."

Provide Lots of Individualized Project Coaching

Recall Martha Denckla's statement that the phrase *on your own* is a death knell to students with executive function deficits (Saltus, 2003). Although it is clearly essential that teachers work to build these students' independent planning, organization, and task completion skills, the least effective way of doing so is to simply insist they do longer-term projects at the same level of independence as most classmates (e.g., "He's got to learn to do these things on his own—he won't always have us to prop him up"). However, when students with executive function weaknesses are compelled to complete large-scale projects with the levels of individualized support provided to all classmates, their neurodevelopmental profiles are often not equipped to manage the resulting task demands.

Teacher: Claudia, why aren't you working on your Maine history project like everyone else? Remember, whatever you don't finish on today's part in school you'll have to do at home.

Claudia (whining):   I need help. You won't help me, and I don't really know what to do right now.

Teacher: I guess I don't understand why you're so confused. We had your topic and planning conference yesterday, right? And even though you got upset I thought we set you up with a good plan. Why aren't you following the plan?

Claudia (whining louder):   I don't remember and we didn't write it down! This whole thing is stupid, anyway. I don't think I'm doing it.

Complete a Structured Project Planning Form

The most practical way of developing the executive skills of all students is to build executive function teaching and practice right into the regular curriculum. Teaching methods that target the needs of students with executive struggles end up improving the project planning and time management skills of all students. Project planning forms, such as the one on provided in Appendix 9.3, can be helpful ways of ensuring that everyone in a class is making reasonable and timely progress toward the completion of long-term assignments. Adapted from a form developed by Dawson and Guare (2004), this planning sheet is meant to be completed by students at the onset of long-term projects to structure the topic selection, materials gathering, and other steps of the assignment completion process. This version of the form also requires frequent contact between the teacher and students to increase the likelihood that children with executive function weaknesses demonstrate their progress on a regular basis and receive the coaching they need as they move from step to step.

Notetaking

The importance of effective notetaking to the learning process, particularly at the secondary and college level, is beyond dispute. Because so much of the important information students learn in school is taught directly by instructors and because most people do not have the memory skill to hold in long-term retention everything of importance that is said in the classroom, notetaking skills are essential to the accurate storage of information needed for tests and projects. Notetaking has the added benefit of teaching students how to summarize and organize information, as well as how to distinguish major ideas from unimportant details.

Some students, because of their strong executive capacities, pick up notetaking skills fairly easily, even in the absence of much formal instruction on technique. These students' minds are able to perceive the organizational structure of a teacher's presentation and accurately represent it in summarized form in their notes. Because of the difficulties many youngsters with executive function weaknesses have with recognizing organizational patterns and saliency determination (i.e., teasing out what is more important from what is less important), they may have a hard time producing effective notes when listening to lectures or reading texts. Purposeful attention and working memory weaknesses can also greatly confound the note-taking process, as these executive struggles tend limit students' ability to hold information online in consciousness while simultaneously transcribing it in summarized form.

Although commonly used classroom accommodations such as the photocopying of the teacher's or classmates' notes do get effective notes into the hands of students who struggle with notetaking, this bypass strategy does little to build the note-taking skills of students with executive function challenges. It is possible to teach productive notetaking to students whose neurodevelopmental profiles tend to inhibit the independent development of this essential learning skill. To do so, however, requires a substantial amount of teacher-directed instruction, explicit modeling, and the use of structured note-taking templates. These intervention principles are discussed more detail in the following sections.

Explicitly Model Notetaking

Probably the best note-taking instruction I have ever witnessed for students with executive function weaknesses was in a ninth-grade Western Civilization class. Because of the rather heterogeneous nature of the academic and executive skill sets among the students in the class, the teacher determined early in the year that the only way she could ensure that all students took effective notes on the content she was teaching was to model the notes she wanted them to take on an overhead projector (as part of her teaching). As I sat in the back of her classroom, observing a student with Asperger syndrome, I saw this highly effective instructional strategy in action and how it benefited even the students whose executive needs tended to make them rather poor notetakers in other classes.

After presenting some specific bit of information and then opening it up to class discussion, the teacher would summarize the essential learning points on the transparencies on the projector while telling the group the reasons for the phrases/keywords chosen for inclusion in the notes. She also paused the discussion every several minutes, directed the students to copy what was on the projector into their notebooks, and then wandered the room to ensure that everyone was doing as instructed. By explicitly teaching notetaking as part of a discussion of key elements of the Roman political structure, this skilled teacher not only achieved essential learning objectives, but also taught her varied group how to summarize and organize the key information from the discussion on paper.

Use Note-Taking Templates

Studies have demonstrated that improved academic performance tends to result from the use of structured note-taking templates (Meltzer et al., 2007). These findings are not surprising when one considers that teacher-developed templates ensure that information conveyed/discussed in class or obtained from other sources, such as textbooks or web sites, is organized for students in ways that are easiest to understand and apply. In the absence of note-taking templates or explicit note-taking modeling of the type discussed previously, students must summarize information on paper on their own, using whatever organization schemes occur to them in the moment—a cognitive demand that commonly overwhelms students with significant executive needs. The best note-taking templates are those that not only make plain the most effective means of organizing information, but are also structured in such a way so that key information is recorded in a format that will ease its recall during upcoming tests and assignments. The following two formats, if ex-

**TWO-COLUMN (QUESTION/ANSWER)
NOTE-TAKING TEMPLATE**

Questions	Answers
What were the main causes of the American Civil War?	• Slavery in the south: the south's agrarian economy was dependent upon the widespread availability of slave labor. A threat to the institution of slavery, therefore, was viewed by southerners as a threat to their livelihoods and lifestyles. • Growing fears among southern politicians that their control over the federal government would steadily diminish as the north's economy and population steadily grew while the south's declined. • Widespread racism and support for slavery in the south (most southerners viewed more moderate northern views of race distinctions and slavery as a threat to the southern culture and way of life). • Cultural and economic distinctions between the north and south: the north in the early to middle 19th century was becoming an increasingly industrialized, heterogenous society comprised of a growing number of immigrant groups, while the south remained an agrarian, homogenous society made up mostly of the descendents of English/Irish settlers.

Figure 9.1.   Example of a two-column note-taking template.

plicitly taught and modeled, may be well suited to the needs of many students with executive function weaknesses.

Two- and Three-Column Templates

Structured around a question-and-answer framework, column note-taking formats can be particularly powerful learning tools because they associate essential information with questions that elicit it (questions similar to those that might be on a test). Figure 9.1 is an example of a two-column format. New information is summarized in a structured manner in the right-hand column, while a question that the information answers is placed next to in the left-hand column.

Three-column templates include a third column that encourages the learner to insert a strategy that will be used to remember the information. Figure 9.2 shows the a three-column template, adapted from the Triple Note Tote presented by Meltzer et al. (2007) and published as part of BrainCogs (Research Institute for Learning and Development and FableVision, Inc., 2002a). The benefit of the additional column is that it encourages students to link new material not just to questions, but also to a strategy that assists its organized storage and retrieval. Students with executive function weaknesses are especially likely to benefit from the explicit memory-strategy cueing because their abilities to develop memorization strategies on their own may be less developed than that of most classmates. A blank version of this template is provided as Appendix 9.4.

Graphic Organizers

Referred to by a variety names, including *mind maps* (Davis & Sirotowitz, 1996) and *thinking maps* (Hyerle, 2004), graphic organizers designed to support

THREE-COLUMN NOTE-TAKING TEMPLATE

Questions/terms	Answers/definitions	Memory strategies (*How will I remember this?*)
What are names of the American great lakes?	1. Lake Michigan 2. Lake Erie 3. Lake Superior 4. Lake Huron 5. Lake Ontario	Use the 'HOMES' mnemonic Heuron Ontario Michigan Erie Superior
Which is the largest great lake?		
Which is the northern-most great lake?		

Figure 9.2. Example of a three-column note-taking template. (From *BrainCogs*, Research Institute for Learning and Development and FableVision, Inc. (2002); adapted by permission.)

notetaking require students to construct visual maps that represent the manner in which main ideas relate to other ideas and supporting information. Although there are now several styles and types of these visual maps, the kinds of note-taking organizers that are most likely to benefit students with executive skill weaknesses are those that have a straightforward, generally linear/sequential flow (see Figure 9.3 and Appendix 9.5). More complex "web-like" organizers (the ones that branch out in an assortment of directions and have many details) may be less helpful to students with significant executive function challenges because of the intense visual organizational demands of these graphics.

Study Skills

Although the reasons that students with executive function difficulties avoid or struggle with studying for tests may be as many as the number of students with executive function weaknesses, the test preparation challenges of this population often center on the following three factors:

1. *Forgetting to remember to study.* As a function of their distractibility and/or impulsivity, many of these students will forget their studying plans after becoming sidetracked by the many more appealing activities available in the home/community setting (e.g., "Shoot some hoops? Dude, that's exactly what I need right now after a long hard day at school. Let's go").

2. *Leaving insufficient time for studying.* See the time management discussion earlier in this chapter for more details.

3. *Feeling overwhelmed by the demands of studying.* For many students, a failure to study relates to an inability to wrap their minds around the organizational elements of the studying process. When presented with a large amount of information to manage and memorize, these students get stuck

MIND MAP NOTE-TAKING GRAPHIC ORGANIZER TEMPLATE

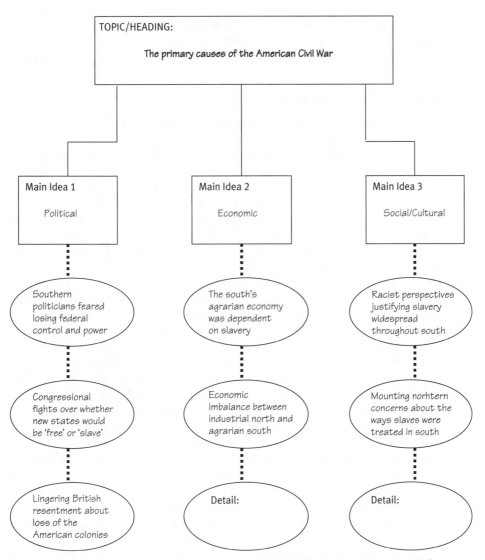

Figure 9.3.   Example of a mind-map note-taking graphic organizer template. (*Source:* Davis & Sirotowitz, 1996.)

on the question, "Where do I start?" They therefore fail to start or get quickly bogged down by anxiety and frustration (e.g., "Forget it. It's all just too much and I'm just gonna fail this test anyway, so why even bother?").

Because students with executive function weaknesses are more likely to struggle than their classmates with structuring the studying process on their own, interventions designed to improve their study skills need to provide scaffolds in the form of highly structured test preparation routines and strategies. These interventions must rely heavily—at least initially—on teachers' and parents' prefrontal cortical capacity to review the range of material that might be on a test and develop schedules/routines and study strategies that are well suited to the information to be learned. Often, once the *when* and the *how* elements of studying are clearly defined for these students, the quality of their test preparation jumps considerably, particularly if sufficient adult supervision is provided to ensure follow-through. The recommendations in the following sections examine this surrogate frontal lobe studying intervention model in more detail.

Establish Study Schedules and Routines

Just as a limited temporal sense will make it difficult for students with executive function struggles to accurately gauge the amount of time needed to complete daily homework and longer-term projects, so too will sense-of-time deficits hamper a student's ability to block out adequate amounts of time to study for tests. Because they are likely to underestimate the hours needed to prepare for examinations, they generally require more adult direction in scheduling and sticking to study time than might be predicted by age and grade levels. Tests that occur on a regularly scheduled basis (e.g., weekly spelling or vocabulary tests, biweekly unit tests, monthly laboratory tests) are the easiest for which to develop study schedules and routines, particularly if they occur with clockwork consistency. For these reoccurring quizzes and examinations, teachers and parents should develop weekly studying schedules that are written into assignment books several weeks in advance and adhered to with unwavering regularity. Thus, if a seventh grader has a science vocabulary test every Friday, then a half-hour of every Thursday evening should be consistently blocked out for science vocabulary review. Similarly, if a fourth grader has midweek spelling tests on Wednesday and final weekly spelling tests on Friday, regular spelling word-review periods should be blocked into every Tuesday and Thursday afternoon. Allowing students to skip one of their regularly scheduled weekly study periods because they claim to already know that week's material is almost always a bad idea, as it creates a precedent for study schedule variation that ends up defeating consistent study routines.

With lots of foresight and planning on the part of parents and teachers, reliable study routines can also be developed for tests that occur on a less frequent basis, such as unit tests, midterms, and finals. Students with executive function struggles may perform better on larger tests like these if the adults in their lives direct them in establishing definite and unwavering blocks of time to be used for test preparation:

Dad: Okay, Jonathan, so both you and your assignment book are saying that your biology midterm is next week. Oh, and we got an e-mail today from your biology teacher saying that she thinks you should devote about 4–5 hours in total studying for it.

Jonathan: Five hours? Come on, Dad, that lady is a freak about work and studying. No one is gonna study that long for this thing.

Dad: Well, freak or no, I think she knows her materials and tests and she also likes you a lot and knows your learning style. Let's block four studying hours into your assignment book between now and the day before the test. I'm also going to put another hour for biology review for you and me into your book for the night before. Got it?

Jonathan: This sucks, but, yeah, I guess I got it.

Show Children Exactly What to Study and How to Study It

One factor that can tank the test performance of students with executive function weaknesses is their difficulties with what Mel Levine (1998; 2002) referred to as *saliency determination*—that is, parsing out the really important information from that which is less important. Because they tend to view all information in a particular unit or course as equally salient, these students often struggle with managing the work and time demands of the studying process (e.g., "How do they expect us to remember all this stuff? It's impossible!"). Therefore, they generally benefit from explicit instruction regarding the information and materials on which they should focus their studying efforts.

Although this accommodation tends to be less important at the elementary school level because of the rather limited range of information that is associated with quizzes and tests prior to middle school, secondary school students with significant executive function challenges face a number of formal assessments of their academic knowledge and skill sets from week to week. Preparing adequately for all of the quizzes, tests, and performance demonstrations taxes the executive skills of even the more organized and disciplined students, and places a particularly heavy management burden on students with self-management difficulties.

Concrete indication by teachers of the information that should be given greatest emphasis during study sessions helps level the playing field for these students, and also provides them with some explicit instruction regarding the prioritization of academic content. This study-skill intervention can be shifted from an accommodation to a form of specialized instruction (i.e., a skill-building activity) when it not only carefully delineates the specific material that should be studied but also provides clear strategies for remembering the information (i.e., shows the *how* of studying). Classroom teachers know the learning objectives that will be assessed by their tests better than anyone, so they are in the best position to help students with executive function weaknesses develop concrete strategies to learn and recall them. Special educators and executive skill coaches (see next section) can also help with the strategy teaching and practice process by helping students construct such study aids as flashcards, mind maps, and two- and three-column note-consolidation systems.

The bottom line is that students with executive function weaknesses often need help studying in more focused, time-efficient, and strategic ways. By completing study plan forms (see Appendix 9.5), teachers can help these students identify the information to prioritize and send them home with clear strategies to learn the material and recall it when needed at test time.

Executive Skills Coaching: Putting It All Together for Middle and High School Students

Developed by Dawson and Guare (1998, 2004), individualized executive skill coaching of students with executive function weaknesses is probably the ultimate expression of the surrogate frontal lobe intervention model in the school setting. Although originally conceptualized by these authors as an intervention approach for students with attention-deficit/hyperactivity disorder (Dawson & Guare, 1998), in their second book (2004) they discussed the method's applicability to students with a range of executive function needs. This approach can be used with both middle and high school students as both a skill-building and daily academic management strategy. Although the approach, as Dawson and Guare noted, only works with students who are willing and able to be active participants in the process, individualized executive skill coaching can be far more effective in improving the general organization, work completion, and work quality of students with executive function struggles than group study-skill or academic support classes.

Unlike group interventions, which often attempt to teach key executive skills using traditional classroom instruction techniques (e.g., "Today, everyone, we're going to focus on using assignment books more effectively"), the executive functioning coaching process is individualized and concretely focused on helping students build strong executive skills via the planning, organization, and completion of their actual assignments (e.g., daily homework and longer-term projects). Educators and school-based clinicians interested in implementing this intervention model are strongly encouraged to obtain these books (Dawson and Guare, 1998, 2004) and adhere closely to the procedures described therein. A summary of their approach follows, as well as some brief recommendations based upon my work with teachers and students involved in the daily executive functioning coaching process.

As conceptualized by Dawson and Guare (1998, 2004), executive skills coaching begins with a structured goal-setting process in which the student, with the coach's assistance, determines the specific goals/objectives that he or she has regarding executive and academic functioning for the school year (e.g., getting my English and Social Studies assignments completed and handed in on time, studying more effectively for tests). Once the goals have been identified, the subsequent daily coaching sessions become structured around the formation of a plan for the day that relates to the student's objectives.

Dawson and Guare (2004) noted that although there obviously needs to be flexibility in how the coach–student interactions are structured, the first portion of each 15- to 20-minute daily session is generally devoted to a review of the extent to which the previous day's plan was achieved. The second portion focuses on the development of a plan for the current day, which includes after-school homework/study periods. The plan may specifically target such things as exactly when different pieces of work will be done and where the necessary resources can be obtained to complete assignments.

It is often the problem-solving element of the coaching sessions that students value most, because these issue-based discussions often allow them to leave the discussion with a way to overcome a problem on which they were previously stuck (e.g., "I've got midterms next week in both chemistry and trigonometry. How am I ever gonna find time to study for both and still do soccer practice every day?"). In addition to serving in this essential problem-solving consultant role, the coach should also serve as an advocate and "cheerleader" for the student, assisting him or her with struggles with teachers and praising all steps toward better executive functioning (Dawson & Guare, 2004). The following additional recommendations may increase the chances of students benefiting from daily executive skill coaching:

1. *Demystify students' executive skill profiles and related academic difficulties prior to the coaching process.* Few strategies are as effective as demystification when it comes to increasing an adolescent's motivation to engage in academic interventions. Demystification involves the careful explanation to the student, using developmentally appropriate language and avoiding jargon to the extent possible, of the specific nature of his or her learning profile (Levine, 2003; also see the articles on this topic available at Dr. Levine's web site, www.allkindsofminds.org). The explicit goal of the process is to make the child an informed part of the treatment team, rather than just the unwitting and potentially resistant recipient of the services adults have deemed necessary. Because it focuses on areas of comparative cognitive strength as well as on domains of weakness, demystification generally leaves students with a more accurate and positive impression of their learning profiles and helps stymie self-defeating perspectives like "I'm stupid" and "I can't do anything right." An added benefit of using demystification in the coaching process is that it is likely to help students participate more effectively in the initial goal-setting step.

2. *Allow students some say in the selection of the coach.* Relationships tend to matter a great deal to adolescents. A teacher may have a spectacular grasp of executive skills and have a wealth of experience improving students' academic functioning, but if she has a personality that links poorly with that of the student, then the coaching process is doomed before it starts. Although the professional role distinctions and staffing patterns in many schools may preclude students from selecting their own coach, it is essential that every practical effort be made to match students with school staff whose company they are likely to enjoy—or at least tolerate (Dawson and Guare, 2004).

3. *Coaching sessions should occur at the same time every day.* Although the rotating schedules commonly used in middle and high schools often make consistent support session scheduling a nightmare, it is extremely important to try to arrange a consistent daily time slot for the coaching session. If held at different times on different days ("Okay, so tomorrow's a blue day, and so we'll meet at 8:30, and then Wednesday is a green day, and so we'll meet at 9:45 . . ."), the odds of students forgetting and otherwise skipping sessions increase exponentially.

4. *Empower the coach to modify assignments to increase their suitability to students' learning needs.* Among the best ways to strengthen the student–coach bond and the sense of trust a student has in the relationship is to build advocacy elements into the coaching role. If a coach is empowered by a planning team or school policy to suggest changes to assignments and tests that make them better linked to students' neurodevelopmental profiles, the coach can be seen by the student as a school-based ally who understands rather than just a professional nag (e.g., "I think Katie can read these chapters on Renaissance culture and write a good reflection paper, but given her reading and writing speed, she's probably going to need a week more than you're giving the other students").

What I Need to Take Home Today

Things to take home	Student checks when done	Teacher checks when done
Reading book or workbook		
Language Arts book or workbook		
Math textbook or workbook		
Science textbook or workbook		
Social studies textbook or workbook		
Other books or workbooks:		
Assignment book or assignment sheet		
Notebooks:		
Binders:		
Gym clothes		
Other clothes:		
Permission slip for parents to sign		
Notices to show parents		
Report card or progress report		
Other:		
Are all these things in my backpack?		

From Dawson, P., & Guare, R. (2004). *Executive skills in children and adolescents: A practical guide to assessment and intervention.* New York: Guilford Press; adapted by permission.

In *Executive Function in the Classroom: Practical Strategies for Improving Performance and Enhancing Skills for All Students* by C. Kaufman.
(2010, Paul H. Brookes Publishing Co., Inc.)

Assignment Book Template

Subject	Monday	Tuesday	Wednesday
	_____ _____ _____ Take Home: _____ _____ _____	_____ _____ _____ Take Home: _____ _____ _____	_____ _____ _____ Take Home: _____ _____ _____
	_____ _____ _____ Take Home: _____ _____ _____	_____ _____ _____ Take Home: _____ _____ _____	_____ _____ _____ Take Home: _____ _____ _____
	_____ _____ _____ Take Home: _____ _____ _____	_____ _____ _____ Take Home: _____ _____ _____	_____ _____ _____ Take Home: _____ _____ _____
	_____ _____ _____ Take Home: _____ _____ _____	_____ _____ _____ Take Home: _____ _____ _____	_____ _____ _____ Take Home: _____ _____ _____
	_____ _____ _____ Take Home: _____ _____ _____	_____ _____ _____ Take Home: _____ _____ _____	_____ _____ _____ Take Home: _____ _____ _____
Initial box	Teacher's initials: ____ Parent's initials: ____	Teacher's initials: ____ Parent's initials: ____	Teacher's initials: ____ Parent's initials: ____

(continued)

*Executive Function in the Classroom: Practical Strategies for
Improving Performance and Enhancing Skills for All Students* by C. Kaufman.
Copyright © 2010 Paul H. Brookes Publishing Co., Inc. All rights reserved.

Subject	Thursday	Friday	Work I'll do Saturday or Sunday
	_____ _____ _____ Take Home: _____ _____ _____	_____ _____ _____ Take Home: _____ _____ _____	_____ _____ _____ *Bring back on Monday!* _____
	_____ _____ _____ Take Home: _____ _____ _____	_____ _____ _____ Take Home: _____ _____ _____	_____ _____ _____ *Bring back on Monday!* _____
	_____ _____ _____ Take Home: _____ _____ _____	_____ _____ _____ Take Home: _____ _____ _____	_____ _____ _____ *Bring back on Monday!* _____
	_____ _____ _____ Take Home: _____ _____ _____	_____ _____ _____ Take Home: _____ _____ _____	_____ _____ _____ *Bring back on Monday!* _____
	_____ _____ _____ Take Home: _____ _____ _____	_____ _____ _____ Take Home: _____ _____ _____	_____ _____ _____ *Bring back on Monday!* _____
Initial box	Teacher's initials: ____ Parent's initials: ____	Teacher's initials: ____ Parent's initials: ____	Teacher's initials: ____ Parent's initials: ____

My Project Plan

I. Select a topic (*must be completed by* _____):

Topic ideas	Good things about this topic idea	Possible problems with this topic idea
1.		
2.		
3.		

After discussing my topic choices with my teacher and parents, I've chosen:

_____

_____

II. Gather what you'll need (*must be completed by* _____)

Resources/materials	Where will you get it?	When will you get it?	Check off when shown to teacher
1.			
2.			
3.			
4.			
5.			
6.			

(continued)

From Dawson, P., & Guare, R. (2004). *Executive skills in children and adolescents: A practical guide to assessment and intervention.* New York: Guilford Press; adapted by permission.

In *Executive Function in the Classroom: Practical Strategies for Improving Performance and Enhancing Skills for All Students* by C. Kaufman.
(2010, Paul H. Brookes Publishing Co., Inc.)

III. All the remaining steps of my project and their due dates

Steps (*things to do*)	Due date	Check off when done and shown to the teacher
1. Will I need help with this? ( ) No ( ) Yes (Helper: _____)		
2. Will I need help with this? ( ) No ( ) Yes (Helper: _____)		
3. Will I need help with this? ( ) No ( ) Yes (Helper: _____)		
4. Will I need help with this? ( ) No ( ) Yes (Helper: _____)		
5. Will I need help with this? ( ) No ( ) Yes (Helper: _____)		
6. Will I need help with this? ( ) No ( ) Yes (Helper: _____)		
7. Will I need help with this? ( ) No ( ) Yes (Helper: _____)		
8. Will I need help with this? ( ) No ( ) Yes (Helper: _____)		
9. Will I need help with this? ( ) No ( ) Yes (Helper: _____)		
10. Will I need help with this? ( ) No ( ) Yes (Helper: _____)		

From Dawson, P., & Guare, R. (2004). *Executive skills in children and adolescents: A practical guide to assessment and intervention.* New York: Guilford Press; adapted by permission.

In *Executive Function in the Classroom: Practical Strategies for Improving Performance and Enhancing Skills for All Students* by C. Kaufman.
(2010, Paul H. Brookes Publishing Co., Inc.)

Triple Note Tote

Question/term	Answer/definition	Strategy

From *BrainCogs*, Research Institute for Learning and Development and FableVision, Inc. (2002); adapted by permission.

In *Executive Function in the Classroom: Practical Strategies for Improving Performance and Enhancing Skills for All Students* by C. Kaufman.
(2010, Paul H. Brookes Publishing Co., Inc.)

Mind Map Note-Taking
Graphic Organizer Template

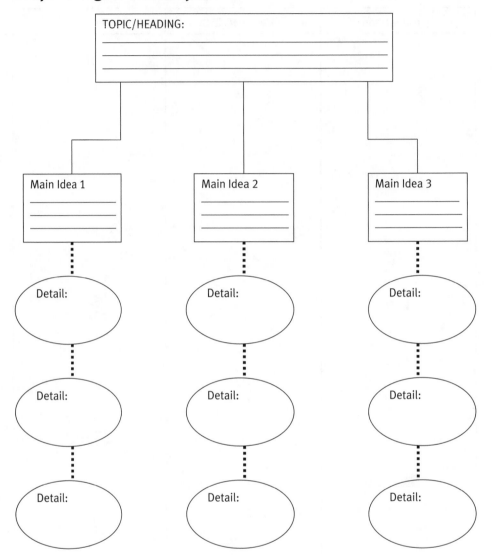

TOPIC/HEADING:

Main Idea 1

Main Idea 2

Main Idea 3

Detail:

Detail:

Detail:

Detail:

Detail:

Detail:

Detail:

Detail:

Detail:

Daily Homework Sheet

Today's date: _____

Subject/assignment	Things I need to take home!!	Things from home I'll need to use:	Priority? Do first, second, third . . . ?	When will I do this?

Teacher's initials: _____   Parent's initials: _____

CHAPTER 10

Unfiltered Comments, Unchecked Actions

Executive Dysfunction and Social Learning Difficulties

> 66 The wise man must be wise before, not after. 99
> — EPICHARMUS, GREEK COMIC POET (~450 BC)

Upon completing this chapter, the reader will be able to

☞ Describe Descartes's error and its relevance to the social-emotional challenges commonly presented by students with self-regulatory deficits

☞ Discuss the relationship between executive functions and Daniel Goleman's concepts of emotional and social intelligence

☞ Discuss the impact of impulse control, working memory, planning skill, and adaptability on students' social-emotional functioning

☞ Discuss the range of strategies that can be effective in preventing (or at least, lessening) the social-behavioral struggles of students with self-regulatory weakness

☞ Discuss the range of strategies that can be effective in building the social and emotional self-modulation skills of students with self-regulatory weakness

☞ Discuss the structure and elements of school-based individual behavior plans that are likely to be effective for students with self-regulatory weakness

Mean Max and Descartes's Error

Have you ever known or worked with a child whose behavioral issues seemed so entrenched and consistent that thoughts like "this kid is bad to the bone" sprang readily to mind? If you have silently labeled occasional students in this manner, know that you are far from alone. Over the years, many veteran teachers have confided to me their private suspicions about the inherent "wickedness" of a child on their caseload and related despair of ever finding ways of improving the situation.

Max (a pseudonym) was such a student. In a consultation meeting hastily convened to address what the principal referred to as Max's *behavioral atrocity du jour,* the classroom teacher complained bitterly about the boy's lack of response to the range of disciplinary interventions she had attempted and apparent lack of remorse for his numerous disruptive and aggressive actions: "He sometimes laughs after he does something mean and lies constantly when I catch him at things. He takes no responsibility for what he does." After the principal had left for another meeting, the teacher admitted to referring to this student in her own head occasionally as *Mean Max,* adding, "I know it's wrong and I'm kind of embarrassed I do this, but that's what the other kids call him sometimes because he's so aggressive and in your face. It's hard not to view him as nasty."

If we are honest with ourselves, most of us can recall at least a few students over the years who we may have dismissed to varying degrees with such pejorative labels as *nasty* and *mean.* Looking back, we may recognize that these condemnations were primarily judgments of a moral nature, with the child in question being found lacking with regard to specific aspects of "character" that greatly influence how one is perceived by society. Rather than viewing these students as showing signs of an emotional or social disability, we saw their failings through a moral lens and maintained—at least to ourselves—that the needed interventions were those that would, in essence, provide a much needed "kick in the pants."

When children are physically disabled in some obvious way, contemporary society rarely hesitates to view their struggles as body centered and provide an array of accommodations to make their lives somewhat easier. We leap with similar speed to the aid of children whose cognitive disabilities are unambiguous, providing whatever levels of specialized instruction and individualized supports are necessary to help them progress in school and in the community. When children's struggles are largely social or behavioral in nature, however, it is amazing how quickly we may view these difficulties as being largely under a student's control. Rather than recognizing the likely neurological contributors to a child's aggression or frequent temper tantrums, society is quick to perceive them as "extracranial" (to use Elkhonon Goldberg's [2001] apt phrase) and condemn the child on moral grounds (e.g., "He's 10 years old and still melts down every day just like a 3-year-old child. What a spoiled brat!"). Overlooking the brain's contributions to the outbursts, we are committing what the esteemed neuroscientist Antonio Damasio (1994) called "Descartes's error."

René Descartes offered the most famous of philosophical statements: "I think, therefore I am." Descartes is also remembered for his convictions regarding mind–body dualism, or the belief that one's thoughts and larger mind exist separate from the body. He maintained that the body, including the brain, functioned essentially as a machine and was controlled by the largely independent mind, or soul (Goldberg, 2001). Although Descartes acknowledged that the mind could be influenced by the body, such as when one acts out of passion, he saw the mind as an entirely separate entity that was housed in the body (in the pineal gland of the brain, to be exact) and basically governed thought and behavior. Thus, if someone tended to act in ways that others found helpful and beneficial, he or she was judged to possess strong moral fiber—"a good soul." Individuals whose thoughts and behavior were problematic, however, were seen as troubled in the mind or soul, and subject to harsh judgments concerning their character and morals.

Cartesian notions of mind–body dualism have had major influence on Western culture and philosophy over the centuries, and continue to shape the ways in which we view elements of behavior. Although, as Goldberg pointed out, few in our society question the neurobiological basis of language, perception, and motor functioning; the larger culture continues to brand elements of behavioral and social functioning as attributes of the mind that exist separate from neurological function, "as if they were attributes of our clothes and not our body" (2001, p. 2).

Descartes's error remains rampant in the educational community, with behaviors such as frequent aggression and noncompliance commonly attributed to "failures of the soul" ("He's such a brat!") rather than to the neurodevelopmental profiles that contribute to them. This chapter examines the influence of what is likely a leading neurodevelopmental contributor to social-emotional struggles across school and community contexts—executive function weakness (Leonard-Zabel & Feifer, 2009). The first half delves into the relationship between executive function challenges and social awareness and social-emotional response, while the second half presents a range of strategies that can effectively prevent, manage, and remediate the social and behavioral difficulties of students with significant executive function weaknessses.

The Role of Executive Function in Social-Emotional Functioning

Consider the following executive function–related social blunders.

☞ Caleb

Caleb, a first grader, wants to be first in line today when his class goes to the gymnasium. Noticing his classmates beginning to gather by the door, he jumps from his seat and rushes headlong for the choice place in line. En route, he inadvertently knocks over a table holding the class's recently finished clay art projects. The assorted paperweights, bowls, and figurines crash to the floor, with most of them shattering to bits. Before anyone can say anything, Caleb runs from the room, screaming "You all hate me!"

☞ Eric

The students in Mrs. Longsufferer's fourth-grade class have been working for the past 20 minutes on the drawing portion of their biography project. When told that they need to start finishing up because it was almost time for math, Eric slams down his markers and shoves his drawing angrily to the floor. When directed to pick up his work and materials, Eric steps on the drawing and kicks the markers across the floor. Later, after calming down, he explains his outburst to the teacher by saying, "I wasn't done and you never give us time to finish stuff."

☞ Emily

Seventh-grade student Emily finishes eating her lunch and gets up to throw away her wrappers into the garbage can. Believing two girls whispering to each other by the door are gossiping about her, Emily flicks her leftover french fries at them, causing the girls to scream such things as, "Oh gross! What the heck? What's your problem, freak?!" Everyone turns to look at Emily, who stomps from the room, yelling "This school sucks!"

☞ Madeline

Madeline, a high school junior, is fired from her summer job with the town's parks and recreation department after only 4 days. When questioned by her mother about the reasons for the dismissal, Madeline responds, "The crew supervisor hates me." Upon calling the supervisor to discuss her daughter's rapid termination, Madeline's mother is told that Madeline was let go because she "just couldn't get along with any of workers on her crew." The supervisor continues, "She kept making all these inappropriate jokes and sarcastic comments, and didn't seem to get that she was making people angry all the time. I warned her about it a bunch of times, and when it still didn't stop I had to let her go."

These scenarios depict just a few of the countless ways in which developmental self-regulation difficulties can impair the social functioning of children and adolescents. Although all students, by virtue of their incomplete prefrontal cortical maturation, remain self-regulatory "works-in-progress" into their early adult years, children with comparative weakness with regard to such executive skills as self-monitoring, adaptability, impulse control, and frustration management are particularly likely to engage in behaviors that others find odd or annoying (Riggs, Jahromi, Razza, Dillworth-Bart, & Mueller, 2006). These students may be saddled by interaction and self-management styles that include a host of socially self-penalizing tendencies (e.g., misreading social contexts, frequently saying the wrong thing at the wrong time, calling out a lot in class, "going ballistic" in competitive games during gym and recess) and are often passively ignored or aggressively rejected by their peers. Even if their other cognitive abilities are such that they are successful in academic domains, substantial executive weaknesses can dramatically limit

Table 10.1. Common social and emotional tendencies among students with executive function weaknesses

Social tendencies	Emotional tendencies
Seeming socially immature relative to age norms	Low frustration threshold (the tendency to experience significant frustration and anger in situations that are unlikely to trigger as much negative emotion in most peers)
A lack of self-awareness and self-knowing	
Immature/limited "theory of mind" (grasping and appreciating that others' have different perspectives from ones own)	
	Low frustration tolerance (the tendency to become overwhelmed by frustration and anger)
The tendency to live very much in the present moment ("Consequences? What are consequences? Full speed ahead!")	Reflexive negativity (the tendency to respond with quick and often intense negative emotion to requests and stressors) (Green, 1998)
Verbal impulsivity (e.g., frequently calling out in class, saying the wrong thing at the wrong time)	Easily explosive behavior (the tendency to exhibit rage and other forms of intense anger/ frustration; "amygdala hijacks")
Motor impulsivity (e.g., often acting without thinking, bowling into and over others and things)	
Verbal overflow (e.g., talking rapidly and excessively, going on and on with little apparent regard to the interest level of the listener, excessive voice volume)	Marked difficulties managing emotions (becomes excessively silly/giddy when happy and aggressive/withdrawn when angry)
Motor overflow (e.g., continuing to roughhouse well after peers have ceased this behavior, continuing recess behaviors after returning to the classroom)	Marked difficulties with alternate thinking (weighing problem-solving options) when stressed
	Limited adaptability (becoming easily "stuck" and overwhelmed by changes in plans and routines, marked difficulties coping with new situations and people)
Troubles with turn taking	
Impulsively inventing or changing game rules for personal advantage	Black-and-white thinking (the tendency to see things or people as all good or all bad)

the emotional and social intelligence with which they operate in school each day (Goleman, 1995, 2006). See Table 10.1 for a more detailed list of social and emotional struggles common among students with executive function weaknesses.

Executive Skill and Social-Emotional Intelligence

What factors predict a child's social and emotional intelligence? Although a comprehensive answer to this question requires a detailed discussion of the range of biological and environmental factors that can shape behavior, a quick scan of the core elements of these essential human abilities as defined by Goleman (1995) and *Social Intelligence* (2006) makes plain their dependence upon executive skills (see Table 10.2). Indeed, the terms *self-awareness, self-management, social awareness,* and *relationship management* are all largely synonymous with the social-emotional regulation elements of executive function. One would certainly not expect a child with difficulties in such core executive functions as impulse control, frustration management, and self-monitoring skills to exhibit much in the way of what Goleman has labeled *emotional and social intelligence.* Therefore, the ability to act intelligently across emotional and social domains of life is dependent on the capacity to simultaneously monitor one's own and others' behavior, keeping a lid on whatever inappropriate impulses might crop up, and responding adaptively or strategically to the numerous challenges inherent in relational life. In sum, socially and emotionally intelligent behavior is most accurately considered to be an expression of executive skill and (with all due respect to Goleman) should be labeled as such.

Table 10.2.   How social intelligence abilities fit into the emotional
intelligence model

Emotional intelligence	Social intelligence
Self-awareness	**Social awareness**
	Primal empathy
	Empathic accuracy
	Listening
	Social cognition
Self-management	**Social facility (or relationship management)**
	Synchrony
	Self-presentation
	Influence
	Concern

From SOCIAL INTELLIGENCE: THE NEW SCIENCE OF HUMAN RELATION-
SHIPS by Daniel Goleman, copyright © 2006 by Daniel Goleman. Used by
permission of Bantam Books, a division of Random House, Inc.

Now that we have identified the range of maladaptive tendencies that
have an impact on the social and emotional intelligence of students with
executive weaknesses, the next section discusses the information processing
factors that underlie executive function-related social cognitive challenges—
more specifically, the roles played by response inhibition (impulse control),
working memory, planning skill, and adaptability/set shifting in social-
emotional functioning.

Response Inhibition (Impulse Control)

The word that best describes the social-emotional style of children with executive function weaknesses is *reactive*. Lacking the self-regulatory capacity
of most peers, they are prone to operate in the social world like ships without
a rudder, tossed this way and that by the emotional tides and situational currents of relational life. In other words, they tend to respond quickly and often
intensely to both the positive and negative events that occur in their days,
giving less apparent regard to the consequences of their actions than would
be expected for a given developmental level (e.g., "Consequences? What consequences? Full speed ahead!").

From a processing perspective, the capacity to look before one leaps
requires the inhibition of what Barkley (1997) called *prepotent impulses*—that
is, impulses that are automatically triggered by particular life events (see Figure 10.1). We all have our range of personal prepotent responses to environmental stimuli, some of which are adaptive (e.g., putting our keys in the same
place without thinking upon returning each evening from work), whereas
others are maladaptive (e.g., snapping impulsively at a loved one when
stressed). The maintenance of civilized society essentially hinges on the ability of people to stifle angry, aggressive impulses (e.g., the urge to throttle the
7-year-old son who has just put an enormous dent in the new car by using it
as a jumping platform) in the interest of maintaining peace and harmony.
Children with marked impulse control deficits are more apt to express their
initial, and often maladaptive, responses to life events because they lack—

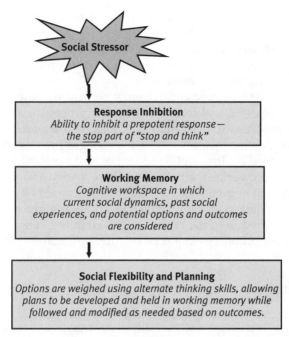

Figure 10.1. The executive processes of social problem solving.

relative to peer norms—the prefrontal cortical capacity to arrest prepotent impulses before they are acted on (Barkley, 1997). This leaves them frequently in the unfortunate position of trying to explain the logic of actions that had no logical basis:

Mom: Theresa! Why on earth did you smash your brother's cell phone on the ground?!? What were you thinking?

Theresa (age 8):   Well . . . I . . . He said I was too stupid to work it.

Thomas (the much-aggrieved brother):   No, I didn't!

Theresa: Yes, you did! And, anyway, yesterday you pushed me out of the bathroom!

Recall the discussion in Chapter 3 about the relationship that exists in the brain between the amygdala (a limbic structure associated with emotional memory and the generation of emotions) and the prefrontal cortex (the brain's primary center of self-regulation). A primary function of the amygdala, working in concert with the hypothalamus, is to generate emotions associated with both fight (anger/aggression) and flight (anxiety). A key self-regulatory role of the prefrontal cortex (particularly its orbital and ventromedial regions) is to review the potential reward value of the impulses triggered by the amygdala (e.g., "If I act on this impulse, are good or bad things likely to happen for me?") and modulate their expression (Feifer, 2009).

Individuals with significant executive skill weaknesses tend to struggle with regulating the prepotent urges that originate in lower brain centers because they lack the prefrontal cortical capacity to suppress them. Their ability to "think on their feet" when confronted by problematic situations is often overwhelmed by what is experienced as a tidal wave of intense emotion.

Goleman (2006) drew a distinction between what he referred to as "high road" versus "low road" emotional processing, noting that although the former (mediated by the prefrontal cortex) is rational and considered, the latter (because it bypasses the prefrontal cortex) operates more automatically and largely below the realm of awareness.

Children with significant prefrontal cortical weakness relative to peer norms may take the low road of emotional processing, particularly when confronted by stressful social situations, making them prone to emotional responses that are "unencumbered by the thought process" (to use the artful phrase employed by Tom and Ray Magliozzi of National Public Radio's *Car Talk* program to describe their own impulsive tendencies). Chapter 3 referred to the swamping of prefrontal cortical thinking capacity by emotional surges from the amygdala as an "amygdala hijack," because the control of behavior is abruptly shifted from the brain's higher cognitive centers (prefrontal cortex) to its more primitive emotional reaction/origination centers.

Working Memory

Working memory, an executive function construct heavily featured throughout this book, also plays a key role in the self-regulation of social-emotional behavior. Barkley (1997, 2006) gave strong emphasis to working memory in his theory of self-control, noting that it is in this provisional form of memory that people hold the elements of any social situation (e.g., a conflict with a peer on the playground over who gets to use a particular swing first) as well as the variety of strategies that might be applicable to address the problem (e.g., grab the swing violently from the other child, offer to take turns, walk away, ask an adult for help).

In the absence of developmentally expected levels of working memory skill, students must function socially without the cognitive workspace in which to sort out the many variables inherent in interactions with others; that is, lacking sufficient working memory capacity to ponder their options, many students with executive deficits often bypass the thinking/planning stage of social problem-solving and respond immediately with some form of prepotent—often aggressive—response. It is working memory, as Barkley noted, that enables the consideration of potential futures associated with the situations at hand:

> This is the special form of memory that I specified would be needed to provide both for the cross-temporal organization of behavior, as in planning, and for the sense of future and its consequent preference for delayed over immediate rewards that are critical to self-control. The working memory system appears to shift behavior away from the moment and away from external control toward the future by way of internally generated information that arises from private, covert behavior (1997, p. 103).

Said more simply, it is in working memory that the *think* element of the "stop-and-think" process of self-regulation occurs, allowing children with adequate levels of working memory capacity the cognitive space and time to consider not just the variables of a given social interaction and their options in managing it, but also the range of potential futures that may occur based on the decisions they make in the moment (Moffit & Lyman, 1994). All of this means that the most honest—or at least, realistic—answer many students with working memory problems can give to the often incredulously stated adult question "What were you thinking?" would be, "I wasn't."

Planning/Organization

Even if students with executive function weaknesses possess the working memory capacity (the cognitive equivalent of a computer's random access memory) needed for social thinking and problem solving, they will still exhibit a range of functional social difficulties if they lack the planning skills needed to quickly establish and adapt social strategies during interactions with others across the day. Consider the following scenario, in which a fictitious preadolescent copes effectively with a fairly typical social challenge as a function of her cognitive flexibility and planning skill.

☞ Elizabeth

Elizabeth, a sixth grader, has been looking forward to her best friend Megan's pool party for weeks. Upon arriving at the party, she learns that Megan's cousin, Stacy, will also be attending. Elizabeth has a strong dislike for Stacy, finding her in past encounters to be a bossy know-it-all who hogs all of Megan's attention. Although disappointed that her time at the party won't be quite as she expected, Elizabeth quickly decides to spend more time with other friends as opposed to challenging Stacy for Megan's attention. Her private thoughts about this plan include, "I'll hang mostly with Carol and Heidi, and will try and spend time with Megan when Stacy's doing other stuff."

The ability to think and act strategically in social settings is among the factors that set socially successful students apart from those who are more apt to engage in socially self-penalizing behaviors. To cope well with challenging social situations like the one that faced Elizabeth, children have to possess the self-awareness and other-awareness to grasp the true nature of the problem at hand ("Darn. I was expecting this party to be a chance for me and Megan to have lots of fun together, but now there's Miss Boss to deal with. Stacy and I don't mix well"). They then must inhibit the expression of maladaptive prepotent responses (e.g., pouting during the party because of the interloper's presence), formulate and hold a plan related to the situation in working memory (e.g., spend time with other kids I like and hang with Megan when the moment's right), and adapt the strategy on the fly as needed. Children who lack planning skills are less likely to think strategically on their own in the face of social challenges, and will therefore be more likely to cope in ways that others find immature and/or aggressive (e.g., "Megan, I can't believe you invited Stacy! You know I hate her! Forget it—now this party's ruined!").

Adaptability

Life is very much about coping with change. Although it sometimes seems that our days progress in an unending stream of sameness and routine, much of the stress we encounter across family, work, and social contexts relates to the unexpected glitches and curveballs that come our way. The ability to flex and adapt with relative grace to the many deviations from the expected that can occur from day to day is a major determinant not just of personal happiness moment to moment, but also of longer-term academic, vocational, and social success. Those who possess the executive capacity to shift well between the expected and unexpected, and among the many activities and tasks that define daily life, tend to remain focused, happy, and productive. As noted in Chapter 1, individuals whose executive function profiles include a "balky cognitive shifter" are more likely to insist on the sameness of their days and react poorly to the new and unanticipated (Moffit & Lyman, 1994).

A dearth of cognitive flexibility not only makes students with executive function weakness cling to the predictable and routine, but also limits their ability to access in social situations what are sometimes referred to as *alternative thinking skills*—that is, the internalized self-talk that allows options to be weighed and social plans developed. Among the reasons it is common for these students to melt down or shut down in challenging academic and social contexts is that they lack the cognitive flexibility needed, when stressed, to quickly summon into working memory from long-term memory a range of problem-solving options. Unable to access a range of alternative strategies to such situations as being called a "loser" on the school bus or tripping and falling in the cafeteria, for example, they tend to quickly access some aggressive prepotent ("low road") response that gets them in trouble with adults and makes them look foolish (or in other ways undesirable) to peers.

Understanding Executive Function Weaknesses as Social Learning Weaknesses (or, Putting Aside Descartes's Error)

When we understand the various ways in which executive function weaknesses can have an impact on the ability to consider and respond to social situations, it becomes easier to accept the neurobiological contributors to many of the social-emotional struggles students exhibit in school contexts. Saddled with neuropsychological profiles that make it difficult to access what Goleman (2006) referred to as the high road of social awareness and problem solving, children with executive weakness lag behind their classmates with regard to both the *stop* and *think* aspects of relational functioning. Lacking the capacity (relative to peer norms) to inhibit their own automatic perceptions and to hold others' perceptions and social options in working memory (Barkley, 1997; Moffit and Lyman, 1994), these children often fail to accurately "read" the social environments in which they are immersed and respond impulsively (prepotently) in ways that are both maladaptive and self-penalizing. How should the educational community label this pattern of social struggles? Given the fairly obvious manner in which executive dysfunction can influence both the learning and demonstration of appropriate social-emotional behavior, it is far more accurate to identify the relational struggles of individuals with executive function challenges as *social learning deficits* in need of therapeutic assistance than as "choice-based" behavioral syndromes (e.g., oppositional defiant disorder) in need of consequence-centered behavior plans.

This brings us back to Descartes's error (Damasio, 1998; Goldberg, 2001) and the many students across this country whose social-behavioral presentation in school is similar to that of "Mean Max." While it would be a gross oversimplification to say that executive function weakness is the sole explanation for the maladaptive relational styles of students like Max, the role played by executive struggles in aggression and noncompliance seem rather difficult to dispute. Children who, because of genetic and environmental influences, bring executive skill profiles to school each day that include rather limited response inhibition, adaptability, working memory, and/or alternative thinking skills will almost certainly display a range of social-behavioral difficulties that peers will find annoying and teachers will find challenging. Unless helped to understand themselves and the reasons they behave the way they do, these students will often feel as bewildered by their behavior as those they affect and may cope with their social difficulties in a variety of maladaptive ways, including the laughing response exhibited by Max. Some students, when at a loss to explain why they do what they do, simply laugh and hope others will laugh as well.

Given what we now know about the biological basis of many social and emotional difficulties, the fields of education and psychology should consign Descartes's error to the trash bin of history. After moving beyond broad-based condemnations of children (e.g., "He's just a brat who's choosing to disrupt my class every day and I'm done putting up with it!"), we can begin the hard work of helping students recognize the nature of their behavioral weaknesses and assist them in developing the skills and strategies necessary to function in a more self-regulated manner.

Strategies

> " Behind every challenging behavior is an unsolved problem, a lagging skill, or both. "
> —ROSS GREENE (2008)

An Ounce of Prevention

When it comes to the effective management of social-emotional struggles associated with executive deficits, Ben Franklin's maxim that "an ounce of prevention is worth a pound of cure" most definitely applies. Because it is almost impossible stop a shutdown or meltdown from occurring once a student with executive weakness has crossed the cognitive divide that separates rationale thought from what Ross Greene (1998) termed "vapor lock"—that is, the point at which the child is no longer able to access effective problem-solving choices and is moving inexorably toward an amygdala hijack—it is crucial to limit the social stressors to which this population is exposed across the school day. As any teacher, clinician, or parent with experience with students with executive function challenges knows, it is far easier to prevent a social crisis from occurring than to try to cope with an affective storm and its fallout. The warding off of social blunders and meltdowns has the added benefit of protecting students with significant executive needs from the social stigma associated with relational awkwardness and emotional dyscontrol. If implemented with reasonable consistency, the strategies discussed in the following sections should limit the frequency and intensity of the socially self-penalizing behaviors to which students with executive function weaknesses are prone.

Keep Nonacademic Periods Well Structured and Adult-Directed

While idle hands may not actually constitute the devil's workshop, a lack of adult-directed structure and consistency in nonacademic school settings may contribute to the social-behavioral struggles that are common among students with executive deficits. In the absence of necessary surrogate frontal lobe support, students with executive function weakness are prone to social blunders and emotional conflagrations that get them rejected by peers and in trouble with school staff. It is not surprising, therefore, that the least structured periods of the school day—passing in the halls from class to class, eating lunch in the cafeteria, and playing or hanging out during recess—are the times in which many behavioral difficulties occur (Bowen, Jenson, & Clark, 2004), as it is in these periods when students with executive skill weaknesses are afforded the least amount of surrogate frontal lobe support. Elementary and middle schools that provide little in the way of structure regarding these nonacademic times of the day are essentially setting up students with executive deficits for social mishaps and emotional blowups. Without adult-directed structure, these students are prone to say and do things that other students find annoying, making them fairly obvious targets for bullying. Indeed, students with executive function weaknesses tend to receive particularly aggressive forms of school-based harassment because peers often view their awkward and impulsive social styles as provocative.

Cody: *Who should I nail with this spitball?*

Ben: *Duh?! Michael's sitting right over there by himself. Everyone hates him, so go ahead.*

To help students with overly rigid, impulsive, or otherwise problematic social styles, an increasing number of schools are electing to increase the levels of adult direction provided in less structured settings. More teachers at the elementary and middle school levels, for example, are eating lunch in the same cafeteria as their students, allowing for greater supervision of peer-to-peer interactions. Students with executive function weaknesses are likely to benefit from social mentoring and adult-led discussions in these settings, as will be discussed later. An increasing number of elementary schools now also provide a range of adult-directed activities, such as games of kickball, basketball, and four-square during recess, to ensure that students with social-skill problems have the opportunity to interact with others in contexts that are safe and supervised. Although such beefed-up adult direction in less structured settings does not guarantee that students with executive deficits will refrain from social blunders and the harassment that often accompanies these self-penalizing tendencies, well-structured activities can help stave off incidents that result in rejection and harassment of children with executive function challenges.

Establish Rules

How do we increase the chances that students with highly impulsive and/or inflexible social styles will access the appropriate methods of managing their own impulses/frustrations and conflicts with others in school contexts? Among the most effective ways of doing so is to develop a set of clearly written rules—ideally with student input and based upon the social teaching activities employed—that specify exactly what students should do when they are feeling frustrated with schoolwork, frustrated with a teacher or other staff member, or angry with one or more classmates (Jones, 2003; Jones, 2007). The following classroom examples target these different social skill and problem-solving domains.

- We raise our hand and wait to be called on before saying something in a class discussion.

- We wait until someone else has finished talking before we start talking. If we absolutely need to interrupt for some reason, we always start with the words, "Excuse me for interrupting" or "Sorry for interrupting."

- We think about the appropriateness of what we say *before* we say it. For example, before making a comment about someone's shoes or shirt (something that we think is funny and only a joke), we stop and think first about how it might make the other person feel.

- Instead of giving up, daydreaming, or acting distracted in other ways when frustrated with schoolwork, we quietly ask a classmate for help or raise our hand and wait for the teacher to come and help.

- Instead of getting into an argument or fight with a classmate if there is a disagreement, we first suggest a compromise (e.g., taking turns, sharing something, or playing together). If we cannot think of a compromise that works, we either walk away from each other and let it go or go to an adult for help (not to tattle, but instead to ask for help).

- We apologize in a sincere way for hurting someone's feelings, even if we did not mean to hurt someone's feelings.

Obviously, the power of any social rules to prevent problematic behavior is dependent upon the extent to which students both understand and remember them on a day-to-day basis. It is all too common for rules to be carefully established for classrooms, cafeterias, hallways, and playgrounds at the start of the year, only to be forgotten quickly by everyone, even if they are artfully posted, by the end of September. Students with impulse control and other self-regulatory problems are particularly likely to forget the adaptive strategies they are supposed to use when stressed. Explicit teaching of the rules during their development certainly helps make them real for students, even those with social learning struggles, but even this approach will not keep them fresh and meaningful for students after a few months have gone by. To increase the chances of desired social behavior being pulled back into students' working memories when needed, teachers should refer to them often by specifically and publicly praising students' prosocial behavioral (e.g., "Wow, Molly and Katie, I just overheard the two of you come up with a great compromise about who would sit next to Eliza on the bus today—that was an awesome display of our compromise rule!") and by periodically reviewing them with more chances for guided practice (e.g., through roleplaying).

Manage Energy and Frustration Levels

As earlier chapters have noted, students with executive function weaknesses may experience physical and cognitive fatigue more quickly in educational settings than their peers. Given the academic and social challenges these students confront throughout the school day, it is not surprising that they are often "fried" by the end of the morning or in the early afternoon. Some of the more spectacular blowups from students with marked executive deficits may come when their physical and/or emotional reserves are exhausted and a well-intentioned teacher insists that they engage in a nonpreferred activity:

Teacher: John, I know you're tired from the field trip and bus ride, but the school day isn't over for another hour and you've got to at least write one paragraph on your field trip reflection sheet.

John: What? Forget it—I'm not doing it! Just give me a zero.

Teacher: Then I guess you're choosing to stay with me after school today until you get it done. I'm not fooling around with this.

John: Forget that! I'm out of here!

Although prefrontal weakness tends to make students more prone to amygdale-driven overreactions (Leonard-Zabel & Feifer, 2009), the swamping of prefrontal self-regulatory capacity by intense emotion will most readily occur when a child's daily supply of cognitive and/or physical energy has been tapped out. Distractibility, rigidity, and impulsivity will also happen with greater frequency and intensity when students with executive function struggles are "out of gas."

To prevent academic withdrawal, social gaffes, and emotional meltdowns, it is important for teachers (working as needed with school-based clinical staff, administrators, and parents) to lighten the academic and social load for these students as necessary across the day. If, for example, a young student with significant executive deficits tends to become overwhelmed and fatigued by very large-group activities such as school assemblies, allowing the student to avoid these events, participate in them only briefly, or participate in an alternative form will likely reap academic and social-behavioral benefits later in the day. At the middle school and high school levels, a reduction in the number of classes taken across the day can dramatically improve the energy and effort students with executive function challenges bring to the remaining classes. Because writing and other production tasks tend to particularly tax the cognitive and physical reserves of this population (see Chapter 7), it is almost always a bad idea to impose significant written language requirements on these students toward the end of the day.

Watch for Red Flags

Most students with executive function weaknesses display one or a series of "red flag" behaviors (Smith-Myles & Southwick, 1999), which can provide some advance warning of an imminent meltdown. Such behaviors include ears and face becoming flushed, breathing becoming rapid, and staring into space—just to name a few. Once these behaviors are observed, it is almost always a good idea to back off from academic and social task demands until the student visibly calms down or, if necessary, until the next day. Each time a fatigued student is triggered to exhibit a full-blown amygdala hijack, he or she will become that much prone to exhibit similar outbursts (as the brain becomes increasingly facile with regard to intense emotional displays) and will be diminished that much more in the eyes of peers. Although far from a cure-all, selective battle picking—particularly when red flags are observed—can go a long way to limiting the behaviors that often result in students with significant executive function weaknesses being moved to more restrictive settings.

Responding Effectively to Amygdala Hijacks

Stay Nearby, But Say Little

The natural inclination of people in the helping professions when confronted by a student in the throes of a major meltdown is to try and talk them through it. Although this response stems from both compassion and a desire to keep things under control, the initiation of an elaborate conversation with a child in the midst of an amygdala hijack is almost always a bad idea. Tony Attwood (2007), psychologist and leading specialist on Asperger syndrome, likens attempts at talking to students who are either in major shutdown or blowout mode to pouring gasoline on a fire.

When an amygdala hijack is in full swing, the portion of the child's brain that is capable of participating in a rational problem-solving discussion (the prefrontal cortex) has essentially "left the building" and has ceded control to more primitive systems associated with fight and flight. While quite capable of storing emotional memories and triggering sustaining survival responses, the amygdala tends to make a rather lousy conversational partner—particularly if the conversation is related to circumstances that triggered the emotional outburst in the first place. This is why well-intentioned problem-solving verbal prompts from school staff such as, "Michael, put the desk down and let's talk about some better choices you could be making right now," tend to only heighten the student's level of emotional distress.

If circumstances permit, it is generally far better to resist the urge to start talking right away about the situation at hand to students who have temporarily lost the capacity for rational thought and instead simply keep them safe and wait for the emotional storm to subside. Once it is clear that a child is back in his or her "right mind"—or at least heading in that direction—initial verbal prompts from adults hoping to start a problem-solving conversation should be neutral (e.g., "Hey buddy") or distracting in nature so as not to arouse the still hypervigilant amygdala. After several minutes of whatever level of neutral banter a student is able to maintain, it is usually safe to offer some nonjudgmental comments about the outburst that occurred (e.g., "Looks like you got pretty frustrated back there, huh?") before allowing the student the chance to tell his or her side of the story. Only after this perspective has been fully vented and the amygdala given another chance to back off should any serious attempts at social problem-solving coaching be initiated.

Remember, Low and Slow

Probably the worst way to respond to the escalating emotional agitation of a student with executive function weakness is to try to threaten or intimidate him or her out of it. When a child's fight-or-flight response has begun to kick in, even well-meaning attempts by school staff to try to manage the situation via chest puffing (e.g., "I'm the teacher. This is my classroom and I will not stand for what you're doing in here. Is that clear?") will almost certainly end badly for everyone involved.

A "low and slow" approach will likely be more successful than coercion when de-escalating student aggression (Peterson & Sheldon, 2006). In such an approach, hold one's body fairly low to the ground (getting down close to eye level if a child is small, seated, or sprawled on the floor) and move with slow, controlled movements rather than sudden, rapid action. The teacher's facial expression should be either a mask of neutrality in these interactions or a reflection of positive concern. Also, speak in a calm, soft manner and keep word amounts to a minimum (see previous section).

Change the Body Before Changing the Mind

> **❝Ain't talking — just walking.❞**
> −BOB DYLAN (FROM THE SONG, *AIN'T TALKIN'*)

A short walk can do wonders to de-escalate students with executive deficits who are in the midst of an emotional meltdown or are rapidly heading in that direction. To borrow an expression from Gerry Molitor, a developmental specialist in the Portland, Maine area with whom I have worked over the years: First change the body, then change the mind. Getting agitated students to move their bodies in a more relaxed (nonaggressive) manner can dramatically reduce the levels of negative emotions that they are experiencing and expressing. By simply taking a student who is teetering on the break of an amygdala explosion on a walk down the hallway or around the school building, a teacher can often change the physiological and emotional dynamic carrying sway in his body—that is, away from intense frustration and anger toward a state that is more neutral and controlled.

Will a walk always produce a predictable de-escalation result? Of course not. Sometimes, the student one is attempting to escort on a calming walk starts off in such a state of agitation that he ends up bolting 50 yards ahead (and sometimes right out of the school) before the startled adult even realizes what has happened. Still, this approach tends to be a successful soothing technique more often than not, probably because it simultaneously moves the student away from the source(s) of frustration while giving his body a chance to move in a way that lets go of tension. The "therapeutic walk" approach, as I sometimes call it, also creates a diversion that allows the student to focus on something other than reasons for the outburst until he has calmed sufficiently to engage in a problem-solving conversation.

Building Social and Emotional Skills

> ❝Your explanation guides your intervention.❞
> —ROSS GREENE (1998)

There is much we can do, as the range of preventive strategies discussed earlier attest, to establish school environments that are less likely to trigger the types of social gaffes and emotional outbursts that can cause grief for students with executive weaknesses and those who interact with them. Effective school-based intervention plans for individuals with executive function challenges, however, need not be limited to improving the goodness of fit between executive skill profiles and the contexts in which they must function (although such efforts to improve the match between students and settings are certainly a strong first step). The other side of the intervention equation should focus squarely on methods of building the social self-regulatory skills of students with executive deficits. While certainly not a quick or even guaranteed fix, the techniques described in the following sections can lead children with even marked weakness across executive function domains of response inhibition, emotional control, working memory, and flexibility toward more adaptive interactions with others.

Collaborative Problem-Solving

Introduced by Ross Greene in *The Explosive Child* (1998) and expanded on in his second book (Greene & Ablon, 2006), the collaborative problem-solving approach is one of the most impressive therapeutic methods for building the self-control and social problem-solving skills of individuals with executive function weaknesses. Based on Greene's theory of the transactional nature of students' cognitive skill deficits and the environments to which they are either well or poorly matched, the collaborative problem-solving model attempts to improve the family interaction and school behavior of students with marked executive deficits by helping students and their caregivers to address conflicts in a problem-solving manner.

The collaborative problem-solving method trains parents (and to some extent, teachers) to abandon autocratic/coercive methods of managing their "easily explosive" youngsters in favor of an approach structured around a spirit of compromise and shared responsibility for arriving at mutually acceptable solutions. Children are trained over the course of the collaborative problem-solving sessions to perceive their parents and teachers not as overly controlling/rigid "jerks" out to ruin their lives, but instead as rational individuals who both understand and want to help them. The process, by modeling lots of proactive and shared problem-solving behaviors, also gives students practice in flexible, proactive thinking and emotional self-control (Greene & Ablon, 2006). Given my positive experience with the collaborative problem-solving philosophy across clinical and educational settings over the years, I can confidently state that those school-based clinicians and family therapists who become trained in Greene and Ablon's methods are unlikely to regret doing so.

Role Playing

Although structured and less formal role playing of social situations is generally unable to create the level of emotional intensity found in actual encounters, it allows students to practice reasoned responses to at least a percentage of the types of real-life social contexts that tend to give them difficulty. Like many school-based clinicians charged with teaching social problem solving to groups of students who would just as soon be doing anything else at the time, I have found dramatic role-play techniques to be a reliable way of bumping up a student's engagement in the training process.

A broad range of commercially published social-skill training programs that emphasize role playing are available. However, many of these (including the still widely used *Skill Streaming* series; McGinnis & Goldstein, 1993) tend to be experienced by students as overly mannered and stilted. As one middle school student once told me, "If you act that stiff and nicey-nice in this school, kids will think you're totally lame and destroy you."

To make social-skill discussions and related role playing meaningful for students, structure both the topics and dialogue around issues of importance to them. Thus, rather than having students with major impulse control problems talk about and practice what social skills curricula refer to as "right of entry" skills, it is more effective to talk first about how hard it can be to join a game or conversation already in progress and then have students recall situations from their own lives (or people they know) in which joining others was hard or scary.

Once a few of these situations have been put up on the board, a clinician now has highly relevant situations to role-play with an individual student or group. To keep the adaptive social techniques practiced via role playing relatively accessible to students' minds when they are away from training sessions, keep cycling through a small number of social skill topics over the course of the school year, putting a new spin on each topic each time its turn comes up again in the rotation.

Social Stories

Developed by Carol Gray in the early 1990s as a method of broadening the social understanding and skills of students with autism spectrum disorders, the Social Stories technique is now increasingly used to benefit the social function of students with a variety of neurodevelopmental struggles, including those with communication disorders and a variety of psychopathological labels. The stories, which can be written about things students do well (to affirm prosocial behavior) and social elements they need help understanding, typically describe a social situation and the relevant skills and cues associated with it (Gray, 2000). The goal of the approach, when used as an intervention, is to help students comprehend social situations they find confusing or to which they respond in problematic ways.

The stories are written in an upbeat, reassuring manner that refrains from criticizing the target child. They spell out in concrete terms such things as the basis for social norms (e.g., why I wash my hands after using the bathroom), people's behavior (e.g., why people cover their ears when other people talk too loudly), and effective ways of managing situations (e.g., good things

I can say when I need time alone). The stories can also be used effectively as a one-time intervention (e.g., for a student with Asperger syndrome who needs help understanding why other children find his nose-picking habit rather distasteful), or can be written as a series for students who needed more of a stepwise approach to understanding a social topic.

The Gray Center web site (http://www.thegraycenter.org) is a terrific resource for those interested in learning more about this powerful approach to building social awareness and competency. By embedding fairly complex social concepts into easily comprehended (concrete, personalized) stories, the Social Stories technique can play a powerful role in diminishing the social challenges confronting students with substantial self-regulatory weaknesses.

Comic Strip Conversations

Also developed by Carol Gray for use with students with autism spectrum disorders and now used with a range of developmental needs, the Comic Strip Conversation approach uses stick figures and other simple drawings to convey the elements of conversations between two or more people (Gray, 1994). Unlike Social Stories, which are largely verbal in nature, Comic Strip Conversations present social interactions in both visual and verbal form, allowing students to see, to the extent possible with simple drawings, the thoughts and bodies of interacting participants,as well as their verbal statements. This visual element increases the concrete nature of the social instruction (and, it would seem, its potential utility with students with executive function weaknesses) because it does not require students to develop and hold in working memory their own mental images associated with the social topic at hand. An example of a simple Comic Strip Conversation is provided in Figure 10.2. Note the "thought bubbles" representing what the characters think as well as the statement bubbles indicating what they say. The inclusion of these different elements provides students with a concrete indication of how their own behavior likely has an impact on the thoughts of others, and therefore builds social awareness as well as social skills.

Figure 10.2. Example of a Comic Strip Conversation.

Superflex: A Superhero Social Thinking Curriculum

Written by Stephanie Madrigal and Michelle Garcia Winner (2008), the *Super-flex* curriculum was developed to provide clinicians and special educators with a fun and motivating way to teach social skills to younger students with Asperger syndrome and other higher-functioning autism spectrum disorders. Structured around a child-friendly comic book and its lead character (Super-flex), the curriculum and accompanying materials are designed to help children recognize the importance of social skills and the ways different maladaptive social thinking patterns (e.g., rigidity, excessive competitiveness, bossiness, irritability, inordinate anxiety) can cause difficulty in people's lives.

The comic book that accompanies the curriculum (*Superflex Takes on Rock Brain and the Team of Unthinkables*) introduces the lead character and presents the array of common social cognitive challenges faced by many children as nefarious cartoon characters (e.g., *Rock Brain, Mean Jean, Worry Wall, One-Sided Sid*) who create challenges for the stalwart *Superflex*. Although explicitly developed to target the social challenges of students with Asperger syndrome and higher-functioning autism spectrum disorders, the program seems well suited to any elementary-age child whose social challenges stem in part from executive self-regulatory weaknesses.

Social Mentoring

Another technique that flows from the core principle of surrogate frontal lobe, social mentoring provides students with significant executive deficits with an adult or more socially skilled peer for specific periods of the school day to serve as a social adviser or coach. This intervention can take many forms, depending upon the intensity of the child in question, but is almost always centered on the goal of improving the skills with which students interact with their peer groups in less structured settings such as hallways, cafeterias, and playgrounds.

For students with autism spectrum disorders with pronounced social learning problems, the social mentor is generally a trained adult who remains close to the target student and takes a fairly direct role in involving him or her in others' conversations and activities. The mentor in these situations might also cue the student to use particular statements (social scripts) learned in social-skill training sessions and to maintain appropriate space between his body and those of others. For students whose self-regulatory and social needs are somewhat less involved, the mentor may act as more of an observer, watching the target student's social interactions from a distance and only intervening when needed or offering feedback in a more private moment (to lessen the stigma associated with the process). It is also common—and often highly beneficial—for the social mentor to meet briefly with the target student just before he or she enters a less structured setting to offer quick reminders of the social and problem-solving strategies that have been worked on in counseling sessions:

Mentor (a school social worker, pulling 10 year-old Adam aside just before he enters the cafeteria):   Okay, buddy, before you go in, let's just quickly touch base on what you're going to work on in the cafeteria and at recess today.

Adam (rolling his eyes and sighing heavily):   I know, I know. I'm really going to try to eat neatly today, not talk with my mouth open and grossing the other kids out with my food and stuff, and at recess I'm going to stay really cool during four-square.

Mentor: And what have we talked about "cool" meaning for you?

Adam: Cool means not changing the rules and just accepting it when I get out and not getting all mad at the other kids. I know! Can I just go in and eat now? I'm really hungry.

Mentor: Yes, go and enjoy, and don't forget that I'll be watching for a while today while you're eating and playing. Oh, and I'm really proud of how well you've been doing. No office referrals in 2 weeks. You rock!

Putting It All Together: Effective School-Based Behavior Plans for Children with Executive Function Weaknesses

Behavioral intervention plans, also called *individual behavior plans* and *positive behavior support plans*, have changed quite a bit over the past 25 years, almost entirely for the good. In the mid-1980s, school-based behavior plans were often rather simple affairs that placed all responsibility for behavior change on the student. Composed of little more than a lists of problem behaviors to be punished and replacement behaviors to be reinforced, these plans had a fairly wretched success rate (generally falling apart in about 2 weeks) because they operated from the naïve assumption that most students with behavioral difficulties would stop "choosing" to misbehave if sufficiently motivated to do so (Greene, 1998).

The growth in popularity of functional behavioral analysis in the 1990s resulted in school districts around the country becoming increasingly focused on the environmental determinants of problematic behavior. With widespread adoption of functional behavioral analysis principles came an important paradigm shift away from behavioral procedures that relied exclusively on incentivized social changes (i.e., "Do this good thing and get this good thing; do this bad thing and reap the whirlwind") and toward plans that tried to change problematic behavior by systematically determining and then altering its situational antecedents and maintainers.

At about the same time that functional behavioral analysis principles and perspectives were beginning to take hold in many sectors of the educational community, *The Explosive Child: A New Approach for Understanding and Parenting Easily Frustrated, Chronically Inflexible Children* (Greene, 1998) was published and quickly achieved significant popularity. Appreciating the logic of the transactional ("goodness-of-fit") perspective it advocated, many school-based behavioral consultants began focusing functional behavioral analysis efforts not just on the apparent environmental contributors of social-behavioral difficulties, but also on the relationship between situational variables and what was known—or at least suspected—about a student's social-cognitive deficits. This more recent paradigm shift, embedded within a larger functional behavioral analysis perspective, has contributed to the development of individual behavior plans far better tailored to a student's cognitive and situational needs than the incentive plans of the past.

Appendix 10.1a provides a positive behavior support plan template that operates from a transactional perspective. (A completed version is also provided.) Shaped by the lessons learned from more than two decades of developing, monitoring, and implementing school-based behavioral interventions, Appendix 10.1a is structured around the following components:

- Description of challenging behaviors

- Functional behavioral assessment summary

- Summary of student's neurodevelopmental profile

- Transactional hypotheses

- Action plan

- Positive reinforcement strategies

- Consequence and safety plan

- Links to family and community resources

This behavior plan development model is meant to be used by school-based team of professionals familiar with profiles of specific students whose behavioral needs have become significantly problematic. A far shorter template has been included in Appendix 10.2a for use by classroom teachers to address less intense social-behavioral challenges. A completed example of this template is also provided in Appendix 10.2b.

☞ CASE EXAMPLE: A SECOND LOOK AT "MEAN MAX"

To bring this chapter full circle, we will return to the case that started it out. "Mean Max," as you recall, was so dubbed by his classmates because of the frequency and intensity of his oppositional, noncompliant, and aggressive behavior. Even his teacher, a seasoned professional who would never tolerate name-calling in her classroom, sheepishly admitted to sometimes referring to Max (a pseudonym) by this unfortunate moniker in the privacy of her own thoughts.

Before applying the positive behavior support plan template in Appendix 10.1a to this case, I will provide summaries of Max's background and neurocognitive profile to enable a more detailed understanding of this child. As with the case study presented in Chapter 4, all potentially identifying information has been changed to protect the privacy of both the student and his family. Some case elements have also been omitted or altered to ensure confidentiality.

Background Information

Max was removed from the care of his biological mother (a chronic substance abuser) during infancy because of substantiated allegations of neglect and placed with a foster family. His biological father was in prison at the time due to a series of assault and theft convictions. Although Max began displaying fairly significant oppositional and aggressive behavior in the foster home as a toddler, he developed a strong bond with the foster mother and was adopted by her at the age of 4 years. He continued to exhibit verbal and physical aggression as a preschooler, resulting in him being removed from two different child care settings before starting kindergarten. Max's adoptive mother also described him at this time as a highly anxious child who frequently clung to her and expressed fear that he would be taken away from his new family.

Max's social-behavioral difficulties continued into his early elementary years, with numerous arguments with school staff and fights with peers reported in school discipline files. He also struggled to a marked extent with literacy skill acquisition, leading to the eventual identification of a learning disability. In his third-grade year, Max's oppositional-defiant presentation in the classroom and frequent verbal and physical aggression toward peers across school settings led to my initial evaluation and follow-up consultation. Teacher and school discipline reports reflected the high frequency of his noncompliant/aggressive outbursts in the classroom and more episodic fights with peers in less structured settings. The classroom teacher complained particularly about Max's tendency to angrily interrupt her when she was presenting assignment instructions (e.g., "This is stupid! Why do we have to do this?!?") and to pick on other students during class discussions. Max's social presentation at recess was characterized by staff reports and discipline logs as highly impulsive and aggressive, with numerous "nasty comments" and more occasional acts of physical aggression being directed at students who frustrated him during competitive games.

Summary of Evaluation Findings

Max's performance on tests of cognitive functioning suggested that although his verbal and nonverbal reasoning skills were generally average to above average, his attention, working memory, processing speed, phonological processing skills, and speeded naming skills were all below to well-below average. Tests of academic skill reflected solidly average math skills, but significant delays were indicated across all domains of reading and written language functioning. Classroom and resource (special education) observations confirmed the frequency of Max's off-task behaviors, as well as his tendency to argue with staff and refuse to comply with directions. He also impressed as anxious during academic activities, particularly literacy tasks, and even reported feeling "nervous" in class when questioned during the student interview.

Although several of Max's student interview comments reflected the tendency to minimize his social-behavioral difficulties and blame others for his aggressive outbursts, he did admit to longstanding "temper problems." Parent and teacher responses to standardized behavior rating scales were indicative of the perception of Max as a highly impulsive, often aggressive child prone to attention and working memory struggles across academic contexts. Elevated levels of academic and social anxiety were also reported, as were a range of apparent peer interaction struggles associated with self-regulation deficits. Max's positive behavior support plan is provided in Appendix 10.1b.

Positive Behavior Support Plan

Student's name: _____ DOB: _____

School: _____ Age: _____

Teacher/house: _____ Grade: _____

1. Describe, in order of priority, the three most challenging behaviors exhibited by the student that have led to the development of this plan.

Behavior	Example	Approximate frequency	Severity and priority
1.			
2.			
3.			

2. Summary of functional behavioral assessment

Behavior	Observed or suspected situational triggers	Observed or suspected or situational maintainers
1.		
2.		
3.		

3. Summarize what is known or suspected about this student's neurodevelopmental profile.

Areas of strength across domains of language functioning, perceptual-motor (nonverbal) functioning, executive functioning, and processing speed
Areas of weakness across domains of language functioning, perceptual-motor (nonverbal) functioning, executive functioning, and processing speed
Does the team suspect that a cognitive or sensory processing weakness is contributing to the target behaviors? _____ Yes _____ No Please explain:

4. *Transactional hypotheses.* Summarize the team's impressions of the cognitive and environmental/situational contributors to the target behaviors and then state hypotheses about the function of each target behavior.

Target behavior	Setting/situational contributors	Cognitive/personal + contributors =	Hypothesized function of behavior
1.			
2.			
3.			

(continued)

ACTION PLAN

5. *Prevention strategies.* What modifications are needed to improve the goodness of fit between this student's social/behavioral needs and school settings in which he or she must function?

Environmental modifications	Staff member(s) responsible	Start date

Instructional modifications	Staff member(s) responsible	Start date

Scheduling modifications	Staff member(s) responsible	Start date

6. Describe the skills/alternative behaviors to be taught to the student and the methods of instruction.

Skills and replacement behaviors to be taught	Method(s) by which skill/ behavior will be taught	Staff responsible	Starting date

7. Specify the methods by the student's exhibition of the target and alternative behaviors will be monitored (i.e., daily tracking sheet or weekly progress sheet). Attach a copy the data collection forms to be used to this plan.

8. Described the individualized reinforcement procedures, if any, to be used in association with this plan.

9. Describe the individualized consequence or crisis (safety) procedures, if any, to be used in association with this plan.

(continued)

10. Describe the methods by which family and any community resources (i.e., outside therapists, case managers, and physicians) will take part in this plan. How will information associated with the plan's effectiveness be shared with the family?

11. List the names and roles of those who participated in the development of this plan.

Name	Role/relationship to student

Example of a Positive Behavior Support Plan

Student's name: Max R****

DOB: ******

School:

Age: 9

Teacher/house:

Grade: 3

1. Describe, in order of priority, the three most challenging behaviors exhibited by the student that have led to the development of this plan.

Behavior	Example	Approximate frequency	Severity
1. Interrupting and arguing with the teacher during instructional periods	"That's stupid!" "Yeah, right—like I'm gonna do that." "No—I'm not doing it!"	Several times daily, as per teacher observations and notations on daily behavior tracking sheets	Severe. Disrupts instruction and class discussions on a daily basis. Contributes to Max's very limited productivity.
2. "Putting down" other students during class discussions	"Ugh, how stupid are you?" "You suck—I was gonna say that!"	Two to five times daily, as per teacher observations and notations on daily behavior tracking sheets	Severe. Affecting other students and leading to significant disruption of instruction.
3. Marked verbal aggression toward peers during games at recess (with occasional shoving)	You guys all suck! F . . . you! I'm doing it anyway I want!	One to three times per day, as per cafeteria/playground behavioral monitor logs and office referral sheets	Moderately severe to severe (5–10 on a scale of 1–10). Leads to numerous time away and office referrals.

2. Summary of functional behavioral assessment

Behavior	Observed or suspected situational triggers	Observed or suspected or situational maintainers
1. Arguing with and interrupting the teacher.	Presentation of tasks requiring substantial written language or cooperative learning component	Sent out of the classroom, either to the office for disciplinary action or resource center for 'cool down' and individual support.
2. Putting down classmates	Whole class discussion and small group work. Often sighs or rolls his eyes before making an aggressive comment	Some students laugh, but most just yell at Max or complain to the teacher. Teacher responds with either a verbal redirection or consequence (Max sent out of room).

(continued)

3. Summarize what is known or suspected about this student's neurodevelopmental profile

Areas of strength across domains of language functioning, perceptual-motor (nonverbal) functioning, executive functioning, and processing speed

Two assessments of Max's cognitive skills have indicated he functions within the above average range across verbal and nonverbal domains. Teacher's have characterized Max as creative and possessing comparatively strong critical thinking skills.

Areas of weakness across domains of language functioning, perceptual-motor (nonverbal) functioning, executive functioning, and processing speed

While Max's oral expressive and receptive language skills are solidly average, his acquisition of literacy skill has been substantially impacted by deficits in the areas of phonological processing, rapid automatic naming, and visual processing speed. A neuropsychological assessment has also identified Max with the Combined Type of ADHD, and emphasized the severity of his impulse control, frustration tolerance, and working memory difficulties. Max also carries diagnoses of reading disorder, generalized anxiety disorder and oppositional defiant disorder.Max's self-reports stress the severity of his distractibility and sensitivity to the 'annoying things' others say in his proximity.

Does the team suspect that a cognitive or sensory processing weakness is contributing to the target behaviors?

___*X*___ Yes _____ No

Please explain: The team concludes that Max's deficits in the executive domains of impulse control and frustration tolerance/control contribute significantly to his frequent displays of verbal aggression across school settings. It is also suspected that Max's slow processing speed contributes to his frustration in classroom discussions by making it difficult for him to answer questions as quickly as many peers.

4. *Transactional hypotheses.* Summarize the team's impressions of the cognitive and environmental/situational contributors to the target behaviors and then state hypotheses about the function of each target behavior.

Target behavior	Setting/situational contributors	Cognitive/personal contributors	Hypothesized function of behavior
1. Interrupting and arguing with the teacher	Presentation of academic tasks Max finds threatening (those placing a premium on literacy or social functioning)	Weakness in the areas of literacy functioning, impulse control, frustration management, and processing speed	Max resists and argues about academic tasks (primarily written language tasks) he finds threatening to avoid/escape from these activities.
2. Putting down classmates (verbal aggression in class)	Others answering questions before he is able to or making comments in class he finds annoying or frustrating.	Low academic self-image combined with slow processing speed, poor impulse control and frustration tolerance.	Max gives impulsive expression to the frustration and irritation he feels in class when others answer before (or better than) he does.
3. Verbal aggression during games and conversations in less structured settings.	Competitive game situations with peers (particularly those without direct adult supervision)	Very limited impulse and frustration control	Unable to tolerate the usual frustrations/ irritations associated with competitive games, Max explodes verbally at peers when things don't go his way to gain control of games.

ACTION PLAN

5. *Prevention strategies.* **What modifications are needed to improve the goodness of fit between this student's social/behavioral needs and school settings in which he or she must function?**

Environmental modifications	Staff member(s) responsible	Start date
For the next 6 weeks Max will be required to only participate in those competitive recess games (i.e., four-square and kickball) that are run and directly supervised by school staff.	School administration, classroom teacher, and recess staff	10/15/2008
Max's desk in the classroom will be moved to a grouping that is adjacent to the teacher's desk.	Classroom teacher	10/15/2008

Instructional modifications	Staff member(s) responsible	Start date
Max will be provided with individualized explanations of written language assignments before they are discussed in class so that he understands the manner in which they have been adapted to suit his skill level.	Classroom teacher and resource teacher	10/15/2008
Max will be provided with one or more questions to answer before classroom discussions begin.	Classroom teacher	10/15/2008
Max will be called on directly to answer at least one or two questions in class discussions and will be given adequate "wait time" before other students are given the opportunity to answer.	Classroom teacher	10/15/2008

Scheduling modifications	Staff member(s) responsible	Start date
Max's twice-weekly sessions with the school social worker will be scheduled to occur just before his lunch/recess period.	School social worker	10/18/2008

6. Describe the skills/alternative behaviors to be taught to the student and the methods of instruction.

Skills and replacement behaviors to be taught	Method(s) by which skill/ behavior will be taught	Staff responsible	Starting date
Academic coping skill (defined in this case as specific ways of coping with assignment-related anxiety and frustration in classroom settings)	Role-play practice in sessions with school social worker, with generalization cuing by the classroom teacher	School social worker, in collaboration with teaching staff	10/18/2008
Social "reading" and empathy skills (focused on how aggressive comments make others feel and how these comments contribute to Max's social isolation)	Relevant portions of the Second Step Program, supplemented by clinician-developed role-plays and Social Stories	School social worker, in collaboration with teaching staff	11/7/2008
Social problem-solving skill, with particular emphasis given to the building of impulse control and frustration management skill	Relevant portions of the Second Step Program, supplemented by clinician-developed role-plays and Social Stories	School social worker, in collaboration with teaching staff	11/20/2008

(continued)

7. Specify the methods by which the student's exhibition of the target and alternative behaviors will be monitored (i.e., daily tracking sheet or weekly progress sheet).

Max's exhibition of Target Behavior 1 (arguing with and interrupting the teacher) and Target Behavior 2 (verbal aggression toward peers in class) will be monitored by the classroom teacher, using a daily "self-control progress" tracking sheet. The teacher will review the contents of the sheet each afternoon with Max before he leaves for the day and a copy will be sent home for his mother's review and signature (to be brought back to school the next day). Max's behavior on the playground will be monitored on a daily basis by school staff running recess games and the school social worker, who will convey an overall rating of his social presentation (using a 10-point scale) to the classroom teacher to include in the daily "self-control" tracking sheet. The recess staff and school social worker will also continue to maintain functional behavioral assessment data regarding all aggressive outbursts Max exhibits, placing emphasis on the situational contributors (antecedents and consequences) to the outbursts.

8. Described the individualized reinforcement procedures, if any, to be used in association with this plan.

All school staff who work regularly with Max (classroom teacher, resource teacher, and recess staff) will be kept abreast by the school social worker of the specific social problem-solving skills Max is working on in counseling sessions so that they can specifically praise his attempts to use these skills in real-life school settings. Max's prosocial behavior will also be reinforced via a positive reinforcement system that provides tokens for each class and recess period in which he refrains from aggressive behavior (defined as requiring no more than one verbal reminder/redirection from staff). For every 10 tokens earned, Max can select one of the reinforcers on his reinforcement menu (e.g., shooting baskets with the school social worker, eating lunch with the teacher of his choice). Max will only earn tokens for those class and recess periods in which he has refrained from aggressive behavior. Although his exhibitions of aggression will not result in the forfeit of tokens already earned, he will be unable to select a reinforcer on any day in which he has committed an act of significant aggression (defined for the purposes of this plan as aggressive behavior that requires an office referral).

9. Describe the individualized consequence or crisis (safety) procedures, if any, to be used in association with this plan.

The first level of response to disruptive defiance of classroom staff or verbal aggression toward peers in the classroom will be a reminder of the relevant classroom rule that must be followed. If the behavior continues (or reoccurs within a few minutes), a second verbal reminder will be issued and the teacher will also cue Max to use a specific coping strategy (e.g., put aside the work that is frustrating him until help is available or moving away from a student with whom he is arguing). If the behavior continues and is significantly disruptive to either the instructional process or the learning of others, the teacher will escort Max to a more private area (i.e., hallway) and make a determination as to whether he is in an appropriate emotional state to engage in a problem-solving discussion. If so, a discussion that centers on understanding and ameliorating the sources of his anxiety and/or frustration will ensue. In those cases in which it is apparent to classroom staff that Max's emotional state is such that the initiation of a problem-solving discussion would only worsen matters, the school social worker or resource teacher will be summoned to escort him to a designated calming space in the school. One of these individuals will also be summoned if Max refuses to leave the classroom with the teacher or becomes significantly belligerent toward the teacher in the problem-solving discussion. On those occasions in which Max refuses to discontinue aggressive/disruptive behavior in the classroom and also refuses to leave the room with either teaching or clinical staff members, an office referral will be made. If necessary at this point, the classroom teacher will remove all other students in the room to the library or other appropriate space so that instructional process can continue and the "audience" for Max's disruptive behavior is eliminated. Once the office referral level of intervention has been reached, school administration will make a determination (with input from clinical and teaching staff) as to if/when Max will be allowed to return to regular instructional settings on the day of the referral.

The sequence of responses to aggression on the playground during recess will be essentially similar to the response cascade discussed above for classroom aggression. Max will receive a reminder of relevant playground rules for initial verbal expressions of aggression as well as explicit cues from staff about the coping strategy he should employ (i.e., stepping out of the game for a few minutes to cool off and prevent heightened levels of frustration). If Max's aggression continues (i.e., continues to yell at other students or does not comply with game rules) and he refuses to engage in cued coping strategies, he will be escorted away from the game by school staff for a set period of time (5 minutes in most cases). If his emotional frame of mind is such upon leaving the game that he can engage in a problem-solving discussion, such a discussion will take place. The staff member will simply walk with Max around the perimeter of the playground for several minutes to assist his calming down if it is apparent that he is unlikely to benefit from a conversational intervention. If Max refuses to leave the game when directed to do so by recess staff or becomes significantly disruptive on the playground (will not respond to staff directions), the assistance of the school social worker or resource teacher will be obtained. Should Max refuse to accompany this individual to a designated calming space in the school, an office referral will be made and school administration (with the input of clinical, instructional, and recess staff) will make determinations regarding when Max can next access supervised recess activities.

10. Describe the methods by which family and any community resources (e.g., outside therapists, case managers, physicians) will take part in this plan. How will information associated with the plan's effectiveness be shared with the family?

As noted above, the classroom teacher will send a copy of the daily self-control sheet home with Max every afternoon for his mother's review and signature. A copy will also be sent to Ms. R**** as an e-mail attachment. Ms. R**** has also duly authorized the school social worker and resource teacher to contact Max's community-based psychotherapist and psychiatrist on a twice-monthly basis to discuss his functioning in school settings.

11. List the names and roles of those who participated in the development of this plan.

Name	Role/relationship to student

Classroom-Based Behavior Plan Template

Student's name: _____   Date: _____

Primary problem behaviors (*Behaviors I would like to reduce or eliminate*)

1. _____

2. _____

Replacement behaviors (*More adaptive alternatives to the problem behaviors*)

1. _____

2. _____

My hypotheses regarding the <u>function</u> of the problem behaviors (*The likely drivers and purposes of the behavior*)

1. _____

_____

2. _____

_____

Accommodations (*Things I can modify or adapt in the classroom to lessen the child's need to exhibit the target behaviors*)

1. _____

2. _____

3. _____

Teaching elements (*How I will attempt to teach this student — to build his or her skills — associated with the problem behaviors*)

_____

_____

_____

_____

_____

Motivational elements (*Ways in which I will attempt to motivate the student to avoid the problem behaviors and replace them with the more adaptive alternatives noted above*)

_____

_____

_____

_____

_____

Example of a Classroom-Based Behavior Plan Template

Student's name: Michael W.   Grade: 4   Date: January 15, 2009

Primary problem behaviors (*Behaviors I would like to reduce or eliminate*)

1. Michael frequently refuses to do class work, particularly if it involves writing, unless I sit right next to him and help him do it. If I move on to someone else, he shuts down or disrupts others.

2. Michael often act in a highly bossy/controlling manner with other kids during cooperative learning activities or will make negative comments about their ideas/suggestions (e.g., "That's stupid!")

Replacement behaviors (*More adaptive alternatives to the problem behaviors*)

1. Michael will engage in writing tasks with higher levels of independence.

2. Michael will exhibit greater willingness to consider others' ideas during shared work activities, and will manage conflicts by appropriately suggesting compromises or seeking adult assistance.

My hypotheses regarding the <u>function</u> of the target behaviors (*The likely drivers and purposes of the behavior*)

1. Michael finds writing tasks to be highly threatening—he has good ideas but can't organize his thoughts and muster the patience and frustration tolerance needed to get them on paper independently.

2. Michael is a bright, but also rather rigid and controlling youngster. He tends to see only one way to do things and struggles with considering alternatives to the "right" idea he has in mind.

Accommodations (*Things I can modify or adapt in the classroom to lessen the child's need to exhibit the target behaviors*)

1. Provide Michael with high levels of prewriting support and then encourage him to attempt to follow the plan we develop on his own, with me checking in frequently but not sitting next to him.

2. Provide Michael with examples of the type of written finished product I'm looking for.

3. "Front load" Michael before cooperative learning activities regarding the types of compromises he needs to make with peers, and group him with students with whom he is likely to reach such compromises.

Teaching elements (*How I will attempt to teach this student—to build his or her skills—associated with the problem behaviors*)

1. I will provide Michael with extra instruction and support with the prewriting elements of writing over the next few weeks (showing him how to make and follow writing plans).

2. I will conduct individual coaching sessions with Michael after school with his parents' support around the types of compromises and shared leadership I expect in groups. I will explicitly model for Michael the development of compromises and have him role play these strategies with me.

(continued)

Motivational elements (*Ways in which I will attempt to motivate the student to avoid the problem behaviors and replace them with the more adaptive alternatives noted previously*)

Reinforcement procedures

1. I will specifically and frequently praise Michael whenever I see him making attempts to write on his own.

2. I will maintain an "I'm doing it by myself" chart with Michael that awards him a sticker or points whenever he has made a good faith effort to write in his journal on his own or complete any other writing assignment on his own after some initial prewriting support from me. He will earn extra recess time for the class or some other classwide privilege every time he amasses seven stickers/points.

3. I will pull Michael aside (quickly) and specifically praise him whenever I see him engaging in the types of collaborative, compromise-based social problem-solving strategies we have discussed.

Consequences

1. Beginning next Monday, Michael will need to complete as homework all writing assignments he has refused to work on in school. His parents have supported the idea and will prevent his access to desired activities (e.g., TV and video games) until he completes the written work.

2. Michael will be provided with a reminder/warning if his behavior in shared activity groups becomes overly controlling or aggressive. I will also cue him with the reminder to use the compromise strategies we've discussed. Any subsequent use of aggressive speech in the same period will result in his being removed from the group for the remainder of the period, 10 minutes off his recess on that day or the next, and a note being sent home to his parents.

Study Guide

Questions and Suggested Discussion Points

Chapter 1

1. Review "Executive Function in a Nutshell" and then discuss the executive requirements of one or two challenging tasks you may have recently confronted in your personal or professional life (i.e., changing a tire, making a soufflé, preparing a curriculum test, developing a presentation for a faculty meeting).

2. Very few individuals go through life exhibiting strength across all domains of executive function (EF). Review the series of metacognitive and self-regulatory executive skills discussed in Chapter 1, and consider your own areas of relative strength and weakness. Discuss a few ways in which your own EF profile has been a source of help and hindrance in your professional life.

3. Chapter 1 presents working memory as the vessel ("stew pot," "desk top") in which conscious cognition occurs and emphasizes that the larger a student's working memory capacity, the more he or she is able to think about at one time in the service of comprehension, problem solving, and production. Select one of your favorite curriculum activities and discuss the relative working memory demands it places on students. How might the activity be altered to lessen its working memory load?

Chapter 2

1. Chapter 2 discusses the development of executive skill across childhood and adolescence. Consider and discuss the developmental norms for various executive skills (e.g., goal-directed attention, planning skill, adaptability, impulse control, self-monitoring) as you have observed them for the grade level you teach. What behaviors have you observed in students at this developmental level that reveal these skill levels. How might these skill levels differ from those of students a grade or two younger and a grade or two older?

2. Consider your instructional style, curriculum, and assignment structure. In what ways might the instruction in your classroom cause stress for

students whose executive capacity across one or more of the core skill areas is significantly delayed?

3. Chapter 2 presents the relative influence of genetics and social/environmental factors on the development of EF. Discuss the extent to which you believe students' executive profiles are a product of nature versus nurture. To what extent can teachers and other school staff members improve the EF profiles students bring into class at the start of the year?

Chapter 3

1. Chapter 3 notes a range of leadership metaphors (orchestra conductor, military general, corporate CEO) in discussing the functional relationship between the prefrontal cortex and posterior cortical structures. Are there educational leadership metaphors that might also accurately reflect this relationship?

2. Among the most important functional distinctions noted in Chapter 3 relates to the neural architecture of the frontal lobe and the other three posterior lobes (parietal, temporal, and occipital). The frontal lobe is wired, essentially, to be a center of self-direction and output, whereas the three posterior lobes are structured to serve more of an input/storage function. List and discuss several ways in which challenges with prefrontal cortical functioning might have an impact on a student's *learning* (not just production) in the classroom. Is it reasonable to consider students "learning disabled" if their profiles of executive weakness substantially affect their learning and production in academic settings?

3. What are the developmental norms for the grade level(s) you teach with regard to the "balance of power" between the amygdala (and related origin points of intense emotions) and the social/emotional regulating structures such as the prefrontal cortex and anterior cingulate cortex. Discuss the common red-flag behaviors students might show as they progress toward an "amygdala hijack" as well the behaviors (verbal and nonverbal) that reflect attempts to rein in the hijack before it reaches full expression.

4. The amygdala is an important site of emotional learning and memory. How might a student learn to experience significant anxiety related to particular academic settings/activities, and what are the implications of such conditioned academic fear for instruction?

Chapter 4

1. Discuss the concept of ecological validity as it relates to the findings of neuropsychological tests of executive skill. Were you surprised to learn that the results of these tests can be fully valid in the testing context but may generalize poorly to real-life learning settings?

2. Select a student from your current or past caseload with significant EF weaknesses, complete the teacher version of the Executive Functioning

Semistructured Interview (see Appendix 4.3), and review the material in Table 4.2 to help clarify the nature of his or her executive skill profile. Based on this review, what executive skills represent areas of relative strength and weakness for this student? What are the implications of this profile for what might be done to improve the student's learning and/or social functioning?

3. Reread the case study ("Ricky") at the end of Chapter 4, paying particular attention to the data obtained from the student, parent, and school staff interviews. Based on this information, to what extent do you agree with the conclusions offered in the Conclusions section of the case study with regard to Ricky's EF profile? What other information would you have liked to have in this case in helping frame hypotheses regarding the scope and severity of Ricky's learning struggles? What additional instructional strategies and accommodations might merit consideration in this case?

Chapter 5

1. A key point made early in Chapter 5 relates to the setting dependency of students' EF profiles; that is, that specific profiles of EF weakness are likely to be more problematic for the student and teacher in some classroom settings than in others. Consider your own teaching style, curriculum, and classroom structure. What executive skill profiles are likely to fit well and less well with your instructional methods and assignment and management structures? Why?

2. Experience tells us that most students with significant executive weakness, regardless of the specific nature of their EF profiles, tend to require higher levels of "surrogate frontal lobe" support than peers with stronger executive capacity. To what extent do your current teaching methods and classroom structure flex to provide students with the levels of individualized monitoring and direction they require? Discuss some ways in which classroom and special educators might increase their ability to provide better surrogate frontal lobe support for kids in the context of their many professional responsibilities.

3. Which of the core strategies resonate particularly for you and the students with whom you work? How might you alter your current teaching and classroom management practices to better exemplify these strategies?

Chapter 6

1. Discuss the role of executive functions as a leading "nonlingusitic" variable in the development of reading skill. Can you recall students with whom you've worked whose difficulties with word reading, fluency, and/or comprehension appeared significantly affected by executive weaknesses? What elements of the students' reading struggles (behaviors, error patterns) cause you to suspect that EF challenges were substantial contributors to their literacy struggles?

2. The National Reading Panel has endorsed guided oral reading as an important method of building students' oral reading fluency skills. Chapter 6 discusses the importance of this approach with regard to students with executive weakness, given that clinical experience shows that many students with EF challenges tend to avoid reading practice. To what extent does your teaching practice reflect the importance of providing individualized guided oral reading practice for students with fluency deficits? How might you work to increase the amount of guided oral reading practice students receive in your classroom and throughout your school? What might be some of the problems with relying largely on sustained silent reading (SSR) practices in trying to improve the reading fluency of students with executive skill deficiencies?

3. Chapter 6 emphasizes the role of working memory as the cognitive "vessel" in which comprehension is constructed and the importance of other metacognitive executive skills to the self-directed development of meaning from text. Discuss how limited working memory capacity and significant attention, self-monitoring, and/or planning/organizational weakness can contribute to a passive reading style and related difficulties with deeper text processing. Review the adapted version of Barrett's Taxonomy of Comprehension (see Figure 6.1) to assist with this discussion.

4. Discuss the ways in which the before, during, and after reading strategies presented in Chapter 6 can help students with executive weakness become more cognitively active, engaged readers. If you've used any of these strategies, discuss the extent to which you've found them beneficial to students with learning deficits. How might you alter or supplement one or more of these approaches to enhance their impact?

Chapter 7

1. Chapter 7 begins with a brief discussion of the reasons most people, even well-educated people, can find writing to be quite challenging. Consider your own experiences with writing as compared with oral language and reading. What challenges have you faced as a writer during the course of your own development (including your professional development)? To what extent have your own executive skills contributed to your past or present writing difficulties?

2. An essential point made early in Chapter 7 relates to the levels of stress placed on students' working memory and other core executive skills by oral and written language. Discuss the reasons why written language, from a cognitive processing perspective, is much more than a written extension of oral language. What are some of the myriad things on which students must focus (hold in working memory) simultaneously as they endeavor to get their thoughts on paper?

3. Chapter 7 emphasizes the importance of interventions at the prewriting phase of the writing process for students with executive weakness. As many teachers know, however, many students with executive and other learning struggles can find structured prewriting activities tedious and

generally to be avoided. What can general and special educators do to increase students' appreciation of the importance of systematic prewriting tasks? Discuss ways to make prewriting activities a required part of the writing process for all students.

4. Clinical experience has shown that many students with EF deficits resist the revision and proofreading elements of the writing process. Discuss the reasons for this resistance and the ways in which the systematic editing/ proofreading approaches presented in Chapter 7 can help. Can you think of ways to enhance these models to make them more acceptable and useful to students with EF weakness?

5. Dictation, also known as *scribing*, is a commonly provided accommodation for students whose writing challenges relate to a range of learning challenges (including executive weaknesses). Discuss the potential benefits and problems associated with this accommodation as well as ways these problems might be overcome.

Chapter 8

1. Constructivist math curricula, such as *Everyday Math*, have a comparatively strong research base and have been widely adopted by school districts over the last several years. Still, many parents and educators have questioned the suitability of these curricula for students with significant executive weakness and other learning challenges. Discuss your own perspectives on the goodness of fit between these programs and students with EF difficulties. To what extent have your classroom experiences informed these perspectives? Have you had success adapting these instructional approaches to increase their effectiveness for students with executive challenges?

2. Discuss the cognitive processing elements underlying the procedural type of math disability. Consider the math struggles of a few students with significant math challenges with whom you have worked over the years. Knowing what you now do about the impact of executive weakness on math performance, to what degree would you attribute the math difficulties of these students to the procedural/algorithmic subtype of math disability?

3. Consider the impact of math fact fluency on working memory load and algorithm use. Chapter 8 presents a range of strategies to build students fact fluency. Which have you tried, and to what extent have they benefitted the students in your classroom with EF challenges? What other methods have you found helpful in building the fact learning and recall of students with EF weakness? Discuss your own observations regarding the relationship between math fact fluency, algorithm use, and problem solving based on your classroom experiences.

4. Chapter 8 emphasizes the impact of working memory limitations and other executive weaknesses on algorithm recall/usage and the solving of word problems. Select two of the strategies presented in this section and discuss the ways in which you would implement them in your classroom

to help students with executive weakness. How might you alter these strategies for a student with whom you are currently working (or with whom you worked in the past)?

Chapter 9

1. Early emphasis is given in Chapter 9 to Mel Levine's concept, *the myth of laziness*. To what extent have you ascribed to this myth in the past and how did this belief influence your work with students? Has your perspective changed since reading this portion of the book (or Dr. Levine's excellent work, *The Myth of Laziness*)? If your perspective on the productivity challenges of students with EF weakness has been changed, how might your altered view affect your instructional approaches and assignment structure?

2. Among the themes running through the recommendations in Chapter 9 is the idea that executive skills such as materials organization, assignment planning, homework completion, and note taking should be explicitly taught and then supported with lots of guided/supervised practice. Consider your own methods of classroom and assignment organization. To what extent do you explicitly teach (and then re-teach, as needed) the organizational structures associated with your classroom and curriculum? Discuss the extent to which you provide the guided and extended practice with these systems/procedures needed by students with executive weakness.

3. Select a student with significant organization/planning, time management, or note-taking difficulties, and then discuss how you would apply at least two of the relevant strategies discussed in Chapter 9 to improve his or her functioning. If you have already attempted similar approaches with the student, consider how you might modify your approaches based on the strategy discussions in this chapter.

4. Discuss your perspectives on individualized coaching as compared with group study skill (or "academic support") classes for secondary school students with executive weakness. What logistical and other factors in your school might support the use of the coaching model and what factors might make it difficult to implement the model? How might these difficulties be overcome?

Chapter 10

1. Chapter 10 begins with a discussion of "Mean Max" and Descartes' error. Can you recall students with whom you've worked who seemed inherently "mean" or "nasty?" Having read Chapter 10, are you able to identify the types of self-regulatory challenges these students may have exhibited? Discuss the potential benefits and difficulties associated with viewing students' behavioral challenges from a brain-based perspective as opposed to a moral perspective. To what extent does Descartes' error

continue to inform the perspectives and treatment of students with significant social/behavioral needs in your school?

2.   Discuss the relationship between self-regulation and Daniel Goleman's concepts of emotional and social intelligence. What role do specific executive functions (i.e., working memory, impulse control, and adaptability) play in enabling socially intelligent behavior?

3.   To what extent is your classroom structured to prevent (or at least minimize) the social/behavioral challenges of student with significant self-regulatory challenges? Are your rules explicit, taught, and practiced on a relatively regular basis? Does your school provide adult-directed activities during recess and other less structured periods of the day?

4.   Consider the range of strategies discussed in Chapter 10 associated with effective responses to "amygdala hijacks." Which school settings lend themselves to approaches such as "low and slow" and "change the body before changing the mind"? In which settings or scenarios might the use of these methods be made more challenging? How might you modify the strategies to increase their chances of success in these contexts?

5.   Select a student from your current class or with whom you've worked in the past and complete the Classroom-Based Behavior Plan Template (see Appendix 10.2a) with this student in mind. Upon completing the form, discuss the Teaching Elements section, focusing on how challenging it was to complete this section as compared with the others.

References

Andrews, D.G. (2001). *Neuropsychology: From theory to practice.* East Sussex, England: Psychology Press.

Attwood, T. (2007). *The complete guide to Asperger's syndrome.* London: Jessica Kingsley Publishers.

Auman, M. (2002). *Step up to writing* (2nd ed.). Frederick, CO: Sopris West.

Baddeley, A.D. (1986). *Working memory.* New York: Oxford University Press.

Baddeley, A.D. (1996). The concept of working memory. In S.E. Gathercole (Ed.), *Models of short-term memory* (pp. 1–27). East Sussex, England: Lawrence Erlbaum Associates.

Baddeley, A.D. (1997). *Human memory: Theory and practice.* East Sussex, England: Psychology Press.

Barkley, R.A. (1997). *ADHD and the nature of self-control.* New York: Guilford Press.

Barkley, R.A. (2006). *Attention-deficit hyperactivity disorder: A handbook for diagnosis and treatment* (3rd ed.). New York: Guilford Press.

Barkley, R.A., & Edwards, G. (2006). Diagnostic interview, behavior rating scales, and the medical examination. In R.A. Barkley, (Ed.), *Attention-deficit hyperactivity disorder: A handbook for diagnosis and treatment* (3rd ed., pp. 337–368). New York: Guilford Press.

Barkley, R.A., Edwards, G., Laneri, M., Fletcher, K., & Metevia, L. (2001). Executive functioning, temporal discounting, and sense of time in adolescents with ADHD and oppositional defiant disorder. *Journal of Abnormal Child Psychology, 29*(6), 541–556.

Barrett, T.C. (1967). Goals of the reading program: The basis for evaluation. In T.C. Barrett (Ed.), *In the evaluation of reading achievement.* Newark, DE: International Reading Association.

Bashir, A. (2008). *Executive and self-regulatory functions and their relationship to oral and written language production.* Paper presented at the 23rd Annual Learning Differences Conference, Executive Function in the 21st Century Classroom: Innovative Strategies for Student Success. Harvard Graduate School of Education, Cambridge, MA.

Beck, I.L. (2006). *Making sense of phonics: The how's and why's.* New York: Guilford Press.

Beck, I.L., & McKeown, M.G. (2006). *Improving comprehension with questioning the author: A fresh and expanded view of a powerful approach.* New York: Scholastic.

Bedard, A.C., Martinussen, R., Ickowicz, A., & Tannock, R. (2004). Methylphenidate improves visual-spatial memory in children with attention-deficit/hyperactivity disorder. *Journal of the American Academy of Child and Adolescent Psychiatry, 43,* 260–268.

Beers, K. (2003). *When kids can't read, what teachers can do: A guide for teachers 6–12.* Portsmouth, NH: Heinemann.

Bell, N. (2007). *Visualizing and verbalizing for language comprehension and thinking* (2nd ed.). San Luis Obispo, CA: Gander Publishing.

Bereiter, C., & Scardamalia, M. (1987). *The psychology of written composition.* Hillsdale, NJ: Erlbaum Associates.

Berninger, V.W., Abbott, R.D., Billingsley, F., & Nagy, W. (2001). Processes underlying timing and fluency of reading: Efficiency, automaticity, coordination, and morphological awareness. In M. Wolf (Ed.), *Time, fluency, and dyslexia.* Timonium, MD: York Press.

Berninger, V.W., & Richards, T.L. (2002). *Brain literacy for educators and psychologists.* San Diego: Academic Press.

Berninger, V.W., & Winn, W. (2006). Implications of advancements in brain research and technology for writing development, writing instruction, and educational evolution. In C. MacArthur, S. Graham, & J. Fitzgerald (Eds.), *Handbook of Writing Research* (pp. 96–114). New York: Guilford Press.

Bernstein, J.H., & Waber, D.P. (2007). Executive capacities from a developmental perspective. In L. Meltzer (Ed.), *Executive function in education: From theory to practice* (pp. 39–54). New York: Guilford Press.

Best, B. (2001). Brain areas supporting cerebral cortex function. In *The world of Ben Best.* Retrieved July 26, 2007, from http://www.benbest.com/science/anatmind/anatmd7.html

Bhardwaj, R.D., Curtis, M.A., Spalding, K.L., Buchholz, B.A., Fink, D., Björk-Eriksson, T., et al. (2006). Neocortical neurogenesis in humans is restricted to development. *Proceedings of the National Academy of Sciences of the United States of America, 103*(33), 12564–12568.

Blair, C., & Razza, R.P. (2007). Relating effortful control, executive function, and false belief understanding to emerging math and literacy ability in kindergarten. *Child Development, 78*(2), 647–663.

Bley, N.S., & Thornton, C.A. (2001). *Teaching mathematics to students with learning disabilities* (4th ed.). Austin, TX: PRO-ED.

Bloom, F.E., Beal, M.F., & Kupfer, D.J. (2003). *The Dana guide to brain health.* New York: Simon & Schuster.

Bos, C.S, & Vaughn, S. (1988). *Strategies for teaching students with learning and behavior problems.* Boston: Allyn & Bacon.

Bowen, J.M., Jenson, W.R., & Clark, E. (2004). *School-based interventions for students with behavior problems.* New York: Springer.

Brady, S.A. (1991). The role of working memory in reading disability. In S.A. Brady & D.P. Shankweiler (Eds.), *Phonological processes in literacy* (pp. 129–152). New York: Taylor & Francis.

Britton, B.K., & Tesser, A. (1991). Effects of time-management practices on college grades. *Journal of Educational Psychology, 83*(3), 405–410.

Brodmann, K. (1909). *Vergleichende Lokalisationslehre her Grosshinrinde in ihren Prinzipien dargestellt auf Grund des Zellenbaues.* Leipzig, Germany: Barth.

Bromley, K., Irwin-De Vitis, L., & Modlo, M. (1995). *Graphic organizers: Visual strategies for active learning.* New York: Scholastic.

Brown, T.E. (1996). *The Brown Attention Deficit Disorder Scales manual.* San Antonio, TX: Pearson PsychCorp.

Brown, T.E. (2002). DSM-IV: ADHD and executive function impairments. *Advanced Studies in Medicine, 2*(25), 910–914.

Brown, T.E. (2005). *Attention deficit disorder: The unfocused mind in children and adults.* New Haven, CT: Yale University Press.

Brown, T.E. (2006). Executive functions and attention deficit hyperactivity disorder: Implications of the two conflicting views. *International Journal of Disability, Development, and Education, 53*(1), 35–46.

Bruns, J.H. (1992). *They can, but they don't: Helping students overcome work inhibition.* New York: Penguin.

Bull, R., & Scerif, G. (2001). Executive functioning as a predictor of children's mathematics ability: Inhibition, switching, and working memory. *Developmental Neuropsychology, 19*(3), 273–293.

Cahill, L., Babinsky, R., Markowitsch, H.J., & McGaugh, J.L. (1995). The amygdala and emotional memory. *Nature, 377,* 295–296.

Cain, K., Oakhill, J., & Bryant, P.E. (2004). Children's reading comprehension ability: Concurrent prediction by working memory, verbal ability, and component skills. *Journal of Educational Psychology, 96,* 31–42.

Campbell, K.U. (2008). *Great Leaps reading program.* Gainsville, FL: Diarmuid Inc.

Carroll, L. (1865). *Alice's adventures in wonderland.* London: Macmillan.

Carroll, W.M., & Isaacs, A. (2003). Achievement of students using the University of Chicago School Mathematics Project's Everyday Mathematics. In S.L. Senk & D.R. Thompson

(Eds.), *Standards-based school mathematics curriculum: What are they? What do students learn?* (pp. 79–108). Mahwah, NJ: Laurence Erlbaum Associates.

Casey, B.J., Tottenham, N., & Fossella, J. (2002). Clinical, imaging, lesion, and genetic approaches toward a model of cognitive control. *Developmental Psychobiology, 40,* 237–254.

Chall, J. (1967). *Learning to read: The great debate.* New York: McGraw-Hill.

Chaytor, N., Schmitter-Edgecombe, M., & Burr, R. (2006). Improving the ecological validity of executive functioning assessment. *Archives of Clinical Neuropsychology, 21*(3), 217–227.

Chomsky, N. (1965). *Aspects of the theory of syntax.* Cambridge, MA: The MIT Press.

Cohen, M. (1997). *The Children's Memory Scale manual.* San Antonio, TX: Pearson PsychCorp.

Connor, D.F. (2006). Stimulants. In R. Barkley (Ed.), *Attention-deficit hyperactivity disorder: A handbook for diagnosis and treatment* (pp. 608–647). New York: Guilford Press.

Connors, C.K., & MHS Staff. (2000). *Conners' Continuous Performance Test, Second Edition.* Toronto: Multi-Health Systems.

Corman, C.L., & Kindschi, C.L. *Test of Variables of Attention (TOVA)* (Version 7.3) [Computer software]. Los Alamitos, CA: The TOVA Co.

Covington, M.V. (1992). *Making the grade: A self-worth perspective on motivation and school reform.* New York: Cambridge University Press.

Damasio, A.R. (1994). *Descartes' error: Emotion, reason, and the human brain.* New York: Putnam Publishing.

Daniels, H., & Zemelman, S. (2004). *Subjects matter: Every teacher's guide to content-area reading.* Portsmouth, NH: Heinemann.

Davis, L., & Sirotowitz, S. (1996). *Study strategies made easy: A practical plan for school success.* Plantation, FL: Speciality Press.

Dawson, P., & Guare, R. (1998). *Coaching the ADHD student.* North Tonawanda, NY: Multi-Health Systems.

Dawson, P., & Guare, R. (2004). *Executive skills in children and adolescents: A practical guide to assessment and intervention.* New York: Guilford Press.

Dehn, M.J. (2008). *Working memory and academic learning: Assessment and intervention.* Hoboken, NJ: John Wiley & Sons.

Delazer, M., Domahs, F., Bartha, L., Brenneis, C., Locky, A., & Trieb, T. (2004). The acquisition of arithmetic knowledge: An fMRI study. *Cortex, 40,* 166–167.

Delis, D.C., Kaplan, E., & Kramer, J.H. (2001). *Delis–Kaplan Executive Function System.* San Antonio, TX: Pearson PsychCorp.

Denckla, M.B. (2007). Executive function: Binding together the definitions of attention deficit/hyperactivity disorder and learning disabilities. In L. Meltzer (Ed.), *Executive function in education: From theory to practice* (pp. 5–18). New York: Guilford Press.

Dingfelder, S.F. (2006). To outline or not to outline: New research sheds light on how people juggle the multiple and often conflicting demands of writing. *Monitor on Psychology, 37*(7), 18–19.

Ehren, B.J. (2000). Mnemonic devices. In B.J. Ehren (Ed.), *Building background knowledge for reading comprehension.* Lawrence, KS: The University of Kansas, Center for Research on Learning.

Elliot, R. (2003). Executive functions and their disorders. *British Medical Bulletin, 65,* 49–59.

Ellis, E.S., & Lenz, B.K. (1987). A component analysis of effective learning strategies for LD students. *Learning Disabilities Focus, 2,* 94–107.

Feifer, S.G. (2007). Know how executive function skills effect reading comprehension. *Today's School Psychologist,* July, 8.

Feifer, S.G. (2009). Social brain circuitry and behavior: The neural building blocks of emotion. In S.G. Feifer & G. Rattan (Eds.), *Emotional disorders: A neuropsychological, psychopharmacological, and educational perspective* (pp. 23–46). Middletown, MD: School Neuropsych Press.

Feifer, S.G., & De Fina, P.A. (2002). *The neuropsychology of written language disorders: Diagnosis and intervention.* Middletown, MD: School Neuropsych Press.

Feifer, S.G., & De Fina, P.A. (2005). *The neuropsychology of mathematics: Diagnosis and intervention.* Middletown, MD: School Neuropsych Press.

Fisher, D., & Frey, N. (2007). *Scaffolded writing instruction: Teaching with a gradual-release framework.* New York: Scholastic.

Flower, L., & Hayes, J.R. (1980). The dynamics of composing: Making plans and juggling constraints. In L.W. Gregg & E.R. Steinberg (Eds.), *Cognitive processes in writing* (pp. 31–50). Hillsdale, NJ: Lawrence Erlbaum Associates.

Foster, G., & Marasco, T.L. (2007). *Exemplars: Your best resource to improve student writing.* East Sussex, England: Pembroke Publishers.

Freedman, S. (2005, November 9). Innovative math, but can you count. *The New York Times.* Retrieved April 1, 2008, from http://www.samuelfreedman.com/articles/education/nyt11092005.html

Freese, G., & Wendon, L. (2003). *Letterland teacher's guide.* Cambridge, England: Letterland International Ltd.

Frey, N., & Fisher, D. (2003). A stitch in time: Increasing literacy achievement in an urban elementary school. *Indiana Reading Journal, 35*(2), 51–59.

Gardner, A., & Johnson, D. (1997). *Teaching personal experience narrative in the elementary and beyond.* Flagstaff, AZ: Northern Arizona Writing Project Press.

Gaskins, I.W., Satlow, E., & Pressley, M. (2007). Executive control of reading comprehension in elementary school. In L. Meltzer (Ed.), *Executive function in education: From theory to practice* (pp. 194–215). New York: Guilford Press.

Geary, D.C., & Brown, S.C. (1991). Cognitive addition: Strategy choice and speed-of-processing differences in gifted, normal, and mathematically disabled children. *Developmental Psychology, 27,* 398–406.

Geary, D.C., Hoard, M.K., & Hamson, C.O. (1999). Numerical and arithmetical cognition: Patterns of functions and deficits in children at risk for a mathematical disability. *Journal of Experimental Child Psychology, 74,* 213–239.

Gentile, D.A. (2009). Pathological video game use among youth 8 to 18: A national study. *Psychological Science, 20,* 594–602.

Gersten, R., & Chard, D. (1999). Number sense: Rethinking arithmetic instruction for students with mathematical disabilities. *Journal of Special Education, 33,* 18–28.

Giedd, J.N., Blumenthal, J., Jeffries, N.O., Castellanos, F.X., Liu, H., Zijdenbos, A., et al. (1999). Brain development during childhood and adolescence: A longitudinal MRI study. *Nature Neuroscience, 2,* 861–863.

Gioia, G.A., Isquith, P.K., & Guy, S.C. (2001). Assessment of executive function in children with neurological impairment. In R.J. Simeonsson & S.L Rosenthal (Eds.), *Psychological and developmental assessment: Children with disabilities and chronic conditions* (pp. 317–356). New York: Guilford Press.

Gioia, G.A., Isquith, P.K., Guy, S.C., & Kenworthy, L. (2000). *The Behavior Rating Inventory of Executive Function professional manual.* Odessa, FL: Psychological Assessment Resources.

Goff, D.A., Pratt, C., & Ong, B. (2005). The relations between children's reading comprehension, working memory, language skills, and components of reading decoding in a normal sample. *Reading and Writing, 18,* 583–616.

Goldberg, E. (2001). *The executive brain: The frontal lobes and the civilized mind.* New York: Oxford University Press.

Golden, C.J. (1978). *Stroop Color and Word Test.* Wood Dale, IL: C.H. Stoelting.

Goleman, D. (1995). *Emotional intelligence: Why it can matter more than IQ.* New York: Bantam Books.

Goleman, D. (2006). *Social intelligence: The new science of human relationships.* New York: Bantom Dell.

Graham, L., & Bellert, A. (2004). Difficulties in reading comprehension for students with learning disabilities. In B. Wong (Ed.), *Learning about learning disabilities* (3rd ed., pp. 251–280). San Diego: Elsevier Academic Press.

Graham, S., & Harris, K.R. (2005). *Writing better: Effective strategies for teaching students with learning difficulties.* Baltimore: Paul H. Brookes Publishing Co.

Graham, S., Harris, K.R., & Olinghouse, N. (2007). Addressing executive functioning problems in writing: An example from the self-regulated strategy development model. In L. Meltzer (Ed.), *Executive function in education: From theory to practice* (pp. 216–236). New York: Guilford Press.

Grant, D.A., & Berg, E.A. (1993). *Wisconsin Card Sorting Test–Revised and Updated.* Odessa, FL: Psychological Assessment Resources.

Gray, C. (1994). *Comic Strip Conversations: Colorful, illustrated interactions for students with autism and related disorders.* Arlington, TX: Future Horizons.

Gray, C. (2000). *The new Social Stories book: Illustrated edition.* Arlington, TX: Future Horizons.

Greene, R.W. (1998). *The explosive child.* New York: HarperCollins.

Greene, R.W. (2008). *Lost at school: Why our kids with behavioral challenges are falling through the cracks and how we can help them.* New York: Simon & Schuster.

Greene, R.W., & Ablon, J.S. (2006). *Treating explosive kids: The collaborative problem-solving approach.* New York: Guilford Press.

Hale, J.B., & Fiorello, C.A. (2004). *School neuropsychology: A practitioner's handbook.* New York: Guilford Press.

Harvey, S., & Goudvis, A. (2007). *Strategies that work: Teaching comprehension for understanding and engagement* (2nd ed.). Portland, ME: Stenhouse Publishers.

Hasselbring, T.S., & Bryan, W.T. (2005). *Research foundation and evidence of effectiveness of FASTT math.* Retrieved January 5, 2008, from http://www.tomsnyder.com/reports/FM_White_Paper.pdf

Hasselbring, T.S., Goin, L., & Bransford, J.D. (1988). Developing math automaticity in learning handicapped children: The role of computerized drill and practice. *Focus on Exceptional Children, 20,* 1–7.

Hibbing, A., & Rankin-Erickson, J.L. (2003). A picture is worth a thousand words: Using visual images to improve comprehension for middle school readers. *The Reading Teacher, 56*(8), 758–770.

Hinshaw, S.P., & Nigg, J.T. (1999). Behavior rating scales in the assessment of disruptive behavior problems in childhood. In D. Shaffer, C.P. Lucas, & J.E. Richters (Eds.), *Diagnostic assessment in child and adolescent psychopathology* (pp. 91–128). New York: Guilford Press.

Hitch, C.J., & McCauley, E. (1991). Working memory in children with specific mathematical learning disabilities. *British Journal of Psychology, 82,* 375–386.

Hooper, S., Schwartz, C., Wakely, M., deKruif, R., & Montgomery, J. (2002). Executive functions in elementary school children with and without problems in written expression. *Journal of Learning Disabilities, 35,* 57–68.

Hyerle, D. (2004). *Student successes with Thinking Maps: School-based research, results, and models for achievement using visual tools.* Thousand Oaks, CA: Corwin Press.

Hyerle, D. (2009). *Visual tools for transforming information into knowledge* (2nd ed.). Thousand Oaks, CA: Corwin Press.

Innovative Learning Concepts Inc. (n.d.). *TouchMath.* Colorado Springs, CO: Author.

Jones, F.H. (2007). *Tools for teaching: Discipline, instruction, and motivation.* Santa Cruz, CA: Frederick Jones Associates.

Jones, S.J. (2003). *Blueprint for student success: A guide for research-based teaching practices K–12.* Thousand Oaks, CA: Corwin Press.

Kamali, C., & Dominick, A. (1998). The harmful effects of algorithms in grades 1–4. In L.J. Morrow & N.J. Kenny (Eds.), *The teaching and learning of algorithms in school mathematics, 1998 yearbook* (pp. 130–140). Reston, VA: National Council of Teachers of Mathematics.

Kaplan, E., Fein, D., Kramer, J., Delis, D., & Morris, R. (2004). *Wechsler Intelligence Scale for Children, Fourth Edition Integrated.* San Antonio, TX: Pearson PsychCorp.

Kaufer, D.S., Hayes, J.R., & Flower, L.S. (1986). Composing written sentences. *Research in the Teaching of English, 20,* 121–140.

Keeler, M.L., & Swanson, H.L. (2001). Does strategy knowledge influence working memory in children with mathematical disabilities? *Journal of Learning Disabilities, 34,* 418–434.

Kiernan, J.A. (2008). *Barr's the human nervous system: An anatomical viewpoint.* Baltimore: Lippincott Williams & Wilkins.

Klein, K., & Boals, A. (2001). Expressive writing can increase working memory capacity. *Journal of Experimental Psychology: General, 130,* 520–523.

Klinger, J., Vaughn, S., & Boardman, A. (2007). *Teaching reading comprehension to students with learning difficulties.* New York: Guilford Press.

Knight, P., & Yorke, M. (2003). *Assessment, learning, and employability.* Berkshire, England: Open University Press.

Korkman, M., Kirk, U., & Kemp, S. (2007). *NEPSY-II: A Developmental Neuropsychological Assessment, Second Edition.* San Antonio, TX: Pearson PsychCorp.

Kyllonen, P.C., & Christal, R.E. (1990). Reasoning ability is (little more than) working memory capacity?! *Intelligence, 14,* 389–433.

LeBerge, D., & Samuels, S.J. (1974). Toward a theory of automatic information processing in reading. *Cognitive Psychology, 6,* 293–323.

Leonard-Zabel, A.M., & Feifer, S.G. (2009). Frontal lobe dysfunction, psychology, and violence. In S.G. Feifer and G. Rattan (Eds.), *Emotional disorders: A neuropsychological, psychopharmacological, and educational perspective* (pp. 107–122). Middletown, MD: School Neuropsych Press.

Lerew, C.D. (2005). Understanding and implementing neuropsychologically based arithmetic interventions. In R.C. D'Amato, C.R. Reynolds, & E. Fletcher-Janzen (Eds.), *Handbook of school neuropsychology* (pp. 758–776). New York: John Wiley & Sons.

Leslie, L., & Jett-Simpson, M. (1997). *Authentic literacy assessment: An ecological approach.* New York: Addison Wesley Longman.

Levine, M. (1998). *Developmental variation and learning disorders.* Cambridge, MA: Educational Publishing Service.

Levine, M. (2001). *Educational care: A system for understanding and helping children with learning differences at home and at school (2nd ed.).* Cambridge, MA: Educators Publishing Service.

Levine, M. (2002). *A mind at a time.* New York: Simon & Schuster.

Levine, M. (2003). *The myth of laziness: America's top learning expert shows how kids and parents can become more productive.* New York: Simon & Schuster.

Levy, F., Hay, D.A., McStephen, M., Wood, C., & Waldman, I. (1997). Attention-deficit hyperactivity disorder: a category or a continuum? Genetic analysis of a large-scale twin study. *Journal of the American Academy of Child and Adolescent Psychiatry, 36,* 737–744.

Lewis, D.A. (2004). Structure of the human prefrontal cortex. *American Journal of Psychiatry, 161,* 1366–1367.

Lezak, M.D. (1995). *Neurological assessment* (3rd ed.). New York: Oxford University Press.

Lloyd, S. (1998). *The phonics handbook: A handbook for teaching reading, writing, and spelling* (3rd ed.). Essex, England: Jolly Learning Ltd.

Loe, I.M., & Feldman, H.M. (2007). Academic and educational outcomes of children with ADHD. *Ambulatory Pediatrics, 7*(1), 82–90.

Luria, A.R. (1973). *The working brain.* New York: Basic Books.

Macan, T.H. Shahani, C., Dipboye, R.L., & Phillips, A.P. (1990). College student' time management: Correlations with academic performance and stress. *Journal of Educational Psychology, 82*(4), 760–768.

MacArthur, C.A., & Graham, S. (1987). Learning disabled students' composing under three methods of text production: Handwriting, word processing, and dictation. *The Journal of Special Education, 21*(3), 22–42.

Macon, J.M., Bewell, D., & Vogt, M.E. (1991). *Responses to literature.* Newark, DE: International Reading Association.

Madrigal, S., & Garcia Winner, M. (2008). *Superflex: A superhero social thinking curriculum package.* Santa Fe, CA: Think Social Publishing.

Malloy, P., & Duffy, J.D. (2001). *The frontal lobes and neuropsychiatric illness.* Arlington, VA: American Psychiatric Publishing.

Marshall, R.M., & Hynd, G.W. (1997). Academic underachievement in ADD subtypes. *Journal of Learning Disabilities, 30*(6), 635–643.

Marzano, R. (2003). *What works in school: Translating research into action.* Alexandria, VA: Association for Supervision and Curriculum Development.

Mayes, S.D., & Calhoun, S.L. (2005). Frequency of reading, math, and writing disabilities in children with clinical disorders. *Learning and Individual Differences, 16*(2), 145–157.

McCardle, P., & Chhabra, V. (2004). *The voice of evidence in reading research.* Baltimore: Paul H. Brookes Publishing Co.

McCardle, P., Chhabra, V., & Kapinus, B. (2008). *Reading research in action: A teacher's guide for student success.* Baltimore: Paul H. Brookes Publishing Co.

McCloskey, G., Perkins, L.A., & Diviner, B.V. (2009). *Assessment and intervention for executive functioning difficulties.* New York: Taylor & Francis.

McCutchen, D. (2006). Cognitive factors in the development of children's writing. In C.A. MacArthur, S. Graham, & J. Fitzgerald (Eds.), *Handbook of writing research* (pp. 115–130). New York: Guilford Press.

McCutchen, D., Covill, A., Hoyne, S.H., & Mildes, K. (1994). Individual differences in writing: Implications for translating fluency. *Journal of Educational Psychology, 86*(2), 256–266.

McGinnis, E., & Goldstein, A.P. (1993). *Skillstreaming the elementary school child: New strategies and perspectives for teaching social skills.* Champaign, IL: The Research Press.

McIntosh, R., Vaughn, S., Schumm, J.S., Haager, D., & Okhee, L. (1993). Observations of students with learning disabilities in special education classrooms. *Exceptional Children, 60*(3), 249–261.

Meltzer, L. (Ed.). (2007). Preface. In *Executive function in education: From theory to practice* (pp. xi–xiii). New York: Guilford Press.

Meltzer, L., & Krishnan, K. (2007). Executive functioning difficulties and learning disabilities: Understandings and misunderstandings. In L. Meltzer (Ed.), *Executive function in education: From theory to practice* (pp. 77–105). New York: Guilford Press.

Meltzer, L., Roditi, B.N., Steinberg, J.L., Biddle, K.R., Taber, S.E., Boyle Caron, K., et al. (2006). *Strategies for success: Classroom teaching techniques for students with learning differences* (2nd ed.). Austin, TX: PRO-ED.

Meltzer, L., Sales Polica, L., & Barzillai, M. (2007). Executive function in the classroom: Embedding strategy instruction into daily teaching practice. In L. Meltzer (Ed.), *Executive function in education: From theory to practice* (pp. 165–193). New York: Guilford Press.

Meyer, M., & Felton, J. (1999). Repeated reading to enhance fluency: Old approaches and new directions. *Annals of Dyslexia, 49,* 283–306.

Meyers, J.E., & Meyers, K.R. (1995). *Rey Complex Figure Test and recognition trial professional manual.* Odessa, FL: Psychological Assessment Resources.

Miller, E.K., & Cohen, J.D. (2001). An integrated theory of prefrontal cortical function. *Annual Review of Neuroscience, 24,* 167–202.

Miller, G.A. (1956). The magical number seven, plus or minus two. *The Psychological Review, 63*(2), 81–97.

Milne, A.A. (1926). *Winnie-the-Pooh.* London: Methuen & Co.

Misra, R., & McKean, M. (2000). College students' stress and its relation to their anxiety, time management, and leisure satisfaction. *American Journal of Health Studies, 16*(1), 41–61.

Moats, L.C. (1999). *Teaching is rocket science: What expert teachers of reading should know and be able to do.* Washington, DC: American Federation of Teachers.

Moats, L.C. (2000). *Whole language lives on: The illusion of balanced reading instruction.* Retrieved March 1, 2008, from http://www.edexcellence.net/detail/news.cfm?news_id=45

Moats, L.C. (2007). *Whole language high jinks: How to tell when "scientifically-based" reading instruction isn't.* Retrieved April 28, 2008, from http://www.edexcellence.net/doc/Moats2007.pdf

Moffit, T.E., & Lynam, D., Jr. (1994). The neuropsychology of conduct disorder and delinquency: Implications for understanding anti-social behavior. In D. Fowles, P. Sutker, & S.H. Goodman (Eds.), *Progress in experimental personality and psychopathology research* (Vol. 17, pp. 223–262). New York: Springer.

Murray, B. (1998). Dipping math scores heat up the debate over math teaching: Psychologists differ over the merits of teaching children whole math. *Monitor on Psychology, 29*(6), 34–35.

National Council of Teachers of Mathematics. (1998). *Principals and standards for school mathematics*. Reston, VA: Author.

National Council of Teachers of Mathematics. (2000). *Principals and standards for school mathematics*. Reston, VA: Author.

National Institute of Child Health and Human Development. (2000). *Report of the National Reading Panel: Teaching children to read: An evidence-based assessment of the scientific literature on reading and its implications for reading instruction: Reports of the subgroups* (NIH Publication No. 00-4754). Washington, DC: U.S. Government Printing Office.

Ogle, D. (1986). K-W-L: A teaching model that develops active reading of expository text. *The Reading Teacher, 39,* 654–674.

Paas, F., Renkl, A., & Sweller, J. (2003). Cognitive load theory and instructional design: Recent developments. *Educational Psychologist, 38*(1), 1–4.

Parkinson, C.N. (1957). *Parkinson's law.* Cutchogue, NY: Buccaneer Books.

Parry, J., & Drogin, E.Y. (2007). *Mental disability law, evidence, and testimony: A comprehensive reference manual for lawyers, judges, and mental disability professionals.* Chicago: American Bar Association.

Pashler, H. (1998). *The psychology of attention.* Cambridge, MA: The MIT Press.

Pelton, M.H. (1993). *Reading is not a spectator sport.* Englewood, CO: Teacher Ideas Press.

Penner-Wilger, M. (2008). *Reading fluency: A bridge from decoding to comprehension.* Retrieved March 1, 2009, from http://www.autoskill.com/pdf/fluency_research.pdf

Persky, H.R., Daane, M.C., & Jin, Y. (2003). *The nation's report card: Writing 2002.* Washington, DC: National Center for Education Statistics.

Pessoa, L., & Ungerleider, L.G. (2004). Neural correlates of change detection and change blindness in visual working memory. *Cerebral Cortex, 14,* 511–520.

Peterson, J., & Sheldon, C. (2006). Treating persistent adolescent aggression. *Current Treatment Options in Neurology, 8*(5), 427–438.

Phenix, J. (2002). *The reading teacher's handbook.* Ontario, Canada: Pembroke Publishers.

Polya, G. (1957). *How to solve it* (2nd ed.). Princeton, NJ: Princeton University Press.

Posner, M.I. (1994). *Images of the mind.* New York: Scientific American Library.

Pribam, K.H. (1992). *Brain and perception: Holonomy and structure in figural processes.* Hillsdale, NJ: Lawrence Erlbaum Associates.

RAND Reading Study Group. (2002). *Reading for understanding: Toward an R&D program in reading comprehension.* Santa Monica, CA: RAND.

Rasinski, T., Blachowicz, C., & Lems, K. (2006). *Fluency instruction: Research-based best practices.* New York: Guilford Press.

Reid, R.C., & Ortiz Lienemann, T. (2006). *Strategy instruction for children with learning disabilities.* New York: Guilford Press.

Research Institute for Learning and Development and FableVision, Inc. (2002a). BrainCogs [software]. Boston, MA: Author.

Research Institute for Learning and Development and FableVision, Inc. (2002b). Essay Express [software]. Boston, MA: Author.

Reynolds, C.R., & Kamphaus, R.W. (2004). *Behavior Assessment System for Children* (2nd ed.). Circle Pines, MN: American Guidance Service.

Reynolds, P.H., Meltzer, L., & Roditi, B. (2001). *BrainCogs.* Watertown, MA: Fablevision, Inc.

Riggs, N.R., Jahromi, L.B., Razza, R.P., Dillworth-Bart, J.E., & Mueller, U. (2006). Executive function and the promotion of social-emotional competence. *Journal of Applied Developmental Psychology, 27*(4), 300–309.

Ritcher-Levin, G. (2004). The amygdala, the hippocampus, and emotional modulation of memory. *The Neuroscientist, 10*(1), 31–39.

Roberts, M.J. (2007). *Integrating the mind: Domain general versus domain specific processes in higher cognition.* New York: Routledge.

Roditi, B.N., & Steinberg, J. (2007). The strategic math classroom: Executive functioning processes and mathematics learning. In L. Meltzer (Ed.), *Executive functioning in education: From theory to practice* (pp. 237–260). New York: Guilford Press.

Russell, S.J. (1996). Changing the elementary mathematics curriculum: Obstacles and challenges. In D. Zhang, T. Sawada, & J.P. Becker (Eds.), *Proceedings of the China-Japan-U.S. Seminar on Mathematics Education* (pp. 174–189). Carbondale, IL: Board of Trustees of Southern Illinois University.

Russell, S.J. (1999). *Relearning to teach arithmetic: Addition and subtraction, a teacher's guide.* Lebanon, IN: Dale Seymour Publications.

Saltus, R. (2003). Lack direction? Evaluate your brain's CEO. *The New York Times,* August 26, 2003. Retrieved November 21, 2007, from http://www.nytimes.com/2003/08/26/science/lack-direction-evaluate-your-brain-s-ceo.html

Samuels, S.J. (1976). Automatic decoding and reading comprehension. *Language Arts, 53*(3), 323–325.

Samuels, S.J. (2006). Reading fluency: It's past, present, and future. In T. Rasinski, C. Blachowicz, & K. Lems (Eds.), *Fluency instruction: Research-based best practices* (pp. 7–20). New York: Guilford Press.

Sborbone, R.J., & Long, C.J. (1996). *Ecological validity of neuropsychological testing.* Boca Raton, FL: CRC Press.

Schenck, J. (2003). *Learning, teaching, and the brain: A practical guide for educators.* Thermopolis, WY: Knowa.

Schneider, M., Grabner, R.H., & Paetsch, J. (2009). Mental number line, number line estimation, and mathematical achievement: Their interrelations in grades 5 and 6. *Journal of Educational Psychology, 101*(2), 359–372.

Schoenfeld, A. (1987). *Cognitive science and mathematical education.* New York: Taylor & Francis.

Schoofs, D., Preub, D., & Wolf, O.T. (2008). Psychosocial stress induces working memory impairments in an *n*-back paradigm. *Psychoneuroendocrinology, 33*(5), 643–653.

Schwartz, J. (1996). *Brain lock: A four-step treatment method to change your brain chemistry.* New York: HarperCollins.

Sesma, H.W., Mahone, E.M., Levine, T., Eason, S.H., & Cutting, L.E. (2009). The contribution of executive skills to reading comprehension. *Child Neuropsychology: A Journal of Normal and Abnormal Development in Childhood and Adolescence, 15*(3), 232–246.

Shanahan, T. (2006). Developing fluency in the context of effective literacy instruction. In T. Rasinski, C. Blachowicz, & K. Lems (Eds.), *Fluency instruction: Research-based best practices* (pp. 21–38). New York: Guilford Press.

Shaywitz, S. (2003). *Overcoming dyslexia: A new and complete science-based program for reading problems at any level.* New York: Alfred A. Knopf.

Shonkoff, J.P., & Meisels, S.J. (2000). *Handbook of early childhood intervention.* Cambridge, England: Cambridge University Press.

Shrager, J., & Siegler, R.A. (1998). SCADS: A model of children's strategy choices and strategy discoveries. *Psychological Science, 9,* 405–410.

Singer, B.D., & Bashir, A. (2004). EmPOWER: A strategy for teaching students with language learning disabilities how to write expository text. In E.R. Silliman & L.C. Wilkinson (Eds.), *Language and literacy learning in schools* (pp. 239–272). New York: Guilford Press.

Smith Myles, B., & Southwick, J. (1999). *Asperger syndrome and difficult moments: Practical solutions for tantrums, rage, and meltdowns.* Shawnee Mission, KS: Autism Asperger Publishing.

Sommers-Flanagan, J., & Sommers-Flanagan, R. (2002). *Clinical interviewing.* Hoboken, NJ: John Wiley & Sons.

Sousa, D.A. (2003). *How the gifted brain learns.* Thousand Oaks, CA: Corwin Press.

Speck, B.W., Hinnen, D.A., & Hinnen, K. (2003). *Teaching revising and editing: An annotated bibliography.* Westport, CT: Greenwood Publishing Group.

Swanson, H.L., & Sachse-Lee, C. (2001). Mathematical problem solving and working memory in children with learning disabilities: Both executive and phonological processes are important. *Journal of Experimental Child Psychology, 79*(3), 294–321.

Swicegood, P. (1994). Portfolio-based assessment practices. *Intervention in School and Clinic, 30*(1), 6–15.

Swick, K.J. (1987). *Student stress: A classroom management system*. West Haven, CT: NEA Professional Library.

Teaching Integrated Math and Science Project. (2008). *Math trailblazers* (3rd ed.). Dubuque, IA: Kendal/Hunt.

Teeter Ellison, P.A. (2005). School neuropsychology of attention-deficit/hyperactivity disorder. In R.C. D'Amato, E. Fletcher-Janzen, & C.R. Reynolds (Eds.), *Handbook of school neuropsychology* (pp. 460–486). Hoboken, NJ: John Wiley & Sons.

TERC. (2006). *Investigations in Number, data, and space* (2nd ed.). Upper Saddle River, NJ: Pearson Scott Foresman.

Thompson, J.B., Chenault, B., Abbott, R.D., Raskind, W.H., Richards, T., Aylward, E., et al. (2005). Converging evidence for attentional influences on the orthographic word formation of child dyslexics. *Journal of Neurolinguistics, 18*(2), 93–126.

Timmann, D., & Daum, I. (2007). Cerebellar contributions to cognitive functions. *Cerebellum, 6*(3), 159–162.

Tindal, G., & Fuchs, L. (2000). *A summary of research on test changes: An empirical basis for defining accommodations*.

Torgesen, J.K. (2004). Lessons learned from research on interventions for students who have difficulty learning how to read. In P. McCardle & V. Chhabra (Eds.), *The voice of evidence in reading research* (pp. 355–382). Baltimore: Paul H. Brookes Publishing Co.

Torrance, M., & Galbraith, D. (2006). The process demands of writing. In C.A. MacArthur, S. Graham, & J. Fitzgerald (Eds.), *Handbook of writing research* (pp. 67–82). New York: Guilford Press.

Tovani, C. (2000). *I read it, but I don't get it: Comprehension strategies for adolescent readers*. Portland, ME: Stenhouse Publishers.

Tovani, C. (2005). *Do I really have to teach reading? Content comprehension, grades 6–12*. Portland, ME: Stenhouse Publishers.

Troia, G.A. (2006). Writing instruction for students with learning disabilities. In C.A. MacArthur, S. Graham, & J. Fitzgerald (Eds.), *Handbook of writing research* (pp. 324–336). New York: Guilford Press.

Troia, G.A., Graham, S., & Harris, K.R. (1999). Teaching students with learning disabilities to mindfully plan when writing. *Exceptional Children, 65*, 215–252.

University of Chicago School Mathematics Project. (2007). *Everyday math* (3rd ed.). Chicago: McGraw-Hill.

van Garderen, D. (2007). Teaching students with LD to use diagrams to solve mathematical word problems. *Journal of Learning Disabilities, 40*(6), 540–553.

Wechsler, D. (2003). *Wechsler Intelligence Scale for Children* (4th ed.). San Antonio, TX: Pearson PsychCorp.

Willcutt, E.G., Pennington, B.F, Boada, R., Ogline, J.S., Tunick, R.A., Chhabildas, N.A., et al. (2001). A comparison of cognitive deficits in reading disability and attention-deficit/hyperactivity disorder. *Journal of Abnormal Psychology, 110*(1), 157–172.

Willcutt, E.G., Pennington, B.F., Chhabildas, N.A., Olson, R.K., & Hulslander, J.L. (2005). Neuropsychological analyses of comorbidity between RD and ADHD: In search of the common deficit. *Developmental Neuropsychology, 27*, 35–78.

Worthy, J. (2005). *Readers Theater for building fluency: Strategies and scripts for making the most of this highly effective, motivating, and research-based approach to oral reading*. New York: Scholastic.

Zentall, S.S., & Ferkis, M.A. (1993). Mathematical problem-solving for youth with ADHD, with and without learning disabilities. *Learning Disability Quarterly, 16*, 6–18.

Zimmerman, B.J., & Risemberg, R. (1997). Becoming a self-regulated writer: A social cognitive perspective. *Contemporary Educational Psychology, 22*, 73–101.

Index

Page numbers followed by *f* indicate figures; those followed by *t* indicate tables.